THE *ROMAN DE TOUTE CHEVALERIE*

Reading Alexander Romance in Late Medieval England

The *Roman de toute chevalerie*

Reading Alexander Romance in Late Medieval England

CHARLES RUSSELL STONE

UNIVERSITY OF TORONTO PRESS
Toronto Buffalo London

Toronto Buffalo London
utorontopress.com

ISBN 978-1-4875-0189-1

Library and Archives Canada Cataloguing in Publication

Stone, Charles Russell, 1978–, author
The Roman de toute chevalerie : reading Alexander romance in late medieval England / Charles Russell Stone.

Includes bibliographical references and index.
ISBN 978-1-4875-0189-1 (hardcover)

1. Thomas, of Kent, active 12th century–13th century. Roman de toute chevalerie. 2. Alexander, the Great, 356 B.C.–323 B.C. – Romances – History and criticism. I. Title.

PQ1533.T74R6678 2019 841′.1 C2018-904341-5

University of Toronto Press acknowledges the financial assistance to its publishing program of the Canada Council for the Arts and the Ontario Arts Council, an agency of the Government of Ontario.

Canada Council for the Arts Conseil des Arts du Canada

Funded by the Government of Canada Financé par le gouvernement du Canada | Canada

For Christopher Baswell

Contents

Illustrations

Acknowledgments

With its sheer volume and widespread textual transmission and influence, the corpus of medieval literature devoted to Alexander the Great has captivated me since I first opened George Cary's magisterial *The Medieval Alexander* in the Pontifical Institute of Mediaeval Studies. To a young scholar, Cary's book seemed a call to arms to pick up where he left off in his brief career, but the reception of Alexander proved, too, to be intimidating in its scope.

So I must first thank Andy Orchard, who introduced me to the Alexander legend nearly twenty years ago at the Centre for Mediaeval Studies, University of Toronto, for encouraging me to explore my research options, and Chris Baswell, the dedicatee of this book, for encouraging me to focus my attention on particular threads within the legend. Without Andy's advice, I would not have applied to the doctoral program in English at the University of California-Los Angeles, and without Chris's intervention, I would not have been admitted. I thank Chris, too, for recommending that I pick up the *Roman de toute chevalerie*, always having the time and energy to cast his critical eye on my work, and fostering my scholarship and career with timely advice and friendship well after we both left Westwood.

At UCLA I had the great fortune to work for V.A. Kolve, whose work ethic and humanism would inspire any young scholar, and once again rely on the guidance of Stephen Shepherd, who first sparked my interest in medieval literature in my undergraduate years and, having relocated to Los Angeles as well, found himself on my dissertation committee. I am grateful to both for their continuing influence on my research into the Alexander legend.

Over the last several years at the University of Nevada, Reno, I have learned to adapt, to shift from a potential career in academics, for which

I had long planned, to one as an administrator, which has proven to be fulfilling in so many, unforeseen ways. Still, defining the role of administrative faculty members in the research enterprise of an institution is an ongoing challenge, and I am grateful to three of my colleagues, in particular, for listening to my concerns while encouraging me to remain active as a scholar: Vice Provost Joe Cline, President Marc Johnson, and Faculty Senate Chair Tom Harrison.

Finally, although the seeds for this book were sown while writing an earlier one on Alexander, *Reading Alexander Romance in Late Medieval England* is the cumulative result of research at several institutions both before and after I conceived of this project, and I am indebted to the many helpful individuals at the Manuscripts Reading Room at the British Library, the Warburg Institute, the Parker Library at Corpus Christi College, Cambridge, and the Huntington Library.

THE *ROMAN DE TOUTE CHEVALERIE*

Reading Alexander Romance in Late Medieval England

Introduction: Reading and Reconstructing the Anglo-Norman Alexander

By the twelfth century, the literary reception of Alexander the Great was largely founded upon the transmission of two distinct corpora of Alexander narratives, the so-called vulgate histories written in Latin and Greek within the Roman Empire and the third-century Greek text known as the *Pseudo-Callisthenes*, which included fantastic anecdotes about Alexander's childhood and campaigns, ultimately circulated in several languages, and inspired various recensions across Europe and the Near and Middle East.[1] Although both branches of this textual lineage were based on the life and career of such a well-known figure of the ancient world, historical fact, long so elusive in recounting Alexander's deeds, was distorted by bias and exaggeration. Of the vulgate histories, the two Latin texts, Quintus Curtius Rufus's *Historia Alexandri Magni* and Justin's epitome of the *Philippic Histories* by Pompeius Trogus, circulated widely in western Europe and promulgated the notion that Alexander was an egomaniacal tyrant whose worst qualities (e.g., megalomania, a penchant for drink) were exacerbated by his journey into the eastern lands that he conquered. Alexander's perceived luxuriousness in the East and his obsession with personal glory and power were considered to be his most egregious faults by Roman philosophers and historians in the late Republic and early Empire, and so the version of the conqueror that they crafted was based upon his moral corruption and increasingly despotic behaviour. So profound was the impact of this reception of Alexander in the vulgate histories, as well as in anecdotes by Cicero and Seneca, that it largely accounts for our modern conception of the figure.[2]

The *Pseudo-Callisthenes* offers, on the other hand, not an extensive examination of the Macedonian Empire and its line of disreputable leaders, but a concise biography of the heroic conqueror, beginning with the sensational story of Nectanabus, a pharaoh in exile and con artist who uses sorcery to seduce Olympias and father the protagonist. Through a range of Greek, Hebrew, and Latin texts stemming from the *Pseudo-Callisthenes* arose an impressively ramified family of Alexander narratives, the recensions and adaptations that George Cary long ago classified as the "derivatives" of the *Pseudo-Callisthenes* and that ultimately informed vernacular romances across Europe.[3] These narratives established a centuries-long tradition of valorizing Alexander and presenting him as a noble-minded adventurer capable of such extraordinary feats as piloting a flying machine and mischievous ploys as disguising himself to visit his enemies' camps incognito. Together, the Latin vulgate histories and the line of Latin texts based on the *Pseudo-Callisthenes* accounted for the Alexander legend in western Europe, the result of a body of literature that had accumulated numerous episodes and attitudes towards the conqueror and that inspired in turn a multi-faceted, at times antithetical, reception of the man and his career, based on an array of interpolations and adaptations in both Latin and the European vernacular languages.

We must not assume that this legend, spanning Greek, Hebrew, Latin, and several vernaculars from southern Italy to England in twelfth-century Europe, was unified, rather than fragmented, or constant, rather than evolving. The reception of Alexander inspired a complicated literary corpus, not simply because it involved so many source-texts and languages, but because it incorporated such diverse perspectives on the conqueror. It has been said of Frederick II that the single most influential factor in the representation of his character and political agenda among poets of his day was the point in his career at which a given narrative was written.[4] This is an effective argument for Alexander as well. As David Williams writes, the extraordinary relevance of Alexander in the Middle Ages rested on his versatility as a figure "pluriculturel et transhistorique" and easily applicable to a range of intellectual, social, and moral agendas.[5] As I argue throughout this book, the evolving reception of Antiquity's most famous conqueror in the late medieval mind made Alexander an adaptable figure attractive to diverse audiences. Although I will ultimately examine four such audiences, Thomas of Kent and his three groups of readers suggested by the three primary manuscripts of the *Roman de toute chevalerie*, I must begin with the larger questions of Alexander's reception in Thomas's century. There is no more appropriate example than the Alexander legend of the necessity to "attend to the rhetorical and ideological functions of twelfth century literature, rather than searching notions of nationalism" or "evidence of some transhistorical fixed national identity."[6] The Alexander legend does not fit neatly into categories based on nationalities, for European geographies determined how it was compiled and transmitted, and Alexander texts, beginning in the languages of Antiquity and giving rise to vernacular romances, migrated gradually in the twelfth century westward and northward from southern Italy and Sicily towards Germany, France, and England.

As this process of transmission occurred over several generations, the various regions of Europe had access to Alexander narratives and episodes at different points in time, and this considerably dictated the conqueror's reception and appropriation by writers from Italy to England. Moreover, twelfth- and thirteenth-century rulers presided over multicultural, multilingual subjects who held distinct attitudes towards the conqueror. Romances written in French under Henry II and his sons and Philip Augustus, for example, not only differed in content but at times represented competing traditions (so Thomas's Anglo-Norman romance is markedly distinct from Continental French narratives of Alexander). Similarly, Frederick II presided over one region, southern Italy and Sicily, previously ruled by the Norman kings, where Alexander was hardly received as an imperial model, and another, Staufen Germany, where Alexander had been idealized as a paradigmatic emperor since the days of Frederick I. It was among similar, conflicting attitudes that the poem known as the *Roman de toute chevalerie* established a narrative of Alexander for Anglo-Norman England.

Obscured in the shadow cast by the more heralded *romans antiques* of the twelfth century both from the court of Henry II and Eleanor of Aquitaine and the European Continent, this Anglo-Norman romance treatment of Alexander the Great raises more questions than it poses answers. There is no extant title provided by the original author but only the explicit preserved in two manuscripts, "ci finist le romaunz de tute chivalerie," an identification that belies the narrative's content. The poem does not necessarily depart from the fundamental narrative bequeathed by centuries of Alexander legends, but its scribes evidently saw in it a record of knightly and chivalric virtues and favoured its battlefield exploits.[7] Covering the mysterious circumstances of the hero's conception and birth, his rise to power through campaigns in Persia and India, and his poisoning in Babylon, the *Roman de toute chevalerie* is nonetheless an ambitious text within Anglo-Norman literature and likely predates more celebrated and oft-discussed Continental French romances of the twelfth century and beyond, yet its author has long remained only a matter of debate.

Identified by earlier cataloguers and scholars as Eustache, he has been known since the early twentieth century as Thomas of Kent, although virtually nothing can be said about him with certainty.[8] M. Dominica Legge long ago pointed out that the earliest illustrator of the *Roman de toute chevalerie* considered its author a monastic, likely Benedictine, writer, as pictured on folio 22r of Cambridge, Trinity College MS O. 9. 34, although Thomas was just as likely a clerical poet.[9] The portrait of an author, whether cleric or monk, working with pen and scraper led Keith Busby to comment on the poem as an object of labour, the result of a "creative act ... which includes the intellectual-verbal process of translation from Latin into vernacular and the physical endeavor of putting quill to parchment,"[10] and in the absence of biographical information Thomas is judged solely by the merits of his work. There is little doubt that he worked as a translator and a reader with a well-stocked library at his disposal in crafting an Alexander for a Francophone audience in England. As for the identity of this audience, Ian Short notes that "seignurs," used throughout the *Roman de toute chevalerie* to address the reader, is common within monastic communities, but that the language of choice, Anglo-Norman French, served as "a ready and natural bridge between the traditionally juxtaposed religious and secular cultures" in the twelfth century.[11] As I will discuss in later chapters, the manuscripts of Thomas's poem fittingly appealed to readerships with a wide-ranging interest in the Alexander legend.

When he wrote his poem is a question that invites further confusion. Over the last century or so, a consensus has evolved from an early argument for the turn of the thirteenth century[12] to a progression of more recent votes, respectively, for the second half of the twelfth century,[13] 1175–85,[14] and the last quarter of the century,[15] a hypothesis corroborated in part by Thomas's interpolation of Jordan Fantosme's Anglo-Norman *Chronicle*. This interpolation provides a *terminus a quo* of 1173–4, but there survives no clear evidence for a *terminus ad quem*. Martin Gosman proposes 1184, owing to the fact that Thomas did not rely on Alexandre de Paris's *Roman d'Alexandre*,[16] but this supposition raises another question concerning the relationship between the *Roman de toute chevalerie* and a prolific century of writing French Alexander romances on the Continent. In basing his work on a range of Latin source-texts, Thomas composed the only surviving Anglo-Norman narrative of Alexander yet disregarded – either wilfully or out of ignorance – this Continental network of French Alexander romances that had been thriving since the early part of the twelfth century. In citing the impressive range of sources on Alexander with which to supplement his own narrative, he includes only those transmitted to him in Latin:

> Nel dy pas pur la moie, assez ay dont diter,
> Car l'estorie en est grant e ly fet sunt plener;
> E ceo poent ly clerk tresbien tesmoigner
> Qui se volent a Cesar e Pompe acointer
> E lire Aristotle e Solin versiler,
> Orosie e Ysidre e Jerome li bier
> E les autres autors mestres de translater
> Qe les fez Alisandre descristrent [al] primer. (1335–42)[17]

> I do not speak for myself; I have enough to put down, because the history is a large one, the deeds many. Those clerics who wish to become acquainted with Caesar and Pompeius Trogus, to read Aristotle and recite Solinus, to translate Orosius, Isidore, the noble Jerome, and the other authoritative authors who first recounted the deeds of Alexander can well attest to this.

As I will discuss in the early chapters of this book, this list – both a works cited and suggested reading for those who wish to learn more about the subject – lends Latin *auctoritas* to Thomas's poem and aligns it, whether intentionally or not, with efforts in England to collate these same sources into Anglo-Latin compendia on Alexander and his empire. Unlike the redactors of these compendia, Thomas relied on sources rooted in the *Pseudo-Callisthenes* line of narratives, namely the Valerius *Epitome* and Alexander's letter to Aristotle, that the Anglo-Latin writers either ignored or explicitly contradicted.

Here again, we must be cognizant of two literary influences, that of the *Pseudo-Callisthenes*, which provided Thomas with his primary source, and that of the vulgate histories, which accounted for the portrayal of Alexander in some of the very Latin works that Thomas cites in the passage above. A third corpus of texts, however, the French romances contemporaneous with him, has inevitably provided a context for discussing the *Roman de toute chevalerie*, even though Thomas does not acknowledge them. No critic has assessed the Anglo-Norman romance more harshly than Paul Meyer, who in his voluminous study of medieval French Alexander narratives declared the poem "equally devoid of originality and style."[18] More recently, the preeminent scholar of French Alexander romance Catherine Gaullier-Bougassas has identified Thomas as one of the first writers in French to compile a historically themed work based on several sources and devoted to the same subject,[19] a distinction that underscores what Legge long ago considered as Thomas's "moral purpose in compiling" his work from so many Latin source-texts on Alexander.[20] To digest the plot as simply as possible, Thomas's poem is about 1) an aging king worried about his scheming family, succession, and the future of his empire, 2) a treacherous wife and a son who uses his mother's influence and father's authority with the barons to take over that empire and expand it eastward, 3) the treachery committed against the son once he is abroad leading military campaigns and exploring unknown lands, and 4) the son's fear of the destruction of what he has inherited and expanded, his barons' inability or unwillingness to maintain his vision of empire, and the public suffering that occurs after the king's death. Although Anglo-Latin writers, relying on the aforementioned Latin texts of the vulgate histories, and Thomas of Kent, working primarily with a source-text that descended from the *Pseudo-Callisthenes* but consulting a wide variety of authorities, could disagree on many factors of Alexander's reign, they concur that the fall of the Macedonian Empire happened because of internal dissent. Unhappy with their leader in his last days, Alexander's officers and governors (according to Latin historians) or his barons (according to Thomas) committed or at least condoned a foul act of treachery that not only killed the conqueror but stoked the flames of civil war and dismembered his empire as well. It is this particular insistence on the causes for the decline of the Macedonian Empire (dissension among Alexander's officers, who would be cast as the baronage of medieval romance) and the moralities to be drawn from this imperial failure that provide an important context for the surviving manuscripts of Thomas's poem.

The Manuscripts and Audiences

The major manuscripts of the *Roman de toute chevalerie* have been variously associated with both monastic and secular scriptoria. Thomas's heroic presentation of Alexander accords at once with *chansons de geste,* the Matter of Britain, and the ancestral histories that sprang up within the Anglo-Norman baronial patronage of literature in the second half of the twelfth century and the first half of the thirteenth,[21] and in at least one manuscript there is indisputable evidence that the poem attracted a feudal audience. At the same time, there remains the possibility that in appropriating so well known a legend, Thomas carried on a long-standing tradition of measuring modern rulers against ancient exemplars.[22] Alexander is easily understood as a paradigmatic figure for medieval rulers, as he had been for Roman emperors, and as Christiane Raynaud argues of the thirteenth and fourteenth century, writers and artists refashioned him to make him relevant to contemporary political trends, whether as a feudal prince surrounded by his baronage or an exemplary warrior-king.[23] Of the few critics of the *Roman de toute chevalerie*, Martin Gosman has been the most insistent on likewise contextualizing it within political trends. Believing that that the poem uniquely reflected Insular questions of kingship, notably those posed by Henry II, Gosman argues for the "réalité littéraire" of Thomas's work in the imperial vision of Henry's reign.[24] Provocative as this suggestion of Anglo-Norman Alexander romance representing Anglo-Norman kingship may be, reading Thomas's poem as a sort of political allegory for the author's England is an exercise reliant purely on assumptions. Historicism certainly has its role in an analysis of the *Roman de toute chevalerie*, but we argue on sturdier ground in first identifying how Thomas appropriated Alexander romance and, to put it simply, made it his own, even as Continental French writers were developing their reception of the conqueror. Thomas wrote in a period when Insular audiences considered themselves more English than Norman,[25] amid an emerging English national identity in the 1170s that involved "a feeling of separation from the Continent,"[26] and this is an important cultural context for discussing his romance as one that was composed in England for *Engleis* readers. At the same time, composing the *Roman de toute chevalerie* in Anglo-Norman may have allowed Thomas to attract a certain type of readership already engaged with French literature – texts, to be sure, not necessarily exported from France but created and disseminated in the French language across Europe. It has been recently argued of this readership that texts written in French in England or elsewhere encouraged them to "participate in a cosmopolitan, supralocal textual culture by virtue of being able to read French,"[27] and Thomas may have responded, then, both to the emergence of Alexander texts in France and to the continuing fashion for literature in French, regardless of its provenance.

The manuscripts of his work, spanning two centuries after its composition, invite us to consider not only how his romance was received and adapted but also how political and literary contexts ensured that the

Alexander legend evolved in England. The oldest surviving copy, Cambridge, Trinity College MS O. 9. 34 (mid-thirteenth century) is incomplete and offers only the second half of the poem. Two manuscripts of the fourteenth century, Durham Cathedral Library C.IV.27B and Paris, Bibliothèque Nationale Française, MS fr. 24364, preserve a complete text, although the latter adapts Thomas's Anglo-Norman into Continental French.[28] A more significant problem for reconstructing Thomas's text is the fact that while he disregarded his French predecessors, all three manuscripts of his poem include lengthy scribal interpolations from the twelfth-century French *Roman d'Alexandre* by Alexandre de Paris, the first an ancillary episode involving some of Alexander's officers (the *Fuerre de Gadres*, the second of the four branches of French romance categorized by Paul Meyer) and the second on the conqueror's division of his lands from his deathbed and the lamentation of his survivors (branch four). The subsequent confusion over what, exactly, Thomas of Kent wrote and intended as the *Roman de toute chevalerie* has further encouraged the neglect of his work, and without a reliable manuscript attesting to some vaunted original state of his poem, it was easily exiled to a scholarly no man's land.

Even when Brian Foster shed considerable light on the poem with his critical edition for the Anglo-Norman Text Society, criticism of his final product attested to the ongoing confusion over the *Roman de toute chevalerie*. Foster's decision to publish a composite text based on readings gleaned from across the surviving manuscripts (while excluding the Continental, interpolated passages unique to each of them) elicited stern responses. As an edition offering a text "only partially accessible to us" and "hiding from us what is truly medieval,"[29] the poem in Foster's edition has nonetheless long provided our access to Thomas's narrative and scribal treatment of it in subsequent centuries. A similar problem plagues the Continental French Alexander romance tradition, composed in individual, smaller texts over the twelfth century and in Alexandre de Paris's composite version in Thomas's generation. The earliest appearances of these Continental romances in manuscript remain so frustratingly obscured that the forty-year series published by Princeton University Press in the twentieth century prompted a less than enthusiastic reception:

> [the series is] an extreme example of the obfuscatory potential of the modern edition ... the [editorial] team have indeed deconstructed the manuscript corpus in order to reconstruct a text which does not survive in any of the surviving medieval copies and which may not have ever existed.[30]

The lineage of original compositions and interpolations generically known as the *Roman d'Alexandre* poses, in other words, the same modern challenge as does Thomas of Kent's *Roman de toute chevalerie*. Manuscripts survive, but the original text does not, and deducing what the author composed and what those who copied his text inserted into it is no easy matter.

Nor was the problem of identifying the "medieval" *Roman de toute chevalerie* alleviated by the facing-page French translation published by Champion in more recent years, a volume that takes as its base text that edited by Foster.[31] What modern readers and scholars receive as the "Roman de toute chevalerie" or the Anglo-Norman Alexander is thus an invention of our era rather than a text of the Middle Ages, and even though Thomas's poem has been recognized as "important ... as a part of the jigsaw puzzle of medieval Alexander material,"[32] what Thomas wrote and what his readers encountered have both failed to generate much interest. The predominance of the French Alexander romance tradition, both in terms of its ponderous corpus of texts and codices and the scholarship devoted to it, has undoubtedly pushed the *Roman de toute chevalerie* to a liminal space of Alexander literature, suggested by a recent assessment of Alexandre de Paris's *Roman d'Alexandre* that "no serious indigenous rival to [it] ever appeared in England" and the Continental romances "left little terrain in which ... English Alexander poems could develop."[33] The challenges of editing the manuscripts have further hindered attention to Thomas and his unique poem. Each of the three major surviving manuscripts offers a different narrative and a different reading experience, for each may feature the basic framework of Thomas's narrative, but each manipulates this narrative with its unique interpolations and arrangement of episodes. My fundamental argument in this book is that without appreciating how Thomas responded to earlier narratives of Alexander, the production of its manuscripts, the interests of their late medieval readers, and the contexts surrounding the reception of the conqueror, it is impossible to assess the *Roman de toute chevalerie* fully or accurately. My challenges, then, are to shed light on the inspirations that Thomas drew from the twelfth century and on the aforementioned readings and readerships in order to analyse the poem not as a modern edition but as a text read, illustrated, and annotated in the thirteenth and fourteenth centuries. And my solution to de-mystifying what sort of poem Thomas wrote is ultimately a simple one: we can only analyse the work that survives, and what survives is not any archetypal poem but three distinct manuscripts, artefacts that attest to the continuing popularity and relevance of Thomas's work in the two centuries after he wrote it.

In the chapters that follow, I attempt to recreate the scribal-artistic production and the experience of reading that particular copy of Thomas's poem, but I also contextualize them within the Alexander legend, as it evolved over the late Middle Ages, and general literary reactions towards key events in English royal and baronial relations, the primary audiences for Alexander romances from the twelfth century onward. On the one hand, I offer what neither Foster in his edition nor Catherine Gaullier-Bougassas and Laurence Harf-Lancner in their translation could, a window into the individual merits of each manuscript, an appreciation of their respective texts, and a recreation of the experience of reading these manuscripts as unique narratives of Thomas's Alexander. On the other, I read these codices within the contexts of Alexander's reception, the portrayal of England's kings and political environment at the time of their production, and as much evidence as can be discerned regarding the scriptoria that made them, their patrons, and their readers. If each copy reveals a disparate agenda on the part of those who filled the folios with verses and drawings, then each readership approached the poem because of a unique interest: that of the Cambridge manuscript, a generation between the thirteenth-century Barons' Wars, for the emphasis on the baronial dissension in Alexander's last days, that of the Paris manuscript, a knight who fought abroad for Edward I and witnessed the uneasy transition to Edward II's reign, for Alexander's onetime glory and relationship with his baronage, and that of the Durham manuscript, a well-read collator of classical and patristic attitudes towards the conqueror, in an age that moralized the ephemeral nature of Alexander's reign.

In an earlier book on Alexander, I surveyed his evolving reception in medieval and early modern England, beginning with the twelfth-century recovery of classical histories, in which he was portrayed as a deranged ruler bent on conquest and self-destruction, continuing in the scholastic praise of a king trained by Aristotle, and culminating in the sixteenth-century insistence that Alexander was an ideal emperor and an enlightened philosopher in his own right.[34] In the present book, I examine how the conqueror was appropriated into vernacular literature for a new audience, the *Engleis*, and how the *Roman de toute chevalerie*, the text responsible for bringing Alexander to this audience in its own language, was read, copied, and treated as a vehicle for other anecdotes and notions of the conqueror in subsequent centuries.

Citations to the *Roman de toute chevalerie* reference the text given in its surviving manuscripts, unless there is sufficient agreement among these versions and no reason to point out a particular variant or characteristic of one codex or another; in such cases, I rely on the text supplied in Foster's critical edition cited above. All translations from the Anglo-Norman and Latin are my own, unless stated otherwise.

Chapter One

Alexander Romance in Twelfth-Century Europe

By Henry II's reign, when Thomas of Kent wrote the *Roman de toute chevalerie*, numerous accounts of Alexander's career had evolved through the interests and perspectives of several preceding generations of writers, particularly active in the twelfth century, when a pan-European interest in the conqueror inspired efforts to translate his legend from Latin into the vernacular. Over the course of this century, Alexander joined the ranks of Arthur and Charlemagne in romances popularized in Norman Italy, Staufen Germany, Capetian France, and, finally, under Thomas of Kent, Angevin England. This flourish of literary activity fostered the composition and copying of Latin and vernacular texts that were transmitted across the Continent via a monastic network that stretched from the Atlantic to Sicily and southern Italy, the gateway for what would become Alexander romances in various languages.[1] Thomas was the benefactor, in fact, of two acts of textual transmission: that by which Anglo-Latin writers received the Latin vulgate histories of the conqueror written in Imperial Rome, which I will discuss in the following chapter, and that which provided him with his primary source-text, a descendent of the *Pseudo-Callisthenes.*

The origins of the latter, the adaptation of the *Pseudo-Callisthenes* into a series of recensions and affiliated narratives that would eventually inspire vernacular narratives, can be located in Italy, to the south of the peninsula, and in Sicily, where scribes in the Norman courts worked with Hebrew, Greek, Arabic, and Latin texts, appropriated aspects of Byzantine and Jewish legends of Alexander, and produced novel conceptions of him that migrated westward through the Staufen Empire towards the Atlantic. Following the same route, manuscripts featuring Alexander's encounter with the Brahmans, which appealed to the conqueror's detractors who wished to contrast his vainglory and belligerence with Christian asceticism, and his letter to Aristotle on the wonders of India, inspired the reception of Alexander as an eastern adventurer. Vernacular romances, on the other hand, began in early-twelfth-century Burgundy and found fertile ground in Capetian France, where, having appropriated in turn many of the aspects of Alexander's reception in Norman Italy over the course of several individual texts and culminating with Alexandre de Paris's composite *Roman d'Alexandre*, they would reflect the ideal of a powerful king supported by his loyal baronage and unflagging army.

The evolution of the Alexander legend in medieval Europe was thus informed by a cis- and transalpine exchange of codices and the ideas therein. Writers of French and Middle English romances appropriated and translated Latin texts originating in Italy, and like the Breton lais and Arthurian narratives popular in Frederick II's Italy,[2] representations of Alexander from the Atlantic travelled to the Mediterranean, where Greek, Hebrew, and Latin tales of the conqueror had originally found a foothold for European audiences and where writers of Latin Christendom mingled with their Jewish and Arabic counterparts.[3] Alexander texts from this time, including Thomas's poem, thus often exhibit a composite arrangement of anecdotes informed by legends of local interest, availability of particular source-texts, or the cultural climates of particular regions and their ruling dynasties.[4] The *Roman de toute chevalerie* incorporates, for example, Latin Alexander texts that had increased in popularity since the Norman Conquest, classical and late antique texts that were commonly found in Benedictine libraries, and Jewish anecdotes that entered the Latin West through Norman Italy, while surely responding to the development of Continental French romance in preceding generations.

Norman and Staufen Italy: Latin Texts

Understanding the niches of Latin narratives in Europe within these routes of westward and eastward textual transmission is thus crucial to assessing the medieval Alexander; the vernacular traditions of Alexander romance that coexisted from the twelfth century to the close of the Middle Ages cannot be fully appreciated otherwise. Yet the transmission of Latin narratives is not without its complications, and we cannot speak of a unified Latin textual tradition in medieval Europe any more than we can of a Greek one that established Alexander romance in the Mediterranean, North Africa, and the Near East.[5] The Latin schema emanated from two primary translations of the Greek narrative known as the *Pseudo-Callisthenes*, which itself survives in several recensions:[6] Julius Valerius's fourth-century *Res gestae* (a translation of the A recension of the Greek text),[7] and Leo, Archbishop of Naples's tenth-century *Nativitas et victoria Alexandri* (a translation of the lost δ* recension of the Greek). Valerius's text had long been popular among monastic readers in Italy,[8] and Leo's translation, produced for Duke John of Campania, began the longtime association of Alexander legends with a secular, especially courtly, readership.[9] The difference in audiences is reflected by the difference in content of Valerius's and Leo's narratives.

The A version of the *Pseudo-Callisthenes*, that behind Julius Valerius, "most closely resembles a conventional historical work" and "contains virtually none of the fabulous elements prevalent in later versions."[10] Leo's version featured, however, episodes more evocative of the romance genre, including Alexander's flight into the heavens and exploration of the depths of the sea in a submarine,[11] and over the twelfth and thirteenth centuries Leo's translation inspired still more episodes, as it was revised into the three *Historia de preliis* recensions.[12] The eleventh-century I^1 recension, the primary source for both the I^2 and I^3 texts (written independently of one another), interpolates anecdotes from Josephus, Jerome, Orosius, Solinus, Isidore, the *Liber monstrorum*, and the Brahman debates,[13] conveys "a tone of moral seriousness lacking in Leo's version, or for that matter the Greek original," and represents "a major step toward transforming the Alexander Romance from entertaining story into a vehicle for the expression of moral ideas."[14] The I^2 recension (1118–19), whose redactor has been recently argued as Guido of Pisa,[15] supplemented the I^1 in turn with its own moralizing anecdotes culled from Orosius, Valerius Maximus, Josephus, Pseudo-Epiphanius, and the Brahman texts, and in the early thirteenth century the I^3 recension (ca. 1218–36),[16] also from southern Italy, added several passages dealing with the dangers of ambition and the vanity of kingship, as well as an epilogue that includes a debate over Alexander's reception between two Greek philosophers and a letter from a Jewish philosopher exhorting the conqueror to embrace monotheism. The *Historia de preliis* recensions were not merely vehicles for the burgeoning Latin Alexander tradition. Through their interpolations, they also helped to convey a multicultural version of him unique to southern Italy and Sicily, where Greek and Hebrew legends of the conqueror had long circulated and where many of the fantastical stories of his career that would ultimately find their way to Germany, France, and England began.

As a conduit for Hebrew, Greek, and Arabic literature to the east and Latin literature to the west, Norman Italy and Sicily supplied Europe with many of the episodes and texts ultimately appropriated for Alexander romances.[17] Critical of his ambition and hubris, the Jewish legends of Alexander that attracted Greek and Latin writers provided a religious element to his story that had not been intended in the earliest recensions of the Greek *Pseudo-Callisthenes*. As versions of this Greek narrative and its Latin descendants interpolated Jewish and Near Eastern Christian anecdotes of the conqueror,[18] they came to reflect the main themes of Jewish writers addressing Alexander, "his pride and arrogance" on the one hand and "his wisdom and justice, [and] his friendliness to the Jews" on the other.[19] Moreover, Talmudic legends, particularly popular among European romance writers, encouraged Alexander's reception as a conqueror protected by Providence or some divine force and one whose expeditions led to didactic encounters with elders and philosophers.[20] His visit to Jerusalem (from Josephus Flavius), his dialogue with sage Jewish elders, his meeting with the Amazons, his failed journey to Eden or another earthly paradise (all from the Babylonian *Talmud*), and the flight and submarine scenes (from the Palestinian *Talmud*), disseminated in Hebrew, Greek, and Latin texts, and through the last they would help significantly to expand romances throughout western Europe.[21] Alexander's reception, particularly as a pagan conqueror who must learn to embrace the Judaeo-Christian God, quickly evolved as a result. The most widely available of these episodes was his visit to Jerusalem, which Josephus included in his *Antiquitates Iudaicae* to temper the biblical hostility towards the conqueror in Daniel and 1 Maccabees[22] and which served a similar purpose in Hebrew legends, versions of the Greek *Pseudo-Callisthenes*, and the Latin *Historia de preliis* recensions where it appears. In Josephus's account, as well as the Latin *Historia*, God sends Alexander a dream vision of Jaddus, the priest of Jerusalem, who announces the Macedonian's impending conquest of Persia, and when Alexander later bows to the Jewish clerics outside of the city, they read for him the prophecy of Daniel and assure him that his victory over the Persians is insinuated therein.[23] Alexander subsequently grants the Jews certain political rights not possessed under Persian rule and marches ahead towards Darius's armies. Importantly, in the *Historia*, Alexander explains that he honours not Jaddus but the priest's God ("non hunc adoravi, sed Deum cuius pontificatu sacerdotii functus est") and that he genuinely believes that the Jewish God will lead him to victory over the Persians ("arbitror divino iuvamine me Darium vincere et virtutem Persarum").[24]

In similar fashion, the story of Alexander's enclosure of the wicked races Gog and Magog in the Caspians, variations of which had developed from a Jewish legend into a Christian one in both Syria (whence came the crucial detail that Alexander succeeds in enclosing the races by praying to God for assistance)[25] and Mesopotamia (where the idea that the races would be released by the Antichrist and announce the Apocalypse was added to the story)[26] centuries before its appropriation by Pseudo-Methodius, was transmitted through Italy to the rest of western Europe and proved immensely popular among later romances.[27] An adapted version of the episode reached a wide readership as well through its inclusion in Peter Comestor's *Historia scholastica*. In this version, Alexander encounters in the Caspian Gates, between the Caucasus Mountains and the Caspian Sea, the sons of ten enclosed tribes who ask him to release their people, but when he hears that they openly rebelled against the God of Israel, Alexander decides to enclose them even more securely.[28] To achieve this, he tries to seal the mountain paths with bitumen, but when this fails he prays to God for assistance, and the Caspian crags straightaway move themselves to surround the tribes.[29] Peter's conclusion of the scene suggests that Alexander's pagan background was admissible under God's plan: "As Josephus asked, 'What would God do for his faithful, if He did so much for an infidel?'"[30] For writers in the Latin West, Gog and Magog represented "polyvalent monsters situated at the margins of Christendom,"[31] including Jews and especially Mongels,[32] and Peter's attitude reflected a considerable reevaluation of Alexander. Although a pagan, he was chosen by God, first in Jerusalem and then in the Caspians, to combat the enemies of Christian civilization.

At the same time, Alexander must understand from philosophers and sages in the Jewish tradition the vanity of fame, fortune, and glory, that he is excluded from paradisiacal lands because he is not spiritually pure, and he must accept limitations placed on him by divine forces (such as the flight scene, in which he is prevented from reaching the heavens).[33] The twelfth-century *Iter ad paradisum*, for example, a Latin adaptation of a Jewish narrative, provided romance writers with a means of rewriting the purpose of Alexander's eastern expedition and to transform him into a hero with Christian moral values. The oldest legends of the expedition had drawn on an appreciation for the marvels of India alongside a sense of foreboding in a journey that ended with the conqueror's assassination. One of the oldest episodes among the tales of Alexander in the years following his death was the prophecy, which he hears in India from the trees of the sun and the moon, that he would fail to return to Macedon and be poisoned in Babylon, and in the aftermath of his assassination his mother Olympias will be murdered in the streets.[34] After Alexander's death, an equally devastating fate awaits his empire and survivors, many of whom will become embroiled in a lengthy civil war. The episode of these trees appears in numerous Latin texts and the vernacular romances that they inspired as an omen of the impending violence that will conclude the campaigns into Asia, but the *Iter* offered writers a distinct alternative. Rather than adding to the sense of failure and imminent disaster of the journey east, the text recasts it as voyage towards spiritual epiphany. In the Latin translation, Alexander is so frustrated at his inability to reach an earthly paradise beyond the Ganges that he proclaims "nichil perfeci in mundo, totiusque ambitionis nichili pendo, nisi hujus voluptatis participium permeruero" (I have accomplished nothing in this world and consider all my ambition as nothing, unless I earn the right to share in this joy).[35] The gatekeeper of the paradise instead sends him a gemstone that only an elderly man named Papas can explain. Placed on scales, nothing can outweigh the stone unless it is covered with dirt, which signifies God's warning that all mortal creatures die. If the conqueror is simply content with his wealth and empire, then he will live free of anxiety, but if he continues his obsession with gain and glory, he will be oppressed unto death. Alexander has here a path to redemption, and just months before dying he takes up a virtuous life and instils in his officers "veritatis et honestatis atque liberalitatis studium" (the desire for truth, honesty, and generosity).[36]

Such a didactic response reflected the tendency to consider Alexander through moralizing reflections on the temporality of his career, and in Norman Italy, where the Jewish legends had significant influence, he was hardly received as an exemplary emperor. Besides the aforementioned anecdotes about his need to respect a monotheistic authority, his pride, and inability to enter a Judaeo-Christian paradise circulating in Hebrew, Greek, and Latin texts, he was also well known in southern Italy and Sicily by visual representations of the failed flight, first translated into Latin by Archbishop Leo. In the episode, a divine force casts down to earth Alexander and his craft led by griffins in his attempted exploration of the heavens, a failure so frequently cast in mosaics that it can justifiably be considered an icon of Alexander's career in the region.[37] The images in these mosaics imply a "sharp condemnation of Alexander's presumption to challenge God," but they also suggest the strained relationship between the Normans and their Byzantine neighbours, as Alexander is frequently represented as a Byzantine *basileus* apparently reaching the limits of his imperial authority and being cast down.[38] These mosaics have even been identified as tools of a programmatic ideology of the Normans' animosity towards the Byzantine Empire, particularly seen in the mosaic completed in Otranto in 1163–5. In this example, Alexander has been interpreted as figuring Manuel I Komnenos in decline, adjacent to an inscription praising the "magnificus et triumphans" William I.[39] Although Roger II had demanded that the Byzantine rulers call him by the title of *basileus*,[40] was crowned wearing a mantle similar to that of Manuel,[41] and relied on "the theocratic framework" of Byzantine imperialism,[42] William I's reign saw a backlash against this appropriation of Byzantine customs,[43] and Alexander's reputation, sullied by association, did not recover enough to make him as esteemed a courtly hero in southern Italy and Sicily as he would be elsewhere in Europe.

When Frederick II united his Staufen and Norman realms and promoted Latin over Greek, Jewish, and Arabic culture in the region, this reputation did not noticeably improve. In the thirteenth century, the redactor of the I^3 recension of the *Historia de preliis* instructs his readers to consider his version of the Latin romance in allegorical terms. Darius and Alexander, he writes, represent, respectively, the need to "superbie vitium abiciendum" (avoid the sin of pride) and "mundanas pompas penitus contempnendas" (utterly contemn worldly grandeur), and Alexander, "qui orbem universum obtinuit nec sibi a mortis impetus valuit precavere" (who won the entire world but was unable to protect himself against death), signifies the futility of pomp and imperial ambition.[44] Throughout the main narrative of the recension, Darius and Alexander encounter a divine force that evolves from pagan Fortune to a *deus* that sounds increasingly Judaeo-Christian, to the point that the epilogue of the I^3 includes a letter from the Jewish philosopher Mardocheus, who exhorts the conqueror to give up his militaristic agenda and consider his spiritual well-being. In 1236, Quilichino of Spoleto translated the I^3 into verse in his epic *Historia Alexandri Magni* yet contextualizes his protagonist's reign therein within the mutability and temporality of all earthly matters, contrasted with the eternal nature of God the creator. Quilichino concludes his work by transforming Alexander into an exemplum to support this lesson that the mightiest conqueror in the world was slain in a moment's notice by a poisoned glass of wine.[45]

Staufen Germany and Capetian France: From Latin to Vernacular Romance

Although the *Historia de preliis* recensions eventually followed Archbishop Leo's *Nativitas* into Staufen Germany and on to France and England, scribes and readers closer to the Atlantic had long known the Alexander legend through the other half of the Latin schema descending from the *Pseudo-Callisthenes*. In the ninth century, Julius Valerius's *Res gestae Alexandri Magni* was abbreviated by an unknown redactor into the so-called Valerius *Epitome*, and while the three recensions of the *Historia de preliis* were still being composed, this *Epitome* enjoyed widespread transmission throughout monastic scriptoria in England and France. Unlike the *Historia* recensions, which accumulated various episodes from Hebrew and Greek sources, the brief narrative of the *Epitome* remained largely unaltered, and it attracted two companion texts, the *Collatio cum Dindimo*, an epistolary debate between Alexander and the Brahman Dindimus, and the *Epistola Alexandri ad Aristotelem*, a letter from the conqueror to his tutor on the wonders of India. We can even establish the contact point of these texts: in 1024, a codex known as the Bamberg manuscript, copied by a Neopolitan scribe and brought to Germany, featuring Latin translations of four Greek Alexander narratives in all, the *Commonitorium Palladii* (an account of the Roman Thebeus, who crossed the river Ganges and met with the Brahmans), the *Collatio*, the *Epistola*, and a further commentary by Dindimus on the Macedonians.[46]

From Germany the *Collatio* and the *Epistola* were disseminated throughout France and England, often collated with the Valerius *Epitome*,[47] and together the three texts accounted for a convenient and comprehensive Latin narrative of the conqueror. The *Epitome* told of Nectanabus's affair with Olympias, Alexander's campaigns in Persia and India, and his death in Babylon, the *Collatio* examined his career in Christian, sermonizing terms, and the *Epistola* offered the definitive aspect of Alexander as a legendary hero, his series of adventures among the exotic peoples and landscapes of uncharted India. As a narrative that contrasted Alexander's belligerence with the Brahmans' asceticism, the *Collatio* complemented the moralizing attitudes cited above. Like the bearer of the Wonderstone and the Jewish elder who interprets it in the *Iter ad paradisum*, Dindimus criticizes Alexander for his obsession with wealth and power, the material and vain aspects of earthly life that detract from spiritual contemplation. "Nos," the Brahman writes the conqueror:

> non sumus incolae huius mundi, sed advenae, nec ita in orbem terrarum venimus, ut in eo libeat consistere, sed transire. Properamus enim ad Larem patrium nullis delictorum ponderibus degravati nec in aliquibus illecebrarum tabernaculis commorantes nec flagitiorum cauponibus obligati.[48]

> We are not inhabitants of this world, but strangers, and we come into the world not to take pleasure in staying here but to pass through it. We hasten to the underworld of our ancestors burdened with no weight of delights, we do not delay in any taverns of alluring women, and we are not ensared by those selling enticements.

The Brahmans are no less ascetic and live no less harmoniously with nature than the inhabitants of other paradises whom Alexander encounters, and as is typically the result, the conqueror finds that he cannot conform with such a radically different lifestyle than his own. The *Collatio* thus situates Alexander within the classical literary tradition of a "confrontation between virtuous Eastern peoples and an ambassador of Western values"[49] – not necessarily the intent of Julius Valerius or the earliest Latin romances of Alexander's journey east[50] – while its companion "Indian" narrative, the *Epistola Alexandri ad Aristotelem*, appealed to the widespread medieval interest in wonders of the eastern world.

Although largely a tale of hardships and marvels encountered in the wilds of India, the *Epistola* concludes in a suggestively deflating manner, especially for medieval readers familiar with the moral didacticism of the *Collatio cum Dindimo* and the *Iter ad paradisum*. Having visited a sacred grove, wherein the so-called trees of the sun and the moon foretell that he will conquer the world but die before he can return home, Alexander becomes determined to surpass the deeds of two other Greek adventurers in India, Dionysius and Hercules. He explains to Aristotle that in the outer reaches of the region, he has his men erect two, twenty-five-foot golden pillars inscribed with his deeds and then an additional five, even taller pillars. The point of the latter is purely bombastic:

quae miraculo futura sunt, carissime praeceptor, posteris saeculis non parvo. Novum perpetuumque statuimus virtutibus monimentum invidendum, ut immortalitas esset perpetua et nobis opinio et animi industriae, optime Aristoteles, indicium.[51]

These will be a wonder, and no little one, my dearest teacher, for future generations. We erected them as a novel, eternal, and enviable monument to our strength, so that we might have a perpetual reputation for immortality and evidence of our spirit of industry, dear Aristotle.

Not unlike the Valerius *Epitome*, which reminds the reader how many Alexandrias the conqueror established in its final lines, the notion of a physical memorial preserving Alexander's reputation in perpetuity is hardly convincing. In these Latin texts so widespread in Atlantic Europe, the dichotomy between admiration for Alexander's accomplishments and his failure to transcend such base concerns as ambition, materialism, and hubris is already apparent. Which of these aspects to privilege in approaching the story of Alexander was a fundamental question for any medieval audience to resolve, and one that would dictate his romance reputation from Staufen Germany to Capetian France and ultimately Angevin England.

Vernacular Alexander romance began in the Kingdom of Burgundy within the Staufen Empire, where in the vanguard of the genre Albéric of Besançon embellished his Latin sources, deriving from the *Pseudo-Callisthenes*, and changed the trajectory of Alexander's medieval reception.[52] Although just over a hundred lines is all that survives of Albéric's narrative, preserved in Florence, Biblioteca Laurenziana, Plut. lxiv 35, fols 115v–16r, it was translated by a German poet named Lamprecht not long after the composition of the French original. Together, these two individuals, about whom little is known, established Germany and France at the vanguard of vernacular Alexander romance, while legends of the conqueror in southern Italy and Sicily still circulated in Latin, Greek, and Hebrew texts. In so doing, Albéric and Lamprecht also established Alexander as a suitable hero for courtly romance. In the late twelfth or early thirteenth century, the so-called *Strasbourg Alexander* romance, the second extant version of Lamprecht's Alexander epic, drew from the *Historia de preliis*, the *Epistola Alexandri ad Aristotelem*, and the *Iter ad paradisum* to present a novel version of Alexander's eastern expedition.[53] Rather than a journey marred by his inability to access forbidden sacred lands and his assassination in Babylon, it becomes one of penance and salvation when Alexander heeds the advice of the Jewish philosopher Papas in the *Iter*, for in ceasing his campaigns to expand his empire, he unexpectedly takes up a life of moral culpability. The *Strasbourg Alexander* is thereby translated into a tale of a hero who rejects the self-interest of his expansionist agenda and "in becoming *rex iustus et pacificus*, he realized the ideal of the Staufen and of Barbarossa in particular."[54] The reconception of Alexander as a pacifist ruler did not end there. By the late twelfth century the conqueror had become a political as well as spiritual model for the Staufen emperors, under whose reigns the idea that Alexander was the first global ruler to accept the Judaeo-Christian God played a significant role in his romance reception.[55]

Forgiveness of Alexander's martial, arrogant behaviour, much less an appropriation of him as a holy warrior, would have been inconceivable in many parts of Europe before the twelfth century. Admiration for Alexander had long before influenced Christian writers throughout Asia and Africa, but their views conflicted with patristic and monastic writers in the Latin West, where romances of his career flourished.[56] Latin Christian writers long considered Alexander the embodiment of pagan immorality, whether from the Orosian perspective of the conqueror as a bloodthirsty tyrant or from that of Christian moralists, who condemned Alexander's ambition and insisted on the exemplum that for all that he accomplished, his life ended in an instant.[57] When Jewish and Near Eastern Christian legends of Alexander made their way west of Italy to influence romances in northern and Atlantic Europe, these were the attitudes with which they clashed. While the former related his acceptance of the Judaeo-Christian God's authority and suggested God's protection of Alexander as an instrument against evil forces, the latter cast him as a pagan ruler incompatible with the tenets of Christianity. Travelling to Germany and France from Italy, the apocryphal stories of his visit to Jerusalem, his battle against Gog and Magog, and his journey to the earthly paradise in particular fostered Alexander's representation as a pagan conqueror who accepted a monotheistic divinity suitable for Christian audiences, a reception that was welcomed by romance writers and their audiences yet conflicted with the traditional sacred criticism of the belligerent conqueror.

As Albéric's original romance circulated across France, it was to help lead this counter-tradition to the traditional Christian stance against Alexander in western Europe, as had Lamprecht's translation of it in Germany. After Albéric's pioneering narrative in the early part of the twelfth century, French Alexander romances flourished until the reign of Philip Augustus in the 1180s, when Alexandre de Paris wrote the *Roman d'Alexandre*, the composite version of the four branches of Alexander narratives (so delineated by Paul Meyer):[58] the first covering from Alexander's birth to the siege of Tyre, the second centring on Alexander's campaign in Gaza, the third from the war against the Persians to the treason of Antipater, who plotted to poison Alexander, and the fourth the death of Alexander and his last will and testament.[59] Collectively, they constitute a textual tradition that Keith Busby calls "frankly, a mess."[60] The actual surviving twelfth-century texts do not quite adhere to so neat a categorization but reflect unique interests in various aspects of the conqueror's legend. We know on account of Lamprecht's translation that Albéric's narrative extended from Alexander's birth to his Persian campaign, the *Alexandre décasyllabique* from Alexander's birth to his battle against one King Nicholas, who attempts to invade the burgeoning Macedonian Empire, and Lambert le Tort's *Alexandre en orient* relates his eastern adventures recorded in the *Epistola Alexandri ad Aristotelem*.[61] Two other works are dated to the 1170s, the *Fuerre de Gadres* (a romance of a foray into Gaza) and the *Mort Alixandre*, of which only eight stanzas survive.[62] The *Alexandre décasyllabique, Alexandre en orient*, and the *Mort Alixandre* were incorporated into the so-called "archetype" *Roman d'Alexandre*, but its original form and date of composition are unknown.[63] Finally, Alexandre de Paris adapted his *Roman d'Alexandre* ca. 1185.

Despite what some have argued as an overall conflicting conception of Alexander in medieval French literature,[64] twelfth-century writers crafted him into an idealized warrior-king enjoying a harmonious relationship with his baronage, celebrated for his bravery and largesse, and a dashing adventurer of the East,[65] and by the 1180s Alexander emerged from the four branches of the French tradition as the paragon of chivalry increasingly removed from the controversies of classical histories and reflective of the values of courtly audiences.[66] More than the Alexander romances developed under the Staufen, Norman, and Angevin rulers; those written across the twelfth century in Capetian lands are largely responsible for our modern assumption that medieval romances unilaterally praised the conqueror.[67] Like their counterparts elsewhere in Europe, however, writers of French romances manipulated their Latin sources to serve their own agenda, reflective of the tastes of their audiences and the political landscape of Capetian society. From Albéric to Alexandre de Paris, these poets maintained a trifold agenda: 1) to refute the story of Nectanabus,[68] 2) to promote Alexander as the model of chivalrous kingship,[69] and 3) to gloss over the Macedonian civil wars in favour of presenting Alexander's death only as a tragedy bemoaned by his surviving barons rather than a *casus belli*.

The Nectanabus story began with the Greek *Pseudo-Callisthenes*, likely composed in Alexandria, and the seeming attempt of its author to unite the myths of two local rulers, Nectanabus III, the last native pharaoh of Egypt, and Alexander, proclaimed a pharaoh in 332 BC. As a sorcerer in the Greek apocryphal text, Nectanabus flees Egypt in the face of foreign invasion and arrives in Macedon, where he impregnates Alexander's mother Olympias and thus gave rise to the legend that the child of two nations would one day return to Egypt to avenge his people.[70] Although the Nectanabus story is the definitive aspect of Graeco-Latin Alexander legends that disseminated from the Mediterranean into Europe, Africa, and Asia, it was evidently too damning for writers of French romance, who insisted on the ideal of a harmonious and highly successful relationship between the king and his baronage and thus created a narrative that appealed to royalist and baronial audiences equally.[71] The suggestion that Alexander was the bastard son of a conniving sorcerer threatened this paradigmatic status, and French writers were keen to deny the rumour.

Albéric begins the stance against this legend by relating that while some "estrabatours" (slanderers) claim that Alexander was fathered by Nectanabus, he simply believes otherwise.[72] To counter this rumour, he argues that as a child, Alexander killed Nectanabus, assigned to serve as one of the prince's tutors, because of the aforementioned slander involving Olympias, and since the celebrated boy cannot be presumed guilty of patricide, Nectanabus cannot be presumed his father.[73] The *Alexandre décasyllabique* follows Albéric's interpretation of Alexander's murder of Nectanabus, as do the manuscripts that attest to the "archetype" *Roman d'Alexandre*:

Quant li .vii. maistre l'orent apris forment,
Un en i ot de greignor escïent,
Sur toz les autres sot cil d'enchantement;
Neptenabus ot nom par escïent.
Per lo reiaune o disoient la gent
Que Al'x. ert sis filz voirement;
Plusor o distrent, mai[s] je n'en croi nïent,
Car pois l'ocist mout engososement,
Desor un mur l'enpeint el fondement,
Pois l'en pesa, si'n ot le cuer dolent.[74]

After the seven masters had been appointed, one of them possessed an especially formidable knowledge, beyond the others, of sorcery. His name was Neptanabus. Throughout the kingdom people said that Alexander was indeed his son – many said it, but I don't believe it at all, for when Alexander killed him and pushed him from a wall into a pit, he would have been upset about it, if his heart were grieving.

The notion that Nectanabus was a teacher of Alexander had circulated since the *Pseudo-Callisthenes* as well, and in the Latin romances that derived from the Greek original, his care for his son leads to the sorcerer's demise. Knowing the boy's future stature and glory, Nectanabus takes pains to assist in Alexander's education, notably in the field of astronomy, but during a lesson, according to the Valerius *Epitome*, Alexander shoves Nectanabus into a pit, and the sorcerer laments:

"Nulli," inquit, "mortalium contra fatum fuga permissa est." Et Alexander: "Cur ista?" inquit. Respondit magus: "Olim quippe per hanc scientiam cognovi, me a filio interfectum iri." Et Alexander ait: "Num ego sum filius tuus?" Ita esse confitetur, tum Aegypti fugam, tum ingressum ad Olympiadem, et quanam arte uxore sit potitus ad similitudinem dei. Et his dictis animam exaestuat. Hinc Alexander comperto quod pater sibi fuerit quem interfecerat, naturali monitus affectu superponit hominem humeris, regiamque revectat.[75]

"No mortal is permitted to escape his fate." Alexander asked, "Why do you say this?" The sorcerer responded, "Because I learned once, through my knowledge [of sorcery], that I would be killed by my son." Alexander asked, "Am I your son, then?" Nectanabus confessed that it was so, that he had fled Egypt, encountered Olympias and, by his art and in the likeness of a god, had known her as a wife. After he spoke these words, he breathed his last. Thereafter Alexander was certain that the man whom he had killed was his father, and moved by a filial piety, he placed [Nectanabus] upon his shoulders and carried him back to the palace.

Albéric and those who followed him dispute the outcome of this scene, when Alexander, touched by the "naturalis affectus" above, carries Nectanabus to Olympias, demands to know whether the man was his father, and buries him when he learns that the sorcerer indeed spoke the truth. By the time of Alexandre de Paris's composite *Roman d'Alexandre*, the sorcerer does not even merit a lengthy role in the narrative, much less a final conversation with the boy who is purportedly his son. In a single stanza in this version, the author mentions that Nectanabus arrived in Macedon, served as Alexander's tutor, was the subject of paternity rumours that created a scandal for the boy ("de lui fu Alixandres mescreüs et blasmez, / Pour ce que de sa mere et de lui ert privez; / Dïent qu'il ert ses fuiz et de lui engendrez"), and is unceremoniously thrown from a tower by Alexander.[76]

Dismissing the story of Nectanabus's paternity as a rumour perpetuated by the conqueror's detractors became emblematic of the regional brand of Alexander romance among Continental French writers. Unlike Thomas of Kent, whose inclusion of the Nectanabus episode (wherein the sorcerer impregnates Olympias and confesses his scheme to Alexander just before dying at his son's hands) conforms to Anglo-Norman romances of illegitimate protagonists who must overcome their inauspicious beginnings,[77] Alexandre de Paris and his predecessors deny this "tâche infamante" and emphasize instead the conqueror's unsullied reputation.[78] As the paragon of kingship, the French Alexander is characterized neither by the story of his disreputable conception nor by the disastrous end of his reign, as I discuss below. He is rather known for what he accomplishes during that reign, both the military victories throughout the Near and Middle East and his adventures and expeditions into India as well.

The centrality of Alexander's accomplishments, rather than his ignoble beginning or the civil war that his death inspired, thus bolsters the Continental French portrayal of him. In Martin Gosman's assessment, the result is an "aggressive, expansionist ruler who succeeds in realising his policy thanks to his vassals' unconditional loyalty," a loyalty that the conqueror must earn and maintain if he is to realize his ambitious military agenda.[79] To the symbiotic relationship commensurate with Capetian feudal politics, reflected in the show of equality between the Macedonian barons and Alexander, *primus inter paribus* and working in harmony with his men appealed to local magnates, Gosman contrasts the Angevin feudal relationship, wherein Henry II's authority was pervasive and unquestioned, as a means of delineating the two political receptions of the conqueror.[80] Such feudal harmony may also explain Alexandre de Paris's lack of political interest in the assassination of the conqueror and the end of his empire, another crucial difference between Capetian and Angevin treatments of Alexander romance in the twelfth century.[81] Before the composite *Roman d'Alexandre* in the 1180s, only one surviving French romance addresses Alexander's death, the *Mort*

Alixandre, which hints at the discord that follows the conqueror's assassination through a well-known prophecy from the Valerius *Epitome*. In the French romance, soon before Alexander is poisoned in Babylon, a woman gives birth to a half-bestial child, and when the conqueror summons a diviner to interpret the marvel, he is told that the top half represents his imminent death, while the bottom represents those whom he will leave behind, his successors, or "douze peers": a lion, a leopard, a bear, a dragon, and a wolf, all of which will fight for sovereignty, in a grim prophecy of civil war that causes considerable sorrow for Alexander.[82] The poem is not extant beyond this passage, but the treatment of Alexander's survivors in the next two French romances suggests that there was no sustained concern for exploring the violence foretold above. In both Alexandre de Paris's composite *Roman d'Alexandre* and the Arsenal manuscript of the "archetype" *Roman d'Alexandre* (early thirteenth century), the successors debate where to bury their fallen leader but maintain peace until the oracle of Jupiter instructs them to bury Alexander in Alexandria, where they erect a lavish pyramid as a monument to his conquests.[83]

Continental French romances of the conqueror may generally gloss over the war that breaks out among his successors as they contend for a larger share of the empire than he bequeaths them, but two texts of the 1180s and perhaps 1190s recount violence of a different sort among Alexander's survivors. Gui de Cambrai's *Le Vengement Alixandre* tells of the mourning and outrage among Alexander's barons that soon unites them against Antipater and Divinuspater, the conspirators behind his poisoning in Babylon. In the battle that ensues, Alexander's brother captures Antipater, the two villains are then given over to Ptolemy, and the barons burn and dismember those who fought for them.[84] The second "vengeance" text, Jehan le Nevelon's *La Venjance Alixandre*, likely written for Henry, the Count of Champagne,[85] features a more inventive narrative involving the love child of Alexander and Candace. When the boy, Alior, is fifteen, he learns the true identity of his father and vows to avenge his murder. After he and Candace unite the barons and restore the bonds broken by civil war, they wage war against Antipater and his army. Jehan is concerned with generational issues more than Gui, and over three battles the narrative focuses on Alior and Antipater's son Florent until the former's men capture the traitors' stronghold and secure victory. As did Gui, Jehan elaborates on the punishments that the barons dole out on those who fought for Antipater, and the narrative ends with mass torture and execution.[86]

The valorization of Alexander by French writers in the late twelfth century was not limited to romance, and under Philip Augustus, the Macedonian became a paradigmatic emperor rather than a mere feudal king. In his epic *Alexandreis*, written for the king's uncle, the Archbishop of Reims, around the same time as Alexandre de Paris compiled his *Roman d'Alexandre*, Walter of Châtillon creates a version of Alexander elevated beyond that in contemporary romances.[87] Over ten books based primarily on Curtius Rufus's *Historia Alexandri*, Walter surveys his protagonist's tutelage under Aristotle and campaigns into Persia and beyond, but he does so not to relate how the magnanimous king and his loyal barons defeat admirable, but decidedly inferior eastern foes, but to insist on Alexander's status as a global conqueror. So successful is he in surpassing the boundaries of mortal man in his transcontinental military campaigns and expeditions into uncharted lands that he draws the ire of the goddess Nature, angry over the revelation of so many of her secrets and determined to cut short Alexander's reign. What served romance writers so well, Alexander's encounters with marvels and monsters in India, becomes for Walter cause for the conqueror's downfall, founded in Christianized, epic machinery. Without gods and goddesses on the battlefield or willingly wreaking havoc on human affairs, in the manner of Homer's Poseidon or Virgil's Juno, Alexander is undone by a divinity symbolic of his ambition. Never satisfied with the limits of his empire and the insufficiency of the lands under his dominion, he finds that the presiding goddess of the natural world is a far greater enemy than any rival ruler's army. Angry that the conqueror has discovered too many secrets of the previously unknown lands of the East and declared the world too small for his ambitions, Nature colludes with Leviathan to hold a council in the underworld to devise proper punishment, the infamous poison that Antipater will have slipped into Alexander's wine.

Walter's intentions in writing either a celebratory epic for a figure long lionized in French romance or what has been termed a "cautionary *exemplum*" are certainly debatable.[88] Contextualizing the *Alexandreis* within the twelfth-century crusading spirit, David Townsend sees in Walter's portrayal of the conqueror a hopeful image of the "bearer of the West's dream of mastery" in the Near and Middle East, effectively a fantasy for a western European audience frustrated with their ability to dominate the Muslim world,[89] and David Ashurst claims that for all of Walter's talk of ambition and provoking Fortune, "admiration for Alexander's sheer splendour and dash ... is the motive force behind the writing of the *Alexandreis*."[90] Walter himself invites both historical and contemporary comparisons with Alexander in a passage that makes it difficult to interpret his admiration for the conqueror as disingenuous:

if you recall with what a meager host
the Macedonian approached such deeds,
in flower of tender youth, against world conquerors,
and in how brief a time the whole world lay
before the knees of Alexander ...
If pious prayers and tearful lamentation
moved mercy from on high to grant the Franks
a king like this, the True Faith would shine forth
unhindered through the earth, and Parthia,
broken by our arms, would beg unbidden
for baptism's renewal, while high Carthage,
which long lay ruined, soon would rise again
at mention of Christ's name.[91]

The fantasy of using Alexander as model for contemporary Crusaders is obvious, but in Walter's primary source, Curtius Rufus's *Historia Alexandri Magni*, the entrance into Babylon signals more than Alexander's establishing his authority over the Persias. The conqueror's time in the city also begins his moral decline into the sort of luxuriousness that Imperial Roman writers associated with the East, and although not as vociferous in his attacks on Alexander as in Justin in the *Philippic Histories*, Curtius Rufus still expresses disappointment over the drunken and licentious behaviour which Walter rather laments than criticizes.[92] This is an admittedly odd moment for Walter to be so effusive with his praise that he longs for a king in France of Alexander's stature, particularly if we understand the conqueror's moral lapse in Babylon as his failure to uphold Aristotle's instruction on virtuous education provided in the epic's first book.[93] Moreover, the occupation of Babylon and the conquest of Persia traditionally mark a crucial turning point in the narratives of both romances and histories, including that of Curtius Rufus. After his victory over the Persians, Alexander begins a series of self-aggrandizing campaigns and expeditions intended not to subdue those inimical to Macedon but to satisfy his seemingly endless ambition.

For the vulgate histories written in Imperial Rome, this altered agenda represents his despotic behaviour, but within the romance tradition the conqueror's ambition invites the moral didacticism seen especially in the Hebrew and Latin texts popular in Norman Italy. Alexander's inability to enter paradise, his thwarted attempt at flight, and the episode of the wonder stone (symbolizing mortality) were appropriated into romances throughout Europe, even if they were not used so explicitly for sermonizing as they had been in Italy. Drawing on the flight scene, for example, Alexandre de Paris may suggest his protagonist's ambition to the point of thinking himself a god before his death in Babylon,[94] but, if so, he does not leave his audience wondering if they might receive Alexander as anything less than heroic. In the *Alexandreis*, Walter seemingly encourages such doubt. His Alexander provokes Nature's wrath, after all, with his ambition, a flaw that the poet chides in his final book ("madman, your works are naught. Though you enclose / all kingdoms in one empire and subdue / the entire world, a pauper you remain").[95] Walter's concluding remarks are even dismissive of his protagonist's accomplishments: for all of his earthly glory, "five feet of carved stone / sufficed for his abode in tunnelled earth, / for whom the world held insufficient space,"[96] a commonplace epitaph for Alexander in the twelfth century and one which Alan of Lille appropriated for Henry II.[97] As Maura K. Lafferty argues, it is easy to receive Walter's Alexander "as a warning against vice, a sinner punished for his hubris and ambition for temporal ambition," although the epitaph simply underscores the conqueror's mortality, not his morality or lack thereof.[98]

Still, the reception of the *Alexandreis* among its intended audience suggests a concern only for a heroic view of Alexander therein. Walter established the exemplum for a group of poets "who wished to lend an air of profane dignity to their panegyrics of rulers" by seeking models in classical texts rather than joining the ranks of contemporary romances.[99] These writers particularly celebrated Philip Augustus, featured in his own epic, the *Philippidos* by Guillaume le Breton, and promoted Alexander as a model ruler for their king second only to Charlemagne.[100] Even when Jean Bodel reasserted Charlemagne as the paragon of French royal virtue at the turn of the thirteenth century and steered classically themed romance away from Alexander towards the Matter of Rome to complement those of Britain and France,[101] the Macedonian conqueror's political relevance did not wane to the point of extinction. With the rise of Old French prose histories under Philip Augustus, Alexander was neither less popular nor any less exemplary.[102]

Such politicizing of the Alexander legend was inevitable. As the ancient world's most famed and controversial conqueror, he offered a versatile paradigm, cautionary or aspirational, and a widely recognized ancient figure applicable to contemporary notions of political leadership for medieval Europe's dynasties. In Staufen Germany Alexander was every bit the exemplary ruler that he was in Capetian France, yet in Norman Italy his association with the Byzantines and the moralizing treatment of his career in Jewish legends may explain his less than admirable reputation there. In France, by contrast, Alexander's heroic status flourished even as animosity towards the Byzantines surged from the Norman siege of Antioch around the turn of the twelfth century to the fall of Constantine in 1204 during the Fourth Crusades, and he remained a decidedly foreign, yet admirable, hero.[103] How, then, did political contexts affect Alexander's reputation in Angevin England? There is no evidence that his ethnicity played a role in his reception among Anglo-Norman writers and audiences in England or France, but his imperialism was surely problematic. The Staufen emperors, for example, were the object of scorn from the Angevins and the Capetians, who criticized their bombastic, imperial show of power and distrusted their political intentions. Western monarchs feared that Frederick I sought transcontinental conquest,[104] and Henry II, in particular, expressed hostility towards him, no doubt spurred on by Frederick's self-identification as "Divus Augustus" and the kings of Europe as mere "reges provinciales."[105] The *Ludus de Antichristo*, a propagandistic text written in the Staufen court in the 1160s, exemplifies the diverging perspectives on the empire, as in Germany it was thought to reflect an emperor "whose *clementia*, *honor*, and *imperium* are a reflection of the divine majesty,"[106] while in England and France Frederick's representation therein signalled his expansionist agenda, a portrayal that would culminate in the 1180s in a supposed letter from Frederick I to the Saladin in which he expresses his desire to conquer the Near and Middle East.[107] His successor, Henry VI, hoped to expand Staufen *imperium* on two fronts, both to Angevin England and down to Sicily, from where he could invade Byzantium,[108] and western European animosity towards the Staufen was exacerbated under Frederick II, whose association with Muslims was a constant source of anxiety[109] and who inspired writers within and beyond his empire to portray him as the Antichrist.[110]

In Norman Italy, however, Roger II and his successors avoided this sort of criticism from the dynasties in Atlantic Europe, owing to an Angevin fascination and growing solidarity with the Mediterranean Normans. Besides the cultural bond strengthened by French as the lingua franca of both the Anglo-Normans and the descendants of Robert Guiscard and Roger I,[111] the deeds of the Normans in Italy found favour with audiences of romances in England. As Peter Noble argues, the Norman conquest of southern Italy and Sicily, their armed hostility against the Byzantines, and the marriage of Henry II's daughter Joan with William II "all made the names of these lands familiar, although they were ... seen as faraway and exotic, which clearly appealed to the audiences of the second half of the twelfth century."[112] That same appreciation for the exotic naturally helped to account for the genesis of Alexander romances in this century, but the affinity that Anglo-Norman writers and audiences felt for the Normans in Italy also helps to contextualize Alexander's reception in England. The aforementioned network of monasteries that connected Angevin England and France with Norman southern Italy and Sicily may explain why historians (and later romance writers) in England were so persistent in their emphasis of the warnings inherent in Alexander's ambition and the collapse of his empire. A moralistic approach to the conqueror, the legacy of Jewish treatments of his legend, is the defining aspect of his reception in Norman Italy and reflective, too, of attitudes that are initially apparent in Anglo-Norman England and later blossomed in the fourteenth century. This assessment of Alexander's legacy is particularly seen, for example, in the latest surviving manuscript of the *Roman de toute chevalerie*, whose scribe and reader saw Thomas of Kent's text as a vehicle through which they could articulate their own conception of Alexander and interest in these episodes originally from the Mediterranean.

Chapter Two

Alexander in Anglo-Norman England: The Latin Texts

Before the Conquest, several perspectives on Alexander circulated in Anglo-Saxon England, including the Latin vulgate histories, the most popular Latin recensions of the *Pseudo-Callisthenes* and companion narratives of Alexander's adventures in the East (notably the Valerius *Epitome,* Alexander's supposed letter to Aristotle, and his correspondence with Dindimus), wonder tales, and ecclesiastical literature. Judging by the surviving evidence, the most common Roman-era histories of the conqueror and his empire were Orosius's *Historiae adversum paganos* and Justin's epitome of the *Philippic Histories,* preserved in monastic libraries across the Continent,[1] although in Anglo-Saxon literature he was also known as an explorer of the East and monster slayer.[2] Between 1066 and the mid-twelfth century, however, two Anglo-Latin texts suggest a pointed, critical reading of these often conflicting sources.

The first, the *Parva recapitulatio de eodem Alexandro et de suis,* the oldest manuscript of which is the late-eleventh-century British Library, MS Royal 13. A. i, is an Anglo-Latin addendum that relies on Orosius's universal history to supplement and correct two primary oversights in the texts of the *Pseudo-Callisthenes* family that were circulating widely in Europe: 1) Alexander was the son not of the Egyptian sorcerer Nectanabus but of Philip of Macedon, and 2) after the conqueror's death (which concludes the Valerius *Epitome,* well known in England), his successors did not merely bury his corpse and lament his passing but turned their arms against each other in a violent civil war.[3] The next surviving attempt to present a broad history of Macedon, again with an emphasis on this civil war among Alexander's successors, is the so-called *St Albans Compilation,* a compendium of classical and late antique sources on the Macedonian Empire. Likely produced during the Anarchy of Stephen's reign, the *Compilation* explores the multigenerational intrigue among the Macedonians, beginning with Alexander's grandparents, continuing with his parents and his own depravity, and culminating with the animosity of his generals in the final two of its five books by relying on Justin's epitome of the *Philippic Histories*, an account of Macedonian vice, self-destruction, and the anarchy that followed Alexander's death.

The Alexander that emerged in England through these two texts was thus founded on Roman *auctoritas*, the authority granted by two sources in particular, Justin's epitome of the *Philippic Histories* and Orosius's *Historiae adversum paganos*, that offered expansive histories of Macedon and an altogether different portrait of Alexander than the heroic version seen in those narratives informed by the *Pseudo-Callisthenes*. The result was twofold. Alexander's worst vices, including his drunken violence, insistence on promoting himself as a god, and his degradation as an "eastern" tyrant from the Roman perspective, suddenly came to light in the historiography of monastic, particularly Benedictine, scribes and chroniclers, clerics, and scholastic philosophers and historians.[4] Twelfth-century writers also came to understand as the causes behind the Macedonian Empire's collapse not simply Alexander's death in Babylon in 323 BC, but the behaviour of his successors as well, as their failure to install a new leader peacefully and their haste to fight for individual power destroyed Alexander's realm in the flames of civil war. While the *Pseudo-Callisthenes* and its recensions had emphasized the glory and the tragedy of Alexander's career, these twelfth-century Anglo-Latin compendia recovered through the *Philippic Histories* and Orosius's universal history a wider, more critical view of Alexander and his empire. No longer was his life, however extraordinary, the sole focus of those interested in ancient Macedon, for in the view of certain Anglo-Latin writers, the establishment of the Macedonian Empire through political machinations and assassinations well before Alexander and the immediate, drastic civil war in the wake of his death in Babylon were made equally important to his historical reception. The empire that Alexander impressively expanded across three continents had shockingly collapsed, because its greatest ruler could not arrange a peaceful succession and because of the greed and ambition of his survivors.

Alexander texts, both the *Philippic Histories* and the Valerius *Epitome*, the most common of the narratives inspired by the *Pseudo-Callisthenes* in Atlantic Europe, were "part of the complement of histories that it was desirable to have" in Norman monasteries at the time, alongside the *Gesta Normannorum ducum*, Paul the Deacon's *Historia Romana*, William of Malmesbury's *Gesta regum Anglorum*, the *Liber pontificalis*, and the *Pseudo-Turpin Chronicle*,[5] but a specific agenda in historical investigation is apparent in the century or so from the composition of the *Parva recapitulatio* to the *terminus a quo* for the *Roman de toute chevalerie*. Anglo-Latin writers surely relied on first Orosius and then the *Philippic Histories* to create a more comprehensive history of the Macedonian Empire than that found in the narratives that would soon inspire vernacular romances, the Valerius *Epitome* and the texts often copied alongside it in manuscripts of the time. The Valerius *Epitome*, in particular, reads as a concise biography focused on the childhood, brief reign, and poisoning of Alexander and so neglects how the conqueror might fit into the larger construct of the history of his people and empire. Orosius and the *Philippic Histories* offered, on the other hand, extensive, highly critical studies of the origins and decline of this empire, and in turning to these source-texts, Anglo-Latin writers compiled a version of Macedonian history that emphasized the egotism, vices, and self-destructive behaviour of Alexander and his successors, who destroyed the empire in civil war. This account of Macedon as a fractured state, owing to internal strife and the ambitions of its rulers and usurpers, resonates with the themes of twelfth-century histories and chronicles of the Normans and Angevins, and while I do not necessarily argue that Anglo-Latin writers sought to compare Macedonian history to events closer to their own time, I maintain that these writers were not coincidentally drawn to their classical sources. Orosius and the *Philippic Histories* both offered a rather dire account of Alexander and his empire, and their themes of ambition, treachery, and political collapse may very well have appealed to those writing histories and chronicles of England at the time and aligned with their interests in political division and the events that threaten political bodies.

The *Parva recapitulatio*

The earliest surviving Anglo-Latin text to redirect Alexander's reception from the influence of the *Pseudo-Callisthenes* to this grim assessment of the Macedonian Empire is the late-eleventh-century *Parva recapitulatio*, which survives in seven manuscripts as an addendum to the very narrative that it seeks to amend, the Valerius *Epitome*.[6] Like Albéric and the French writers whom he would inspire in the subsequent century, the *Parva recapitulatio*-redactor considers the Nectanabus story (that he flees an incoming invasion of Egypt, arrives in Macedon, and uses sorcery to seduce Olympias and sire Alexander) to be the primary misconception of the conqueror's life within the romance tradition. However, whereas the Continental writers reject the story because it slanders an otherwise idealized hero, the Anglo-Latin redactor does so in order to conform with the account of Macedon in his patristic source, Orosius's *Historia adversum paganos*, identified by the term "true history" below:

> Hic Alexander secundum ueram hystoriam Philippi et Olimpiadis fuit filius Aristotelis philosophi et Nectanebi phisici discipulus cuius etiam falso creditus est filius propter familiaritatem nimiam quam filii karissimi gratia habebat Olimpias ad ipsum Nectanebum et propter studii precipuam diligentiam quam Nectanebus exercuerat in Alexandro matris sue pio instinctu. Unde etiam sicut fertur hic idem Nectanebus animositate adolescentis discipuli interiit dum quadam uice equo asperius discipline intuitu in eum exarsisset. Philippus itaque Alexandri pater filius habebatur Amin et Olimpias mater eiusdem soror erat Alexandri Epyrotarum regis.[7]

> According to true history, this Alexander was the son of Philip and Olympias, and he was the student of the philosopher Aristotle and the scientist Nectanabus. He was falsely believed to have been the son of the latter, on account of the excessive familiarity between him and Olympias for the sake of her dearest son, as well as the extraordinary diligence in studies that Nectanabus demanded of Alexander, who was motivated by his devotion to his mother. Hence it was also said that this Nectanabus was killed because of his young student's animosity, for on a certain occasion the teacher had railed against him with a look more vehement than that merited in teaching. Philip, Alexander's father, was recognized as the son of Amyntas, and Olympias, his mother, was the sister of Alexander, king of the Epirotans.

Besides the implication that the Valerius *Epitome* does not merit consideration as a *vera historia*, this passage spins the relationship between Alexander and his sorcerer-tutor in an unusual manner. The redactor does not explicitly exonerate Olympias from her role in the possible affair (surely "propter familiaritatem nimiam" hints at a sexual relationship), and he paints Alexander as a tempestuous child so unwilling to face criticism that he murders his teacher. Orosius's account of Alexander expounds on the conqueror's unpredictable temper, drunken paranoia, and self-destructive egomania, so the cause for Alexander's violence against Nectanabus in the *Parva recapitulatio* is explicable. So, too, is his suggestion of Olympias's involvement with the sorcerer, for Alexander's mother is never free of scandal in the classical tradition.[8] A more difficult question to answer is that of scribal intention. That all of the copies the *Parva recapitulatio* are written in codices following upon the Valerius *Epitome*, the *Collatio cum Dindimo*, and the *Epistola Alexandri ad Aristotelem* tells us that it was seen as a companion text, if not part of a self-contained Anglo-Latin corpus of Alexandriana, for the standard Latin texts read in Atlantic Europe. If one were to read the Valerius *Epitome* and its wholly positive portrayal of its subject we might suppose the redactor and the scribes of his work to presume, then one ought to know a little of what a Christian historiographer thought of the conqueror as well. Orosius offers a broader survey of Alexander's empire, even as he undercuts the heroic reception of Alexander in the Valerius *Epitome*. Moreover, the classification of *vera historia* and what the redactor must have considered untruthful history implies a reaction against the Valerius *Epitome* and its companion texts that circulated in eleventh-century England but would soon expand their influence exponentially among both the Normans in Mediterranean and Atlantic Europe in the twelfth century. While Thomas of Kent relied on the Valerius *Epitome* as his primary source, the same motivation as that of the *Parva recapitulatio*-redactor is apparent in the *Roman de toute chevalerie* as well. Like the redactor of the Anglo-Latin text, Thomas does not exonerate Olympias from sexual intrigue in the Nectanabus story, and even though he retains this scandalous story in his narrative (likely to appeal to an Insular audience for romance, as I discuss below), he, too, is keenly aware of the discrepancies and boundaries of credibility among true and fanciful histories.

The *Parva recapitulatio* also established a long Insular interest in the fate of post-Alexandrian Macedon, a fate that I believe monastic and clerical historiographers recognized as ominously reflective of the first period of political strife over succession in Anglo-Norman England, that following the death of William I and the sort of fears for the kingdom as retold by Orderic Vitalis below. The redactor begins his survey of this tumultuous period in Macedonian history, for example, by adapting a passage from Orosius, whose imagery of civil lay informs Orderic's tone as well:

> Quo mortuo [Alexandro] Macedonum principes diuersas sortiti sunt prouincias et ueluti opimam predam a magno leone prostratam auidi

discerpsere catuli seque ipsos inuicem in rixam irritatos prede emulatione fregerunt et mutuis bellis sese consumpserunt.[9]

After Alexander died, the leaders of Macedon divided up his various provinces, and just as ravenous cubs tear apart sumptuous prey killed by a great lion, they crushed themselves, were incited to violence against each other by their greed for booty, and consumed themselves in civil wars.

The redactor then explains that Alexander's royal family (his mother Olympias, his widow Roxane, the daughter of Darius, the Great King of Persia, and their half-Persian son Hercules) remain at the centre of the conflict among the successors. The eventual ruler of Macedon, Cassander, has Olympias punished for an attempted coup to seize control of Macedon and, fearing popular support for Alexander's fourteen-year-old son, has the royal family imprisoned and executed, but to no ultimate avail. Along with his fellow successors, Cassander soon succumbs to the perils of continuous fighting:

Deinde ipse Cassander paruo post tempore uiuens defungitur simulque omnes Alexandri regis duces triginta et quatuor numero uix quatuordecim [the final folio of the text is missing in British Library, MS Royal 13. A. i; the following is from MS Royal 15. C. vi, fol. 130v] annis in omnibus substiterunt miseriarum enormitatibus inuicem inuidentes inuicem prouocantes et turpiter adinuicem morientes. Et qui arbitrabantur totius mundi terminos sibi angustos fore sic infra breue tempus et magnus ille qui dicitur Alexander et magni illi principes successores interierunt suis ipsis armis.[10]

Thereafter Cassander died, after living just a little while longer. All of King Alexander's officers, thirty-four total, withstood the totality and enormity of their miseries for scarcely fourteen years. They were envious of each other, they provoked each other, and they shamefully died together. So they who thought the ends of the world were too narrow for them – that Alexander called "the Great" and his mighty leaders and successors – died by each other's arms within a brief amount of time.

This portrait of a king fearing the anarchy that will plague his survivors and the justification of those fears in the civil war that tore apart Alexander's empire would resonate in the twelfth-century Insular reassessment of the conqueror. This may be partly accounted for by the general proclivity for Roman authorities among writers of the twelfth-century renaissance, particularly those historians eager to delve into classical source texts. Orosius's *Historiae adversum paganos* and Justin's epitome of the *Philippic Histories* were indispensible in helping historians in Angevin England expand their knowledge of ancient Macedon. In so doing, they found a means of rejecting the incredible content, especially the Nectanabus story, and the more focused narrative of the Valerius *Epitome*, which, although it covered only Alexander's life rather than the span of Macedonian history, remained popular within cloistered libraries even as writers and readers interested in what the *Parva recapitulatio* identifies as "true history" understood its errors and limitations.

The *St Albans Compilation*

While the *Parva recapitulatio*-redactor turned only to Orosius to emend and expand the story of Alexander, Ralph Gubiun, abbot of St Albans in the mid-twelfth century, interpolated passages from Justin's epitome of the *Philippic Histories*, Orosius's *Historiae adversum paganos*, Josephus's *Jewish Antiquities*, Jerome's commentary on the Book of Daniel, Solinus's *De mirabilibus mundi*, Augustine's *De civitate Dei*, Bede's *Chronica maiora*, and Isidore's *Etymologiae* to produce the earliest surviving Anglo-Latin history of the Macedonian Empire.[11] His *Compilation* thus befits a historian working with a wealth of classical sources on Macedon in "one of the most important – if not, in fact, the largest – libraries within the Benedictine congregation,"[12] and although Gubiun never challenges what he perceived to be false histories in the manner of the *Parva recapitulatio*-redactor, his compendium reflects a similar interest in digesting his source texts in order to craft a reliable narrative of the Macedonian Empire. Gubiun's five-book narrative survives complete in the twelfth-century Cambridge, Corpus Christi College MS 219 and the late-twelfth or early-thirteenth-century Cambridge, Gonville and Caius College MS 154/204, as well as a fourteenth-century Anglo-Norman translation in Cambridge, Fitzwilliam Museum, CFM 20, and partially in a fifteenth-century fragment in Cambridge, University Library MS Dd. 10. 24,[13] but he went unidentified as the author of the work until a passage on the flyleaf of Oxford, Bodleian Library MS Greaves 60 (ca. 1600) came to light.[14] Gubiun held the abbacy from 1146 to 1151, and as an educated, former head of the St Albans scriptorium, he surely would have been well versed in classical histories.[15] Primarily reliant on the *Philippic Histories* and its narrative of Alexander's degradation into a temperamental, egomaniacal, besotted tyrant corrupted by Persian wealth, Gubiun offered a well-researched alternative to the Valerius *Epitome* and the epistolary narratives from Alexander to Aristotle and Dindimus and told quite a different story than that found in the other three narratives. Besides the sordid details of Alexander's devolution into a tyrant, the *Philippic Histories* provided a broad survey of Macedonian internecine violence and ambition. Beginning with Alexander's grandmother, who plots to kill her husband and later murders two of her sons to secure her own political authority, continuing with his father Philip, a tyrant in his own right (and so egregious that his wife Olympias colluded in his assassination), and concluding with Alexander's successors, who dismembered his global empire and killed each other in civil war, the *Philippic Histories* offered Gubiun a thorough exploration of the rise and fall of a famed but ultimately short-lived empire.

Within this scheme of Macedonian history, the portrait of a mind corrupted by power would especially alter Alexander's reputation in England for the next several centuries, but for a historian who wrote during the Anarchy, Gubiun's presentation of the Macedonian civil wars best illustrates how his compendium reflects his own turbulent times. At the end of his third book, for example, Gubiun announces the extraordinary shift in history as Alexander lies on his deathbed and foresees the violence that awaits his empire:

> Dimissis militibus circumstantes amicos percontantur uideanturne similem sibi repperturi regem. Tacentibus cunctis tum ipse hoc nesciat ita illud scire uaticinarique se ac pene oculis uidere dixit quantum sit in hoc certamine sanguinis fusura Macedonia, quantis cedibus quo cruore mortuo sibi parentatura [...] Cum deficere eum amici uiderent querunt quem imperii faciat heredem. Respondit dignissimum [...] Hac uoce ueluti bellicum inter amicos cecinisset aut malum discordie misisset ita omnes in emulationem consurgunt et ambitionem uulgi tanti cum fauore militum querunt.[16]

> When the soldiers were dismissed, Alexander asked his friends standing around him whether or not they supposed that they would find another king like him. They fell silent, and he told them that he did not know if they would, but he did know and could prophesy – and could almost see it with his eyes – how much blood Macedon would spill in the oncoming struggle, and with what slaughter and gory death it would avenge

his murder ... When his friends saw that he was dying, they asked him whom he would name his heir to the empire, and he responded "the most worthy" ... It was as if by these words he had given his friends the call to attack or had tossed among them the apple of discord, for they all rose up in rivalry and sought popularity among the great masses and the favour of the soldiers.

The Valerius *Epitome* does not present the civil wars that would prove the conqueror's prophecy true, and Gubiun took considerable care in unfolding these events. His reasons for spending two books on the wars between Alexander's successors must lie in large part with the wealth of information provided by his newly recovered classical source. The *Philippic Histories* had long circulated in England, but there is no evidence that earlier redactors had interpolated it for a narrative devoted to the rise and fall of ancient Macedon. Unlike Orosius, who tends towards exaggeration of Alexander's pagan belligerence, Justin's epitome provides a Marlovian account of a man corrupted by his obsession with power and excess, and in terms of storytelling alone, it is understandable why Gubuin would have been drawn to it, particularly as it, too, offers an exhaustive account of Macedon's disreputable history.

These concerns over uncertain leadership, anarchy, and the collapse of a kingdom occupy the fourth book of Gubiun's *St Albans Compilation*, which relates that when Alexander dies at the height of his power, his nobles yield to their emotions and individual desires in dismembering the empire. With Alexander dead, his military finds itself ideologically divided:

Huc accedebat, quod principes regnum et imperia, uulgus militum thesauros et grande pondus auri uelut inopinatam predam spectabant: illi successionem regni, hi opum ac diuitiarum hereditatem cogitantes ... Sed [nec] amici Alexandri frustra regnum exspectabant. Nam eius uirtutis ac uenerationis erant ut singulos reges putares ... Neque enim unquam ante Macedonia uel ulla gens alia tam clarorum uirorum prouentu floruit. Quos primo Philippus, mox Alexander tanta cura legerat ut non tam ad societatem belli quam in successionem regni uiderentur electi. Quis igitur miretur talibus ministris orbem terrarum uictum, cum exercitus Macedonum non tot ducibus, sed regibus regeretur? Qui numquam sibi repperissent pares, si non inter se concurrissent, multosque Macedonia prouincia Alexandros habuisset, nisi Fortuna eos emulatione uirtutis in

> perniciem mutuam armasset ... Inter ipsos uero equalitas discordiam augebat nemine tantum ceteros excedente, ut ei aliquis se submitteret.[17]
>
> So it happened that the generals looked to gain the kingdom and power over it, including the ranks of soldiers, treasures, and the great amount of gold, as unexpected booty: the first thought about succession to the throne, and the second about the inheritance of wealth and riches ... However, Alexander's friends were not looking in vain to take the kingdom, for they so possessed his strength and demanded his reverence that you would have thought all of them were kings ... Never before had Macedon or any other foreign nation flourished with such an abundance of outstanding men. First Philip, then soon afterwards Alexander, had appointed them with such care that they seemed chosen as much to fight together in war as to take over the kingdom. Who, then, can marvel that the world was conquered by these seconds-in-command, when the Macedonian army was led not by officers but by kings? They would never had found their equals, if they had not fought among each other, and the kingdom of Macedon would have had many Alexanders, if Fortune had not armed them with an envy of each other's authority and set them towards their mutual destruction ... Their very equality, for no one so surpassed the others that they would submit to him, exacerbated the discord among them.

Two debates further divide the generals over the matter of succession. Alexander's pregnant Persian bride may have a son, yet it is unlawful for a foreigner to take the Macedonian throne, and Alexander's brother Aridaeus is encamped with the men in Babylon, yet he is dismissed as the son of a courtesan. Alexander's survivors prefer leaders truly worthy of replacing him and consider it better to be ruled by men "qui prouineias regant, quibus bella mandentur quam sub persona regis indignorum imperio subiciantur" (who could rule the provinces and be entrusted with making war rather than being subject to the authority of unworthy men under the aegis of a king), and the voice of authority soon becomes Perdiccas.[18]

Endearing himself to the Macedonian infantry with the practical argument that civil war would provide "egregium hostibus suis spectaculum, ut quorum armis uictos se doleant eorum mutuis cedibus gaudeant" (an egregious spectacle for their enemies, such that they would lament that they had been conquered by [Macedonian] arms and rejoice that the Macedonians were slaughtering themselves), Perdiccas quickly divides the provinces of Alexander's empire among the deceased conqueror's generals.[19] Far from pacifying the volatile situation, however, this decision merely exacerbates the animosity of his countrymen:

> Haec itaque Alexandri commilitiones ... diuisio ueluti fatale munus singulis contigisset, ita magna incrementorum memoria plurimis fuit. Siquidem non magno post tempore, quasi regna non praefecturas diuisissent sic reges ex prefectis facti magnas opes non sibi tantum parauerunt, uerum etiam posteris reliquerunt.[20]

> This division among those who fought with Alexander occurred as if it were a gift of fate for each of them, as it was for many of them a great time to increase their lot. Indeed, not long afterwards, as if they had divided kingdoms rather than lands to be governed among themselves, so they were made kings instead of prefects and obtained great power not only for themselves but for their descendants as well.

Over his final two books, Gubiun explains the progress of the civil wars through these individuals, until four remain: Demetrius in Macedon, Lysimachus in Europe, Seleucus in Asia, and Ptolemy II in Egypt. After the first is attacked and defeated by the other three, Lysimachus and Seleucus engage in the final battle of those who had served under Alexander:

> Ultimum hoc certamen commilitonum Alexandri fuit et uelut ad exemplum fortunae par reseruatum. Lisimacus annos natus quatuor et septuaginta erat, Seleuchus sex et septuaginta. Sed in hac etate utrique animi iuueniles erant imperiique cupiditatem insaciabilem gerebant. Quippe cum orbem terrarum extinctis iam triginta et quatuor Alexandri ducibus duo soli possiderent, angustiis sibimet inclusi uidebantur uiteque finem non annorum spacio sed imperii terminis metiebantur.[21]

> This was the last battle among the fellow soldiers of Alexander and one reserved, as it were, as an appropriate example of Fortune. Lysimachus was seventy-four and Seleucus seventy-six. Even at that age each man was youthful in spirit and led by an insatiable desire for power. Although they two alone – with all of Alexander's thirty-four successors dead – possessed the world, they seemed too close for comfort in its narrow confines and assessed the end of their lives not by the number of years but by the extent of their empires.

As a compendium of ambition, vice, and the destructive lure of power, Gubiun's compendium showcases unlike any other Alexander text in England at the time the totality of Macedonian corruption and failure to maintain an empire after the death of its ruler. Thomas N. Bisson argues that the mid-twelfth century defined itself as "an age of tyranny, for no other contemporary concept in such general use so well summed up the prevailing experience of power" in a range of texts of the time,[22] an assessment that suits the tenor of the *St Albans Compilation* well and helps to contextualize it within other responses to political instability at the time.

Latin historians from this period frequently rely on the trope of political crises fuelled by internecine and feudal violence that arises when an authoritative king dies, particularly when his survivors and claimants to the throne take up arms against each other, subvert the peace and prosperity of the kingdom, and bring about public suffering. Paul Binski associates such a scenario with the common presentation of a ruler's death in medieval literature that occurs on the battlefield, or otherwise unexpectedly, and inspires further violence, as opposed to death scenes that portray a peaceful succession dependent on the king's will.[23] In the retrospective telling of twelfth-century writers, William I's death elicits, for example, a decidedly emotional response, owing to the inability of his nobles to agree on succession and their attempt to wrest control of England and Normandy by force. In his redaction of the *Gesta Normannorum ducum*, Orderic Vitalis hints at William's concern over the fate of his lands, for while "he did not grieve at his approaching death, [he] lamented the future that he foresaw, asserting that after his death his homeland of Normandy would be plunged into misery."[24] In the *Ecclesiastical History*, Orderic has William articulate his anxiety over his successors further:

> If the Normans are disciplined under a just and firm ruler they are men of great valour, who press invincibly to the fore in arduous undertakings and, proving their strength, fight resolutely to overcome all enemies. But without such rule they tear each other to pieces and destroy themselves, for they hanker after rebellion, cherish sedition, and are ready for any treachery, so they need to be restrained by the severe penalties of law, and forced by the curb of discipline to keep to the path of justice. If they are allowed to go wherever they choose, as an untamed ass does, both they and their ruler must expect grave disorder and poverty.[25]

The portrayal of William I as fearful of pending anarchy persists in vernacular texts as well. Benoît de Saint-Maure depicts a worrisome ruler in his *Chronique des ducs de Normandie*, in which William sees his bickering sons from his deathbed and "out dotance / Qu'en Engleterre eüst turbance, / Tribous e noise e destorbier" (was afraid that in England there would be an uprising, pillaging and uproar and confusion).[26] So, too, speaks Wace's William I, who grants Robert Curthose Normandy before the issuing the caveat from his deathbed:

> If the Normans have a good chieftain, their company is greatly to be feared; if they have no fear of a lord who constrains and represses them, they will begin to give bad service. The Normans are arrogant and proud, boastful and overweening; they should be repressed the whole time, for they are very hard to discipline. Robert, who has to watch over such men, has much to do and to think about.[27]

The theme of broken societal and political bonds following an authoritative ruler was hardly limited to historians writing about William. Henry I likewise appears in Anglo-Latin histories and chronicles as the paragon of kingship, a ruler who ushered in a halcyon era in England,[28] and his passing inspired a reaction among historians that reflects an emotional depth lacking in the response to William's I death, although the response to Henry's death was equally profound for the Normans in the Atlantic. As praiseworthy as Henry's reign is in contemporary histories, his death signals a renewed era of despair for mid-twelfth-century writers.[29] The Benedictine monk Robert of Torigni thus laments both the demise of a paternal king and the suffering of his people in his addendum to the *Gesta Normannorum ducum* of the 1140s:

> After the father of his people, who brought peace and love, defence of the weak,
> Himself a devout man succumbed, impious men raged, oppressed and burned.
> On this side mourn the English, on that the Normans weep.
> O, Henry, now you perish; once your name meant peace, now mourning for both people.[30]

Orderic Vitalis laments in similar fashion the socio-political breakdown after Henry I's death:

> Every man now seeks to plunder the goods of others
> And abandons himself to unbridled lawlessness.

See how hellish furies drive on mortals!
They take up arms, incite to war, and distribute javelins;
The Normans abandon themselves to robbery and pillage,
They slay and capture each other, and bind with fetters;
They burn buildings and everything that is inside them,
And neither spare monks nor show respect for women.[31]

Finally, the anonymous *Gesta Stephani* echoes Orderic's scorn in a scene that resonates in turn with both the final book of the *St Albans Compilation* and the end of the *Roman de toute chevalerie*, as discussed in chapter 4:

> The sacred obligations of hallowed friendship were at once broken among the people; the closest bonds of relationship were loosened; and those who had been clothed in the cloak of an enduring peace were assailed by the noise of war and the fury of Mars. For each man, seized by a strange passion for violence, raged cruelly against his neighbour and reckoned himself the more glorious the more guiltily he attacked the innocent. Likewise, utterly disregarding, or rather bringing to naught, the enactments of law, whereby an undisciplined people is restrained, and abandoned to all things unlawful, they were executing most readily any crime that occurred to their minds.[32]

In the accounts of this generation of historians, domestic order yields to the Anarchy of Stephen's reign, when the Normans, as Orderic Vitalis writes, "rushed out hungrily like ravening wolves to plunder and ravage mercilessly,"[33] and, in John of Worcester's words, "the bonds of peace were torn apart ... each man plundered the goods of others" and "the strong violently oppressed the weak" so that "the rich nobles of the kingdom … [were] not in the least bothered by the way the poor are unjustly treated."[34]

Expressions of anxiety and anarchy after the death of a powerful king are hardly relegated to twelfth-century literature, but the number of writers addressing the difficulties with succession among the Normans in England should give us pause when considering the Anglo-Latin recovery of the classical Alexander. In rejecting the fallacy that Alexander was fathered by an Egyptian pharaoh-sorcerer and in expanding the story of the conqueror beyond his death to recount the intrigue among his successors and the civil war that ended his empire, the *Parva recapitulatio*-redactor and Ralph Gubiun may have been motivated, in part, by a desire to produce compendia on Macedonian history, and their interpolation of Orosius and the *Philippic Histories* imposed classical and patristic authority on a legend that was becoming both myopic in its focus on Alexander and eulogistic in its presentation of his death. In the Valerius *Epitome*, which was transmitted in several copies in England in the eleventh and twelfth centuries, the narrative extends from Nectanabus's arrival in the Macedonian court to Alexander's tragic death by poisoning in Babylon, and the body of the narrative presents a series of premonitions, adventures, and battles. However, as records of the vices and intrigue of so many generations of Macedonian leaders, culminating in the war among Alexander's survivors, the *Parva recapitulatio* and the *St Albans Compilation* also present the conqueror and his empire as a collective exemplum for succession crisis and baronial in-fighting precisely at a time when such themes were prevalent in historical writing in England. At once, then, these Anglo-Latin texts re-situate Alexander within a monastic approach to historiography that is founded on classical and patristic sources and insists on the violence that he perpetuated and that ultimately undermined his empire, tellingly resonant within late-eleventh- and twelfth-century representations of political instability.

In this expanded view of history, Alexander was thus to be remembered in a rather dichotomous fashion. His martial heroics and extraordinarily quick rise to power were counterbalanced by his erratic behaviour and failure to secure a peaceful succession, just as the vastness of his empire was undermined by the internal strife that followed upon his death in Babylon. It was this final aspect of his reception that especially informed, I believe, the twelfth-century reconsideration of the history of the Macedonian Empire; perhaps contemporary events, too, played an influential role. Between the composition of the *Parva recapitulatio* and the *St Albans Compilation* (and, for that matter, the *Roman de toute chevalerie*), Latin and vernacular historians in England were clearly accustomed to commenting on the deaths of powerful kings, the backbiting and violence among those who strove to succeed them, and the damage inflicted on the populace of the kingdom.[35] Alexander's story was an ideal one to be rewritten and read within the corpus of Anglo-Latin and Anglo-Norman histories of the long line of kings whose deaths gave rise to the threat of anarchy, a literary and historical context that may not have been lost on Thomas of Kent.

Chapter Three

The *Roman de toute chevalerie*: Sources, Influences, and Innovations

The *Roman de toute chevalerie* lies between the twelfth-century developments of Anglo-Latin Alexander history and Continental French Alexander romance, the one based on the recovery of classical sources and the other indebted to the *Pseudo-Callisthenes* and its later recensions and adaptations. As the first writer in England to compose a full-length Alexander narrative in vernacular poetry, Thomas of Kent undoubtedly responded to Continental French efforts at telling Alexander's story earlier in the century, and at least three individual French Alexander poems had preceded him and could, if he had so desired, have served as a model: Albéric's pioneering romance, the *Alexandre décasyllabique*, and Lambert le Tort's *Alexandre en orient*. The *Fuerre de Gadres* and the *Mort Alixandre*, both from the 1170s, may have been contemporaneous with Thomas's work, and the "archetype" *Roman d'Alexandre*, which incorporated *Alexandre décasyllabique*, *Alexandre en orient*, and the *Mort Alixandre*, seems to have held no influence on him, nor did Alexandre de Paris's *Roman d'Alexandre* (ca. 1185) or Walter of Châtillon's Franco-Latin epic, the *Alexandreis*. Thus stands the impressive French corpus that surrounds Thomas's Anglo-Norman romance, and it is unlikely that he was ignorant of this Continental development of vernacular Alexander romances. Even if he was unfamiliar with each of the texts, the interchange of French literature across both sides of the Channel would likely have alerted him to the fact that Alexander, like the heroes of Arthurian narratives and the *chansons de geste* of Charlemagne and his knights, had already inspired his own corpus of vernacular literature. Throughout the second half of the twelfth century, French-speaking poets on the Continent and in England shared patrons among the nobility,[1] and with the composition of a good deal of literature in French in

England,[2] these poets maintained an awareness of each other's works.[3] Moreover, Insular readers and audiences evidently maintained a long-standing interest in French *chansons de geste*, judging by the number of Anglo-Norman copies of them and the well-known case of the twelfth-century copy of the *Chanson de Roland* in Oxford, Bodleian Library, MS Digby 23, the oldest surviving version of a work that may very well have originated in England.[4]

Thomas also composed his narrative on the threshold of the "golden age of historiography in England,"[5] the last twenty years of the twelfth century (when contemporary histories began to flourish),[6] and he often cites his role as a researcher of classical, late antique, and medieval works on Alexander. Although he undertakes a French verse translation with the justification that "romanz est ennoius quant un poy n'est rime" (romances with only a little rhyming verse are dull [414]) and cites at least one other such work as a precedent to his own (a vernacular translation of Alexander's letter to Aristotle),[7] Thomas avoids any mention of the French romances of Alexander fast gaining popularity in western Europe. Instead, he emphasizes the authority of the Latin sources that encourage "treat[ing] translation and interpretation as essentially the same because they have the same purpose, the recovery of meaning."[8] In explaining the necessity for a translator to fashion a truthful narrative and avoid corrupting his original text with falsehoods and superfluous material, Thomas maintains a critical distinction between his own work as a translator and those Latin *auctores* whom he consults. While the Norman poet Wace refers to himself in the vanguard of vernacular verse histories in the 1160s as a "maistre" to promote his scholarly authority,[9] Thomas designates only his source authors as such. However, in encouraging his audience to read these authors for themselves, Thomas relies on a motif associated with such histories in the twelfth century,[10] and there is no doubt that he knows which Alexander sources would be considered the authorities of the day. Relying on and promoting this knowledge gleaned from multiple authors, he situates himself within the intellectual context of Gubiun's *St Albans Compilation*, the incipit of which cites many of these same writers (e.g., Pompeius Trogus, Isidore, Jerome, and Solinus), and even if Thomas departs from Gubiun in basing his narrative on the Valerius *Epitome*, he is certainly aware of the corpus of Alexander authorities interpolated in the earlier Anglo-Latin compendium.

Catherine Gaullier-Bougassas argues that these references to ancient texts distinguish Thomas from other romance writers of the twelfth century, for not only does he rely on this Latin corpus to lend authority to his own narrative, but he also refuses to refer (much less defer) to his French predecessors, although several Continental texts had already presented the story of Alexander "en romanz."[11] The fact that Thomas did not admit any other French work on Alexander into his poem, whether as an implicit influence or an explicit source, is perhaps due not to ignorance of his competition, but to the air of authority that he derives from relying on Latin, rather than vernacular, material. That he and writers of Continental French Alexander romances adapted some of the same texts, namely the Valerius *Epitome* and the letter to Aristotle, was better left unsaid. If Thomas was to promote the *Roman de toute chevalerie* as a pioneering vernacular narrative, he had to both remain silent on those poets who preceded him and pay more than lip service to recognizable Latin works. Throughout his poem, in fact, he interpolates these texts to construct a narrative that is no less varied in its synthesis of authoritative texts than the *St Albans Compilation* without undermining the authority of his own primary sources, the Valerius *Epitome* and the *Epistola Alexandri ad Aristotelem*, collectively signified by the term "estorie," as discussed in the introduction.[12] By the later twelfth century, this had become a common term among verse historians for their source material, but it was also a self-referential term for the level of scholarly research invested in composing a vernacular history, one used by Gaimar, Wace, and Benoît de Sainte-Maure, the preeminent poets of such histories in Norman and French literary culture.[13] Thomas likewise suggests his research into and translation of these, his primary Alexander texts – he refers to the *Epistola Alexandri ad Aristotelem* as a "bon livre en latin" (194) and,[14] in citing the physical space of research, "l'estoire de l'almaire" (the history from the book cabinet [195])[15] – but he, like the *Parva recapitulatio*-redactor a century earlier, understands these texts' questionable credibility.

Nowhere is this more evident than in the section of the *Roman de toute chevalerie* that narrates Alexander's Indian campaign, with its extensive record of wondrous flora and fauna. Translating the *Epistola Alexandri ad Aristotelem* for this section, Thomas twice goes on the defensive against a potentially incredulous audience. In the first, he again cites an array of ancient authors:

Solum [ceo] qe ceus dient qe avant sont nomez,
Qui escristrent ceo qu'il virent en autoritez,
Jerome le dit e Solin li alosez,

Li bon Magastenes e autres auturs assez,
Qui pur veer merveilles furent en Inde alez,
Car des diz de lur liveres est cesty translatez.
Si vous de ceo qe dis, seignurs, ne me creez,
Jerome sur Ethike e Solin reversez,
E Troge e Pompeie: ceo qe di troverez;
Si le tenez a mensonge, a ceus vos pernez! (4604–13)[16]

I write according to those whom I have already named, those who said these things and wrote down what they saw as authoritative: the aforementioned Jerome and the celebrated Solinus, good Magastenes and many others who went to India to see marvels. My work is a translation of the contents of their books. If, sirs, you do not believe the things that I say, turn to Jerome, Ethicus, Solinus, and Pompeius Trogus, and you'll find therein what I am saying. If you hold my work a lie, then consult them!

Although this passage again recalls the sources cited in the incipit of the *St Albans Compilation*, such explicit, acknowledged reliance on Latin *auctores* also has a long-standing tradition in twelfth-century vernacular literature.[17] Establishing one's literary authority in such a manner had been established, in fact, by Gaimar, Wace, Benoît, and the clerical writer Jordan Fantosme, the four Anglo-Norman and French poets who may not only be conveniently compared with Thomas but may also be seen as those who codified the sort of narrative "en romanz" that he produced. These poets had lent credibility and authority to narrating historical subjects in vernacular verse, and by the time Thomas wrote the *Roman de toute chevalerie*, in the years after 1174, he may have relied on their literary models in approaching a substantial figure within ancient history. Gaimar had written in Anglo-Norman "as a self-conscious scholar anxious to assure his audience of the authenticity of the material they have been listening to,"[18] and in the *Roman de Rou* Wace had both announced the merits of writing history ("if documents were not composed and then read and recounted by clerics, many things which transpired in times gone by would be forgotten")[19] and faithfully rendered his Latin sources "with a view to establishing the true course of events, as a serious historian."[20] In writing on the Matter of Britain, either or both had possibly provided Thomas with a model to apply to Alexander.[21] Another possible influence is Jordan Fantosme, whose chronicle Thomas seemingly knew, and who begins his work by declaring it as "veraie estoire" (true history), an authoritative account of the rebellion that had just been raised against Henry II.[22] The promotion of truth and authorial credibility was a key topos for twelfth-century writers dealing with historical subjects in either Latin or the vernacular,[23] and to write an Anglo-Norman narrative filled with battlefield exploits of a well-known ancient ruler and his barons (many of whom were also recognizable figures in classical history), Thomas required a model determined by these poets in England as much as that set by French poets establishing Alexander romance.

Composing the *Roman de toute chevalerie* after the "age of *vulgarisation*, of history for a wider public"[24] and the flourishing of Anglo-Norman literature,[25] Thomas demonstrates a keen awareness of the need to assert his authority as a vernacular translator of an "estoire" notoriously filled with exaggerations and incredible scenes.[26] While Ralph Gubiun never assesses truth versus fiction in his *St Albans Compilation*, he does not incorporate the Valerius *Epitome* into his work either, and the *Parva recapitulatio*-redactor begins his addendum, approximately a century before Thomas, by citing the "uera hystoria" of Alexander against the claims of the Valerius *Epitome*. However, writers who translated the Latin Alexander on the Continent shared neither Thomas's notion of sacrosanct sources nor his insistence on citing their authority for his audience. As D.H. Green argues, writers engaging with the Alexander legend could rely on the "historicity" provided by a corpus of ancient and medieval texts on his career, as well as, and perhaps more importantly, the biblical allusions to him in 1 Maccabees and Daniel. New narratives relying on these older, often canonical works on Alexander could more easily be promoted as truthful.[27] Thomas, however, self-consciously explains his task as a translator of Latin works who seeks to complement the Alexander story with these very types of authoritative sources, while French romance writers before and after him tended either to amplify their sources into a model of chivalric *courtoisie* or use what they perceived as gaps or unresolved issues in the Alexander legend as inspiration for composing elaborate fictions (e.g., the romances of the conqueror's son and devoted followers avenging his death).[28] Alexandre de Paris, who arranged his composite *Roman d'Alexandre* in the 1180s, thus acknowledges the conflicting accounts of Nectanabus but avoids any explicit discussion of historical veracity and maintains a didactic narrative that values heroism over historical accuracy.[29] The *Roman de toute chevalerie* is didactic in its own right, noted for its "serious, moralistic, and philosophical bent,"[30] and likewise designed to appeal to audiences with an interest in marvels of the ancient world, and in its detailed battle scenes and lengthy descriptions of the East the text invites its readers to engage in the fantasy of joining in the adventures of Alexander and his barons, traits reflective of both epic and romance.[31] Writers adapting the *Pseudo-Callisthenes* and its recensions in Norman Italy had done much to impose moral readings on the conqueror by interpolating Jewish anecdotes that condemned his worldly ambition and emphasized the necessity of his recognizing a higher power, just as writers of vernacular romances in Capetian France had established Alexander as a warrior-king hero in the manner of Charlemagne and an ideal classical figure for an audience valuing chivalric themes, and Thomas seems to have appreciated both approaches.[32]

His Alexander is an authoritative king, and he is often, although not always, a beloved one, as his barons share in the benefits to be gained from his adventures and offer him a formidable army that guarantees him victory for twelve years. Their mutual glory ensures that Thomas's romance can be read at once as a continuation of the success of the *romans antiques* of an earlier generation, a suitable text for the baronial audience for romances in his own time, and evidence of the popularity in England of the *chansons de geste*. Owing to the influence of the Continental *romans antiques*, including the *Roman de Troie*, the *Roman de Thèbes*, the *Roman d'Enéas*, and the Alexander romance tradition begun by Albéric,[33] Thomas may have been inspired to draw moral lessons from Antiquity,[34] and if he considered his work a response to these earlier narratives, he clearly also respected literary tastes in England that leaned towards romance and epic, both of which informed his own style. It has recently been argued that French *chansons de geste* and Anglo-Norman romances were not distinguished as separate genres in England and that with their stories of campaigns in the East, Thomas's poem and others represent the development of the latter from the former.[35] The *Roman de toute chevalerie*'s sustained focus on Alexander as a warrior and leader determined to achieve "advancement through his military prowess,"[36] Thomas's lack of any amatory digression other than the requisite Candace scene present in the Valerius *Epitome*,[37] and the hero's eastern adventures could all have appealed to various audiences. Ian Short argues that the "influence of epic discourse is very much in evidence" in the *Roman de toute chevalerie*,[38] Rosalind Field assigns it to a group of three Anglo-Norman romances, including *Horn* and *Boeve de Haumtone*, that rely on the *laisse* to convey a narrative of "heroic or epic nature,"[39] and Judith Weiss reads Thomas's work within a group of Anglo-Norman hybrid, epic-romance narratives, alongside

Tristan, Ipomedon and Protheselaus, and *Boeve.*[40] Spanning the second half of the twelfth century, these surviving Anglo-Norman romances written before or contemporaneous with the *Roman de toute chevalerie* help to delineate the type of narrative that Thomas envisioned for an audience with increasingly varied options. He was clearly more influenced by the classical themes of the Continental *romans antiques* than by the amatory ones of the *Tristan* romances of Thomas and Béroul, but the romances of the last quarter or so of the century, his own generation, suggest the interests of writers and their audiences that invited an Anglo-Norman narrative on Alexander.

Horn's tale of revenge against Saracens and adventures abroad parallels Alexander's journey into Asia primarily to conquer the Persians, who have long held dominion over Macedon and shamed his father, Philip, by demanding tribute, and Hue de Rotelande situates the stories of love and hidden identity in *Ipomedon and Protheselaus* in Norman Italy and Sicily, a hotbed of Alexander literature in the twelfth century and an evocative location in Thomas of Kent's generation. M. Dominica Legge attributes *Ipomedon* to "the vogue for Classical and Byzantine romances" after the betrothal of Henry II's daughter Joan to William II of Sicily in 1164 and marriage in 1176,[41] a fashion with which we can also associate the *Roman de toute chevalerie.* Unlike earlier Anglo-Norman romances, Hue's and Thomas's narratives move the action from Atlantic Europe to the Mediterranean. While the former uses Norman kingdoms as his backdrop, the latter follows Alexander's expedition from the empire of the Normans' rivals ("Greece"), lands that recall the Second Crusade ("Greece" or Byzantium, again, and the Levant and Jerusalem), and more speculative, eastern locales of romance (from Persia to India). As Judith A. Green argues, this Crusade encouraged the Normans in England to expand their global political view from one restricted by a sense of isolated nationality on the Atlantic to "wider ... international horizons – the world of crusades and of chivalry" on the other side of Mediterranean Europe and the Near East.[42] Having been transmitted through Greek and Jewish to Latin culture from Norman Italy to Capetian France, Alexander had grown increasingly acceptable to European audiences as a ruler compatible with their global view. Although a pagan of the Greek-speaking Mediterranean, he conquered the forerunners of twelfth-century Europe's enemies in the Levant and beyond.

Finally, the ending of Thomas's narrative recalls the interest in succession crises among Insular romances[43] and perhaps satirizes the structure of baronial romances, in which an idealized, paternal figure's reign has to be recreated or restored by the hero.[44] In the *Roman de toute chevalerie,* Alexander's father is hardly an imitable figure, and the young conqueror, beloved by his barons, establishes an imperial exemplum that cannot be recreated, owing to the civil war that consumes his survivors. This conclusion is also evocative of the *chansons de geste,* notably that of Roland, and considers both the royal and baronial implications of Macedon's fall. As Alexander's survivors argue where to bury his corpse, God intervenes and instructs them to inter their fallen emperor in Alexandria, and although the moment cannot prevent the subsequent civil war over control of Alexander's lands, it alleviates the initial tension among his barons, each of whom wants the privilege of burying his leader in his inherited province. An act of divine intervention to defuse one potential conflict while not another, more destructive one after the protagonist's death situates the conclusion of the *Roman de toute chevalerie* within the expectations of both *chansons de geste* and romance.[45]

Although Alexander romances did not generally promote genealogical myths or national myths in the manner of the Trojan, Arthurian, or Charlemagne cycles of the late Middle Ages[46] or present their hero as a paradigmatic ruler of local, familial history in the manner of *chansons de geste,*[47] they could still serve as veiled expressions of political commentary. It has been suggested that the *Roman de Thèbes,* "a pessimistic story about a fratricidal war in which the best die and the land is ruined,"[48] had already responded to the chaos and violence of the Anarchy, and the *Roman de toute chevalerie* has been called "a romance of uncertain, multiple, and absent fathers, almost an anatomy of the weak points in patrilineage," an aspect of the narrative that mocks the very theme on which the *romans antiques* were founded.[49] In similar fashion, although the extent to which Chrétien de Troyes intended his Arthurian romances to reflect contemporary dynasties remains debated, his transformation of Arthur from a powerful king reminiscent of Henry II in his earlier romances to an increasingly impotent one and "mocking caricature of the descent claimed by the ... Plantagenet dynasty" in *Lancelot* and *Perceval* provides a compelling context for Alexander romances in the twelfth century.[50] Chrétien's later romances are likely contemporaries of the *Roman de toute chevalerie,* and while Insular audiences did not yet share the Continental interest in Arthurian narratives, Thomas was certainly aware of literary traditions and tastes well beyond England.[51] Chrétien was by then portraying in his Arthurian narratives "a world ill regulated by its customs, chronically prone to crisis, and repeatedly destabilized in the absence of effective upholders of its institutions,"[52] effectively an unravelling of the myth of a stable, idealized kingdom, and it is not inconceivable that Thomas approached the Alexander romance favoured by Continental French audiences in similar fashion.

Like Arthur, Alexander was established in both French and Anglo-Norman romance as a warrior-king known for his generosity towards his barons and soldiers,[53] but in the twelfth century it was Thomas, not his counterparts on the Continent, who emphasized that like Arthur, Alexander's story ended with the ramifications of ambition and imperial failure reminiscent of Chrétien's later Arthurian romances and thirteenth-century Arthuriana.[54] While we know nothing of the original reception of the *Roman de toute chevalerie*, its surviving manuscripts span a period when Arthurian romances starkly evolved for both Continental and Insular audiences, as I will argue in the following chapters. In the generation after Thomas, French writers of prose romance began to develop "a new eschatological history" for the Arthurian cycle, characterized by the gloominess of the incestuous Mordred story, the affair between Lancelot and Guinevere, the Grail quest, and Arthur's death.[55] The Durham copy of the *Roman de toute chevalerie*, featuring the version of the text that is most insistent on moralizing the collapse of Alexander's empire, was produced when these grim Arthurian episodes inspired "the mutability, failures, and infidelities surrounding the sovereign" in Middle English romances,[56] themes that likewise colour Thomas's portrayal of Alexander and his family.

Thomas of Kent and French Alexander Romance

As discussed in chapter 1, beginning with Albéric, French romance writers denied the story of Nectanabus and cast Olympias as the victim of slander, regarding the affair with the exiled king-sorcerer, in order to preserve Alexander's idealized stature. These writers long rejected the notion that Nectanabus fathered Alexander, a central claim of the *Pseudo-Callisthenes*, but they did not join in the investigation and advertisement of the Latin vulgate histories or Orosius's universal history, an intellectual exercise undertaken in England by the *Parva recapitulatio*-redactor and Ralph Gubiun. Rather, in denying this sordid story of Nectanabus, French poets sought to resolve the paternity scandal within the Alexander legend for the purpose of moral didacticism. This is not to say that the *Parva recapitulatio*-redactor and Gubiun (and Thomas) were not interested in didacticism of their own – all three evidently saw the pedagogical value of collating older sources on Alexander – but they had disparate conceptions of their subject's cause for infamy than the French poets of the twelfth century. The Anglo-Latin writers emphasize Alexander's tyrannical behaviour and the ambition of his successors that would dismember the Macedonian Empire, while Thomas emphasizes the futility of Alexander's earthly rule, and all three underscore the transience of his empire.

He does not share the antagonism towards the conqueror as that seen in the *Parva recapitulatio* and the *St Albans Compilation*, but neither does Thomas hold the Macedonian Empire in the paradigmatic regard as seen in the French romances of his century. While Alexandre de Paris would present Alexander as a "roi-chevalier exemplaire, conformément à l'idéal politique du XIIe siècle,"[57] Thomas is more cautious in his view of the conqueror, especially when recounting his childhood and the last days of his empire. Rather than simply appropriating the figures of Olympias and Philip from earlier twelfth-century French romances, for example, he refashions them into players in a domestic drama that now dominates the narrative of Alexander's childhood. Olympias, the aging queen desperate for power and vengeance against her husband, and Philip, the increasingly impotent king who must acquiesce to a son whom he knows is not his own, are brought into relief in the *Roman de toute chevalerie*. Although both are scheming and duplicitous in their efforts to wrest control over each other, Thomas grants them a depth of character by establishing them as victims as well, Olympias that of her husband and Philip that of his son.

He was not the first writer to cast Olympias as a *femme fatale*, but Thomas's portrayal of the Macedonian queen recalls the twelfth-century Anglo-Latin compendia on the empire more than it does the French romances that sought to exonerate Olympias from the scandal involving Nectanabus. In his *St Albans Compilation*, Ralph Gubiun appropriated a damning portrayal of Alexander's mother in his primary sources, Justin's epitome of the *Philippic Histories* and Orosius's *Historiae adversum paganos*. Besides implicating Olympias in her husband's assassination (as does Thomas), Gubiun thus depicts the Macedonian queen as a vicious power-player in the anarchy that follows her son's murder. Attempting to consolidate her authority in Macedon immediately afterwards, Olympias is initially welcomed by her one-time subjects "seu memoria mariti seu magnitudine filii et indignitate moti" (either owing to the memory of her husband, the greatness of her son, or the indignity of the rebellion),[58] but this favour soon devolves into resentment over her increasingly violent behaviour, typical of Macedonians in the *Philippic Histories*. "Nam cum principum passum cedes muliebri magis quam regio more fecisset, fauorem sui in odium uertit" (For when with more womanly than regal behaviour, she widely committed the slaughter of noblemen, favour towards her turned into hatred), the *St Albans Compilation* reads, and the citizens, despite the previous glory of her husband and son, are compelled to execute Olympias.[59] Still, in a scene extraordinary for the stoicism that it grants Olympias, the executioners find that divorcing the fallen queen from the exalted past of the empire is a difficult matter indeed:

> Qua uisa percussores attoniti fortuna maiestatis prioris, et tot in ea memoria occurentibus regum suorum nominibus substiterunt, donec a Cassandro missi sunt qui eam confoderent non refugientem gladium sed ad uulnera haud muliebriter uociferantem uirorumque fortium more pro gloria ueteris prosapie morti succumbentem, ut Alexandrum posses etiam in moriente matre cognoscere. Compresse insuper expirans capillis ac ueste crura contexisse fertur, nequid posset in corpore eius indecorum uideri.[60]

> When Olympias was seen by her executioners, astonished at what had happened to her former majesty and recalling the names of so many kings associated with her, they stood still, until Cassander sent others to stab her through. She did not flee the sword or cry out over her wounds in a womanly fashion but succumbed to death in the manner of brave men, adding to the glory of her ancient race, so that you would have even recognized Alexander in his dying mother. Moreover, she is said to have combed her hair while dying and covered her legs with her garment, lest anything seem indecent about her corpse.

Whereas Gubiun followed his sources closely, Thomas was clearly interested in adapting the portrait of Olympias found in the Valerius *Epitome* and French romances alike, although he, too, sought to disparage her character in creating a dynamic of marital unease between a queen and her king and the son as her means of vengeance. Like his distrust of Alexander's barons and dismissal of earthly vanities, Thomas's occasional misogyny attests to what Catherine Gaullier-Bougassas terms "un discours clerical médiévale."[61]

The last of these is particularly useful in considering Thomas's treatment of Alexander's birth and formative years in the Macedonian court and the degree to which he holds one figure especially culpable in the domestic crisis of Alexander's youth. He presents in Olympias the story of a conniving queen and a woman whose reputation is marred not so much by a philandering sorcerer (the basis of the Nectanabus episode in the Valerius *Epitome*) as by the temptation of power and vengeance on her husband that Nectanabus offers. In the Anglo-Norman poem, as in its Latin source for this episode, the sorcerer clearly dupes the queen into believing that she conceives Alexander with an actual god. Thomas clarifies this both before Olympias sleeps with the disguised Nectanabus, whom she quickly assumes has divine powers, and after Alexander kills his father and reports his dying confession.[62] When Olympias hears that Nectanabus has admitted to his ruse, Thomas exculpates her from any suggestion of collusion with her speechless reaction, "mult se merveille de ceo qu'il disoit" (she very much marvelled at what he said [508]). Yet the queen remains provocative in her own right, despite her gullibility in falling for Nectanabus's schemes. Thomas suggests, in fact, that this gullibility arises from her desire to combat Philip's increasingly public abuse. When the sorcerer first addresses Olympias and asks for a private meeting, "pour ad du vassal, ne siet sa volenté / E velt qe s'il rien en siet qe seit a celé" (she was afraid of the man and did not know what he wanted, and she wished to remain secret anything that he could know [152–3]), and Nectanabus soon realizes that political and domestic power offer an easy means of controlling her.

Olympias is introduced in the *Roman de toute chevalerie* as a queen who revels in the temporary power granted her when Nectanabus arrives. Presiding over a birthday celebration, she arranges feasts, games, and spectacles, which Thomas describes in considerable detail. This superficial and extravagant show of authority is all the more conspicuous, as Thomas clarifies that with Philip off on a campaign Olympias reigns in his stead ("la reyne Olimpias governoit la cite" [95]), and the world that she creates is one of leisure and delights that also attracts Nectanabus. Following a traditional blazon of the queen, Nectanabus is seized by physical desire and quickly plans his seduction of Olympias, who encourages his supposed ability to foretell the future by expressing her most pressing anxiety. When Philip returns, Olympias confides in Nectanabus – he will attempt to divorce her and marry another. Provided with the means of manipulating the queen's emotions, Nectanabus relates a prophecy that both captivates her and accurately predicts the narrative of Alexander's career:

E dit: "Qui ceo vous dist, de rien ne vous gaba.
Le roy guerpera vous, autre muiller avera,

> Mes un enfant ançois de vous, dame, istra.
> Dieu de terre ert nomé, voz hontes vengera,
> Les regnés d'environ trestoz governera,
> Desqu'al chef d'orient les terres conquera;
> Si hardiz ne si pruz unques armes ne porta." (207–13)
>
> He said, "He who says these things to you is not at all lying. The king will reject you and marry another, but a child, my lady, will be born to you nonetheless. He will be named a god of the earth, he will avenge the dishonour committed against you, he will govern kingdoms in every direction, and he will conquer the earth unto the ends of the Orient. Neither a man as strong nor one as valiant will ever bear arms."

Although Nectanabus promises Olympias what she most desires, a son who will protect her from Philip, Thomas faithfully renders the Valerius *Epitome* and maintains not only that Olympias is genuinely deceived but even feels an amatory connection towards the alleged god who sleeps with her. He thus uses the Nectanabus story in a traditional manner: as in the Latin source-text, the sorcerer naturally provides the paranormal intrigue surrounding Alexander's conception, and while he deceives Olympias and later Philip, he outlines Alexander's career in impressively accurate terms.

For Thomas, however, it seems that the more important aspect of Nectanabus and Olympias's first conversation is the anxiety expressed over Philip and his intentions to replace his queen. Olympias's susceptibility to the Egyptian's trickery surely results from her knowledge that Philip seeks a divorce and that, as Nectanabus predicted, a powerful son represents her best opportunity for political survival. After the murder of Nectanabus, Thomas emphasizes the escalating tension between the Macedonian king and queen by fulfilling both Olympias's fears of divorce and the sorcerer's vision of their child's prowess. In returning to Philip's plans to rid himself of Olympias, the Valerius *Epitome* bluntly states that "Philippum spreto consortio Olympiadis in Cleopatrae nuptias demutantem" (after he spurned his marriage to Olympias, Philip turned his mind to marrying Cleopatra [23]) and relates how Alexander publicly challenges his father's plans to remarry by killing one of Philip's wedding guests, wounding Philip himself, and convincing his parents to reunite.[63] Thomas expands this sparse narrative of family drama into another elaborate scene of festivity and provides Olympias with an emotional reaction not included in the Valerius *Epitome*, the first time in the *Roman de toute chevalerie* that he explicitly departs from the framework of his primary source.[64]

In his telling, the animosity between Olympias and Philip is exacerbated anew by the rumour of the queen's affair with a Trojan lover (Pausanias, who later assassinates Philip), a scandal that leads Philip to hold council with his barons and divorce Olympias for the hand of one Cleopatra.[65] The grounds for the royal couple's divorce elicit a curious interjection from Thomas:

> Car quant l'om se sent honiz de sa moiller,
> Ne siet qu'il en face ne cum se deit venger
> Sanz sey memes honir e les soens laydenger.
> Ce sevent bien celes qe l'em voit trop fol[oi]er,
> E pur ceo ne volent lur folie lesser.
> Olimpias ne deit pas aver reprover,
> Car plus sage de ly put l'em bien enginer.
> Ne voy qe s'en puisse totes houres gaiter,
> Neqedent l'em se deit par autre chastier (653–61)

> When a man feels that he is dishonoured by his wife, he does not know how to react or avenge himself without dishonouring himself or putting his own people in danger. Those women who do not wish to quit their folly but wish to continue it know this well. It is not right to reproach Olympias, for wiser women than she can well be tricked. I do not think that one can be on guard all the time, but one must chastise oneself by following others.

After acknowledging Olympias's innocence (or perhaps naivety) in the Nectanabus episode, Thomas here tempers his attitude towards the queen. His parental attitude that women should not be misled by young men ("pur ce dy as dames k'ont le quer leger, / Qe a ces bachelers solent tant don[oi]er" [648–9]) would seem to exonerate Olympias once again from the ramifications of adultery, but Thomas uses this passage to transform her character. Olympias has already fallen victim to "folie" in her dealings with Nectanabus, but whereas in that affair she played the role of the passive, deceived woman, she is duplicitous in her tryst with Pausanias. Thomas rejects the French portrayal of Olympias as the virtuous and faithful wife and seizes instead the opportunity to cast aspersions on the king and queen, the one through increasingly disreputable, uproarious behaviour and the other through her involvement in her husband's assassination.[66]

Philip's mishandling of his divorce and planned second marriage becomes public when he ushers his new fiancée, Cleopatra, into the royal palace and sends Olympias "a un chastel la hors … / Car ne put de honte la cite chevacher" (to an outlying house … because she was not able to ride through the city without shame [681–2]). Replaced by another woman in her position of public extravagance that begins Thomas's romance and removed from the seat of power, Olympias can only hear "les timbres e les tabors" (the tambourines and drums [692]) that signify her exile, hope for Alexander to return home and avenge her, and yield to desperation:

Vest s'en Olimpias dolente e irascue,
De la honte qe ele ad fremist e tresue.
Si grant dolur en ad, a poy qe ele ne se tue.
Sovent se fust occise si hom ne l'eu[s]t tenue;
E dit: "Lasse e cheitive, grant joie en ay perdue!
Si n'est, bel fiz, par tey, jamés ne m'ert rendue.
Par petit[e] achaison grant peine m'est cr[e]ue,
E jeo en reprover e en vilté [sui] chaeue.
Jamés n'averay honur, fiz, s'il n'est par ta ayue.
Si tu poez longes vivere, ma peine ert [cher] vendue.
Ore m'appellent my home Royne abatue.
La dehors me covient vivere en un[e] mue;
Ceo fet Cleopatras qe m'onor m'ad tolue." (701–13)

Grieving and angry, Olympias leaves, and she trembles and bristles at the insult. She felt such great sorrow that she was not able to keep silent. Often she would have killed herself, if someone had not prevented her, and she cried, "Wretched and unfortunate, I have lost all my great joy! If not through you, my dear son, then it will never be returned to me. I have been brought to ruin by a small accusation, and I have been renounced and have fallen into dishonour. Never will I have my honour back, son, if not through you. If you are able to live a long life, then you will sell my pain for a dear price. Now my men call me a queen laid low. I have to live outside the city in a prison, because of Cleopatra, who has stolen away my honour."

Thomas here adapts the story of Olympias into one of a disgraced queen, pushed from court by a husband wishing to marry another, kept in a prison tower, and hoping for deliverance from her beloved son, saviour, and avenger – a son, to be sure, who seemingly held little filial devotion towards his father. At the same time, in both the Valerius *Epitome* and the Roman histories of Macedon disseminated in the twelfth century, he would have seen Olympias as an unmistakable model of feminine duplicity and treachery. Quickly granted her freedom by her son's intervention, her vengeance in Thomas's telling is swift and lethal, and it comes not from Alexander, who is emboldened enough to force Philip to release her and ultimately overshadows his father's legacy with his own accomplishments, but from her lover, Pausanias.

In returning to the matter of Olympias's infidelity, Thomas narrates a dangerous romance, as he explains that Pausanias falls in love with Olympias, finally able to exact vengeance on Philip and resolved to do so:

> Quant la dame le seit e son voler entent,
> Au desir qu'il ad la dame ly consent
> Qu'aprés la mort le roy fra son comandement.
> Ore oiez de femme quel est son vengement!
> Mult cele son voler par aise qu'ele atent,
> Mes quant vient al venger, mult se venge crualment. (985–90)

> When she knew and understood [Pausanias's] intent, because of her desire for him, she consented that after the king's death, she would do his will. Now hear how this woman got her vengeance! For a long time she hid with ease what she intended, but when it came time for vengeance, she cruelly and thoroughly achieved it.

Once again, Thomas exaggerates the sparse depiction of her in the Valerius *Epitome*, wherein Pausanias only discusses with the queen his plans to marry her before violently attacking Philip and seizing Olympias, who later implores Alexander to kill her crazed lover once he assaults her as well.[67] While Thomas translates this sequence of events from Pausanias's attack against Philip to Olympias's cries for her son to kill the Trojan (in her words, "vengez mon marrement," avenge my misfortune [1003]), Thomas reflects on Philip's assassination as a crime of domestic treachery, as "mort est li rois qui tint de Macedoigne l'empire, / Car sa femme le fist, cum dist est, occire" (Dead is the king who ruled the Macedonian Empire, because his wife, as it is said, had him killed [1040–1]). In fact, the Valerius *Epitome* does not implicate Olympias in the murder but presents an act of violence orchestrated by Pausanias, a crime of passion committed by her lover. As discussed above, the Roman sources known to Thomas do implicate the queen, and the poet could easily have found this version of the assassination in the *Philippic Histories* itself or the *St Albans Compilation*, which relies on the classical history. Why Thomas chose to interpolate and amplify this portrayal of Olympias is, however, the more intriguing question.

Thomas's Olympias is not wholly defined by her scandalous relationship with Nectanabus, as she is in the Valerius *Epitome*, but also by her persistent faith in her son as a ruler of Macedon and personal protector, her loss of power, and her schemes to avenge Philip's attempted divorce. Prophecies and premonitions regarding the boy equally incite the consternation of Thomas's Philip in the *Roman de toute chevalerie*. While the *Philippic Histories*, consulted by Ralph Gubiun for his compendium of Macedonian history, presents Philip as an erratic and drunken tyrant, the *Pseudo-Callisthenes* established the portrayal of him as an aging, helpless king at the mercy of Nectanabus's stratagems and the destiny of Alexander. Thomas underscores both of these facets of Philip's role in his narrative, as he becomes a king who ultimately cannot help but yield to the intrigue and increasing authority of the Egyptian sorcerer, Olympias, and their son while acknowledging the limits of his own authority. This weakness encourages Olympias to use Nectanabus and his talk of a divine son to her advantage against her husband; as long as she is able to deceive Philip and raise a son who will both protect her and outshine the king, he will remain in a precarious position.

The first indication that Philip must struggle to maintain his authority against this new royal family within his court is apparent in a dream vision conjured by Nectanabus. In the Valerius *Epitome*, the king describes it to his soothsayer as such:

> "Vidi per quietem deum quondam formosum et canitie capitis caesariatum arietisque cornibus insignitum supervenisse Olympiadi, coniugi meae, seseque illi nuptiis miscuisse. Quibus peractis haec etiam verba addiderat: 'Excepisti, o mulier, ex me filium vindicem.' Tum mulieris virginal contegere biblo ac consignare annulo aureo videbatur, cui insculpta erant solis effigies et leonis caput hastili subiecto."[68]

> "I saw in the dead of night a certain handsome god, distinguished by long white hair and ram horns on its head, come upon my wife Olympias and copulate with her. Afterwards it said: 'You have received from me, woman, a son and an avenger.' Then I saw him cover her vagina with a

> book and seal it with a golden ring, on which were engraved images of the sun and the head of a lion with a spear beneath it."

Thomas amplifies the vision to bring both Alexander's might and Philip's fear into relief:

> "Dist ly qe enceinte estoit d'un riche empereur
> Qui ma mort vengera, ma peine, ma tristur.
> Desur le nombril prent jus d'une verte colur,
> La moité d'un lion forma [enz] en la flur.
> Orgoillus chef avoit, unc ne vit greignur,
> La forme du soleil i esteit od sa luur,
> Le lion le fereit de son pié en l'ur,
> E la [ou] jeo estoie en si faite errur
> Un ostour m'esveilla; mult ai grant freur." (313–21)

> "[The dragon] told her that she was pregnant with a wealthy emperor, who would avenge my death, my pain, and my sorrow. He put a green coloured juice on her navel, and he drew there half of a lion in the nascence of its power. It had a proud head – you have never seen a greater lion. There was also a drawing of the sun and its light, and the lion struck it with its paw, and while I was dismayed by these things, a goshawk woke me up, and I was very much afraid."

Philip's interpreter deduces that the colour green signifies Alexander's divine father, the lion represents the child's strength and pride, and the sun is a symbol of the East, where Alexander will seek to expand the Macedonian Empire. For Philip, however, the import of the vision and this interpretation is not so much the grandeur of the child's future reign as the emotions suggested in the rhyme of "errur"/"freur." From the moment of Nectanabus's arrival in Macedon, Philip's political efficacy and legacy are threatened, for the sorcerer provides Olympias with a means of thwarting his attempts to remarry in bearing a son who will both denounce and exceed Philip's sovereignty. The king himself has little choice but to recognize this eventuality of Alexander's greatness. Although he curses the child as an ominous "faiture" (conception [418]) upon his birth, Philip is haunted by dream visions of Alexander's extraordinary destiny and told by the gods that the boy must be his rightful heir if he can tame the legendary man-eating horse Bucephalus. In sum, Nectanabus's sorcery, Olympias's animosity, Alexander's passion for defending his mother, and even the gods themselves conspire to end Philip's reign prematurely.

This tension within the royal family culminates in the wedding scene discussed above, as Philip exiles Olympias from court and celebrates the arrival of his fiancée Cleopatra in grand fashion. The occasion marks Philip's boldest attempt to reassert his power over his wife and son, but it ends in public humiliation. When Lysias provokes Alexander to violence at the wedding feast, Thomas identifies a clear disparity between the mentally unstable father and the physically imposing son:

Quant ceo voit Phelippe, a poy qu'il n'est desvez,
E saut vers Alisandre, a ly s'en est medllez.
Le deis est abatu, li manger reversez,
La sale estormie; tuit crient: "Montez!"
Des chevalers i ad bien tost cent mil armez,
Lur seignur ont rescuz car mult sunt airez.
Li rois est d'un espié en la quisse navrez;
En sa chamber fu puis a grant peine portez.
Alisandre ert pruz e fort e alosez
E tint le brant al poing qe ert ensanglentez.
N'est qui le requerge, tost ne seit affolez. (778–88)

When Philip saw this, he nearly went mad, and he jumped towards Alexander to fight him. The table was overturned and the food thrown back; the room was filled with fighting, and everyone cried out, "To arms!" Nearly a hundred armed, furious knights came in to help their lord. The king was wounded in the thigh by a spear and carried, with considerable effort, into his room. Alexander was valiant, strong, and praiseworthy, and he held his sword covered in blood to the hilt. There was no one who attacked him who was not wounded.

The theme of a father in decline and a son asserting his physical and political dominance continues shortly thereafter, as Alexander, after chasing Cleopatra out of Macedon, turns his attention to foreign rulers who freely defy Philip and would presumably continue doing so, if not for Alexander's increasingly commanding presence in the Macedonian court. The young prince successfully battles a potential rebel against his father and casts the Persian ambassadors (who demand tribute from Philip) out of court, but the last defiant subjects, in an anonymous city subject to the Macedonians, justify their rebellion in a telling manner.

Thomas writes that the citizens therein renege on their tribute money "pur ceo qu'il [i.e., Philip] est vielz" (because Philip was old [977]). Once again, Alexander defeats those who would challenge his father, and two lines later, Thomas begins the Pausanias episode, in which Philip is murdered and Alexander is hastened to the throne.

Even with this succession, the young ruler faces incessant ridicule over the rumours of his conception, as everyone around him (both at home and abroad) seems to have some inkling that Philip did not father him, or at least of Olympias's infidelity. In Thomas's version, Alexander makes a genuine effort to expunge Nectanabus from the record, as it were, to exonerate his mother from the charges of adultery, and to assert Philip as his father in a crucial adaptation of its Latin source. In the Valerius *Epitome,* Alexander encounters in one of his earliest excursions abroad a statue of Nectanabus in Tripoli, and he weeps upon seeing the likeness of his father and even proclaims that the onetime ruler was, in fact, his father.[69] While Alexander spins his emotional reaction to his own advantage in this account, for he very well knows that he must demonstrate his lineage from the pharaohs in Egypt, and Nectanabus fits the bill, in the Anglo-Norman version Alexander cannot afford embarrassing rumours about his paternity as he consolidates his empire across North Africa. Here, Alexander weeps at the memory of his father but says nothing to those around him. Rather, he publicly makes sacrifices to the gods and bribes the priests of the town to make the following proclamation: "roy, Phelippe t'engendra. / A grant tort est blamee cele qe te porta, / Car onques coupes nen ot de ceo dont blame en a" (king, Philip sired you. Most wrongly is that woman who bore you blamed, for she never committed that crime of which she is accused [1154–6]).[70]

Still, although Alexander publicly denies Nectanabus as his father, he achieves for the sorcerer the same objective desired by his nominal father Philip – vengeance against the Persians. It was the Persians, after all, who invaded Egypt and sent Nectanabus into exile in Macedon, and who continually compel Philip, powerless against their mighty empire, to pay tribute. Alexander, who learns of Nectanabus's story upon seeing his statue and who witnesses Philip's shame first hand, dedicates the first phase of his career to seeking revenge for his fathers and establishing his own glory in the east. While the *Roman de toute chevalerie* does not explicitly present Alexander on any expedition dictated by piety and vengeance, it is, in the end, constructed around a series, beginning with Nectanabus, of fallen kings and father figures who will forever lie in the shadow of their son. Over five hundred lines after he consoles the dying Nectanabus and buries him honourably, for example, Alexander finds himself in a parallel situation with Philip. Having been mortally wounded by Pausanias, the young Trojan noble who commits regicide in his lust to bed Olympias, Philip is assisted by Alexander, who helps his father drive a sword through the assassin's head and body.[71] The gruesome death of Pausanias causes Philip such happiness that he forgets his troubled history with Alexander, and with his dying words he tells his supposed son of his confidence that he would avenge his murder.[72]

For the second time in the poem, Alexander sees a father take his last breath, and once again he sets about performing an honourable burial. Unlike Nectanabus, however, Philip receives the honours of a king, as Thomas describes in splendid detail the embalming and ornate sarcophagus that Alexander commissions for his father, an act of textual and visual memorializing to which Thomas pays particular attention. An epitaph on the tomb states that "Ci repose li roys qui tant ama mesure. / Sanz renable achaison ne fist a nul laidure, / Ne tort ne volt suffrir ne orgoil ne sorfaiture" (Here lies the king who dearly loved moderation. He committed no malfeasance without a good reason, nor was he willing to suffer a wrong, either pride or arrogance [1,025–7]), yet nowhere in the *Roman de toute chevalerie* does Philip exhibit such admirable qualities. On the contrary, he has (in the Anglo-Norman text and elsewhere) a reputation for intemperance, a violent disposition, and is quick to divorce his wife for political advantage. Even more puzzling is the statue that Alexander erects of his father:

> "Corone d'or au chef, entaille sanz jointure, / E tenoit en sa destre un brant par la heudure, / Ovec l'autre un escu dedenz par l'enarmure. / Le vis avoit mult fier e la barbe meure, / E quarré fust par piz e grant par forch[e]ure, / E manance orient tant cum brant li dure." (1034–9)
>
> It had a golden crown, sculpted in one piece, on its head, and it held a sword by the helm in its right hand and a shield by the strap in its left. It had a proud face with a manly beard, it was barrel-chested and broad-shouldered, and it menaced the East with the length of its sword.

While the epitaph memorializes Philip the governor, this likeness depicts him as a warrior, and an awkward exaggeration (and inconsistency with the narrative) is apparent, for Philip never realized his dream of threatening the East. He remained subject to the Persians, and he never even waged battle with them. The memorial thus raises two contradictions, for it represents Philip as a greater ruler than he was, and it suggests the sort of king that Alexander himself wants to be, once he can officially step out of his nominal father's shadow. This statue of Philip also stands in obvious contrast to that of Nectanabus, which Alexander soon finds in Egypt. Although this second statue is similarly decorated and executed, the only story associated with it is that unflattering one told by the locals, who claim that the statue depicts a pharaoh, who, having learned by sorcery of an imminent Persian invasion of his country, stole away in the middle of the night. Naturally, Alexander cannot associate himself with this sort of father and tale of cowardice, but he can present his supposed bloodline in the story of Philip as a fair and just warrior-king. That, we are to believe, is the Macedonian exemplum, and it is in the land towards which Philip's sword points and Alexander will soon lead his army that the new ruler will find his greatest opportunity to achieve this standard.

The present ruler of the East, Darius, the Great King of Persia, is strikingly analogous to Alexander in the *Roman de toute chevalerie*. The Persian ruler represents precisely what Alexander desires – a geographically massive, politically powerful empire and immeasurable treasure – and he represents what Alexander strives to become, for while the young Macedonian succeeds to the throne and replaces Philip, he will ultimately elect to stand in for Darius and adopt his eastern empire rather than returning to his own. For his part, however, Darius arrogantly considers Alexander as nothing more than a young imitator of Philip, an upstart king to whom he sends silken reins (to restrain his aspirations), a golden ball (to amuse himself with a likeness of the *orbis terrarum*), and two sacks of gold (to fill his presumably barren coffers).[73] The Great King fails to see Alexander as anything more than a boy playing dress-up in royal robes, and Thomas occupies himself for over two thousand lines in exploring the Persian king's realization that he, like so many others, will have to yield his position of power to Alexander, but also that he, unlike other kings, will accept Alexander as both a political and familial successor. Other similarities are obvious as well. Both argue with their barons to assert their respective agenda (perhaps most ominously when the Persian nobles warn an arrogant Darius that Alexander represents a genuine threat), both lead a multicultural coalition of subject and allied nations, and both are killed by treacherous factions within the ranks of these barons.

It is this last commonality that played so vital a role in the characterization of Alexander throughout Antiquity and the Middle Ages. In the previous chapter, I examined the centrality of Alexander's conquest of Persia in the burgeoning interest in the twelfth century in the *Philippic Histories* and its stark portrayal of Alexander as a tyrant. In his *St Albans Compilation*, Ralph Gubiun pays, for example, considerable attention to Alexander's warm treatment of Darius's family after he captures them in battle, and how that act wins not only the king's wife, mother, and daughter over to the Macedonian's dream of a unified empire, but indeed all of the Persians. At the same time, this victory on the battlefield and act of filial kindness off of it signals Alexander's transformation. No longer does he seek the glory of conquest, but its wealth, and no longer does he seek to overrun Persia, but to adopt it as his own nation. Latin legends, having no intent to vilify Alexander for his foreign policy in Persia, had long treated the conqueror's affection for the Persian royal family in altogether different terms. In the Valerius *Epitome*, the report of Alexander's compassion for Darius's mother, wife, and daughters culminates in a scene in which the dying Great King personally commits his family and his empire to his Macedonian enemy whom he has come to respect as one of his own:

> "En mihi in tali fortuna constituto magnum adest obitus huius solatium, quod in tuis manibus, o Alexander, fortissime regum, spiritum effundam. Quare quaeso, ne invideas mihi sepulturam, quam mihi cum Persis tui Macedones exsequantur. Tum Rogodunen, matrem meam, et Cilito uxorem in manus tuas commendo; filiam vero Roxanen hec prece tibi commendo, ut eam coniugio tuo dignam censeas; erit enim ei largiter ad solatium, nihil sibi de regia coniunctione defuisse."[74]

> "Alas, with such a fortune befalling me, it is a great comfort in death that I shall breathe my last in your arms, o Alexander, strongest of kings. Wherefore I beg you not to begrudge me a burial, which your Macedonians along with the Persians can perform for me. I commend unto your hands my mother Rogodunes, my wife Cilito, and my daughter Roxane, with the wish that you will deem her worthy of being your bride. It will be a great comfort for her, and neither of you will find anything wanting in this royal marriage."

In translating this death scene, Thomas grants a more expansive and emotive final speech to the conquered Persian. Besides asking Alexander to bury his corpse and protect it from scavenging animals, Darius requests a personal favour from his former enemy:

"Ma mere ne mes filles, roy, ne honissez.
Sur tote rien ma feme pri qe conseillez.
Pernez la [a] moiller e si sires soiez,
Donc ert ses honurs granz e ses pris eshaucez.
D'onur ne de mari n'ert ses los abessez,
E vous ne serez, sire, point desparagez,
Car plus franche ne quid qe jamés prengez.
Jeo sui naffrez a mort, sire, de deus espiez,
Si vous rent ma terre, mes honurs e mes fez.
Par ma moiller seront mes tresors enseignez.
Des plaies qe jeo ay suy forment angoissez,
Mes par vostre venue suy mult alegez.
De ceo qe moer entre vos meins en sui jeo mult lez.
Tut le mal qe jeo sent est par ceo obliez." (3690–703)

"Dishonour neither my mother nor my daughters, o king. Above all else, I pray that you help my wife. Take her as your bride and be her husband – her honour is great, and her esteem is renowned. The honour of having you as a husband will not lessen her stature, and you, sir, will not at all be married below your station, because I do not think that you will ever take a more noble bride. I am wounded nearly to death, sir, by these two lances, and so I render my lands, my domains, and my fiefdoms to you. My wife will show you to my treasures. I am in considerable anguish due to my wounds, but your arrival greatly relieves me. I am so happy dying in your arms that I forget all of the hardship that I have suffered."

Rather than bestowing his daughter upon Alexander and making him a son-in-law and heir-apparent to the Persian throne, in the *Roman de toute chevalerie* Darius thus asks the Macedonian to *become* him, to *become* a second Darius at the head of Persia. Alexander is, in the king's parting request, to marry his wife (not his daughter) and appropriate his lands and treasures, so that Darius ensures continuity in the transferral of power within both Persia and his own family. Not only does he hand the throne over to a man whom he respects as a competent ruler, but he also bequeaths his family to a man whom he clearly respects as a new *pater familias* for his family and empire. Much of Darius's confidence in Alexander – and indeed his paternal devotion to his new successor – is

Figure 3.1 Alexander has Darius buried (Cambridge, Trinity College MS. O.9.34, fol. 21v). Reproduced with permission of the Master and Fellows of Trinity College, Cambridge.

apparent in his last statement, his admission that he finds such comfort dying in Alexander's arms that he forgets his other troubles. This touching sentiment occurs at the moment when Darius and Alexander find themselves physically and ideologically conjoined, when Alexander is appropriating Persia as his own empire, with its lands, fiefdoms, treasures, and even a ready-made family, and accepting Darius's blessing, while the dying Great King repeats the posturing seen in Nectanabus and Philip's final scenes. In Alexander's arms and devoting the future of his family and empire to him, Darius inspires a third moment of filial piety in the young man. Darius's confidence in his former foe and Alexander's piety are equally figured in the burial scene featured in the earliest surviving manuscript of the *Roman de toute chevalerie*, Cambridge, Trinity College MS O.9.34.

As the caption reads "Coment Alisandre fist enterrer le cors Darie" (How Alexander had Darius's corpse buried), the Macedonian conqueror fulfils his promise of an honourable interment to a fellow king, yet he also proves his genuine concern for a man long known as Macedon's chief enemy (and one who effectively bullied Alexander's nominal father Philip). With his hands on his chest and his downcast face full of compassion for the royal corpse, Alexander's gestures recall the earlier intimacy between the two men, when Darius entrusted his empire and family to his former enemy and proclaimed his relief at dying in his arms. However, as the new Great King of Persia looks down mournfully on his predecessor, a serious threat lurks in this illustration. To either side of the coffin stand men (presumably Persian) yielding to laments and weeping, and in their physical division and in their unmitigated grief, these figures anticipate the Macedonian reaction upon Alexander's death depicted later in the manuscript, when the conqueror's successors will stand united in their own anguish before retreating to their respective lands and waging a long and bloody civil war. Persia, too, rests on the edge of factionalism and civil war, as Darius's barons, who argued with his defence plans for the invading Macedonians and committed an egregious act of regicide by running their leader through with lances, now bicker over the future of their once great empire. However, Alexander, standing in the centre of this picture of lamentation, will punish the traitors who murdered Darius and unify his officers, soldiers, and his people, and he will not only continue the Persian empire but transform it into something greater, a coalition stretching from the Mediterranean to India – until, that is, his own death at the hands of traitors will repeat this scene with direr consequences. Along with his treatment of Olympias and Philip, this reminder to the audience that one of Antiquity's most famed and seemingly most successful empires collapsed because of a succession crisis represents Thomas's most significant departure from his Latin source-text, the Valerius *Epitome*, which concludes simply by lamenting the conqueror's death and praising his accomplishments. This was the conclusion favoured, too, by Albéric and French romance writers in the twelfth century, and so rather than adhering to the traditional narrative promulgated by the *Pseudo-Callisthenes* textual tradition and vernacular romances inspired by it, Thomas continues an interest in Alexander's disreputable parents and ambitious barons that began with the *Parva recapitulatio* and the *St Albans Compilation* in previous generations.

Readers of his narrative (as it survives in the Cambridge, Paris, and Durham manuscripts) would encounter, however, novel views of Alexander that did much to alter the conqueror's legacy in the century after Thomas composed his romance. Various Anglo-Latin portrayals of Alexander, in particular, were soon to change from the damning accounts of his degradation, influenced by Orosius and the *Philippic Histories*, of the twelfth century towards anecdotes that tended rather to emphasize his role as a divinely ordained ancient ruler who was victorious over agents of evil in the East and defended European civilization. As the political landscape changed, too, in a period of royal-baronial conflict in the thirteenth century, a time when lamenting the sad state of political affairs and misguided kingship inspired a myriad of literary expressions, Alexander became an idealized king – at once God's chosen warrior and a leader who valued and rewarded his baronage – for audiences of the legend and of Thomas's romance.

Chapter Four

The Two Deaths of Alexander in Cambridge, Trinity College MS O. 9. 34

As the oldest surviving copy of the *Roman de toute chevalerie*, Cambridge, Trinity College MS O. 9. 34 has long inspired more questions than answers among textual critics and codicologists. Produced approximately seventy-five years after Thomas composed his poem, the manuscript was associated in the nineteenth century with St Albans (M.R. James even assigned its "excellent" final product, including the 152 drawings, to Matthew Paris),[1] although recent scholars have convincingly attributed it to a secular workshop.[2] The only record of provenance is that of scholar and antiquarian Thomas Gale, who donated the codex to Trinity College in 1738.[3] Questions of quality aside, the generic designation of the manuscript's text has clearly vexed its cataloguers. James's title, which remains in use on Trinity College's online catalogue, is simply the "Romance of Alexander," yet Heinrich Schneegans, who published his notes on the copies of the poem in 1930, noted that a modern hand had recorded the Trinity College codex as "The History of Alexander the great" at the top of the first folio.[4] Then there is the matter of the far older title, the *Roman de toute chevalerie*, which is the modern form of the explicit found in both this copy and Paris, Bibliothèque Nationale MS 24364: "Ci finist le romaunz de tute chivalerie."[5] This leaves us with an author about whom little is known, a work influenced by diverse sources on Alexander, and an Anglo-Norman poem whose manuscripts were interpolated with lengthy sections of its French predecessors and successors, resulting in a state of textual amalgamation that frustratingly obscures our view of what Thomas actually intended.

None of these problems are alleviated by the Trinity College copy of the *Roman de toute chevalerie*. Its forty-six surviving folios (featuring roughly the latter half of the text) begin with the end of the *Fuerre de*

Gadres, a French narrative interpolated into each of the major manuscripts of Thomas's poem. As a *chanson de geste*-inspired text, the *Fuerre de Gadres* recounts a doomed expedition by Alexander's generals into the Levant, where they encounter the forces of two enemy leaders, Betys of Gadres and Balés of Tyre. Outnumbered but too proud to retreat, Alexander's men send for reinforcements, and the conqueror's arrival tilts the battle in his army's favour. Still, the Macedonian general in charge of the expedition, Emenidus, is killed by the Egyptian Gadifer, and the narrator ends with Alexander's vengeance on Gadres and the sack of Tyre. Thomas's original poem begins immediately thereafter, seven folios into the manuscript in the middle of Alexander's campaign against Persia, and it continues (with the occasional lost folio) until his death and the beginning of the baronial wars that would decimate his empire. At this point, the scribe appended five folios of material from the *Roman d'Alexandre* covering Alexander's partitioning of the Macedonian Empire from his deathbed and scenes of mourning and eulogizing from his barons.[6] The most distinctive feature of this copy of the romance is, then, that it features two confusing series of images depicting Alexander's death and his division of the empire among his successors. The first series, from Alexander's consumption of the poison on fol. 38v to his burial on fol. 39v, corresponds to Thomas's text (and figures the narrative up to *laisse* [stanza] 545 in Foster's edition); the second, from folios 39v to 43r, corresponds, however, to Alexandre de Paris's redaction of the fourth branch of the *Roman d'Alexandre*, which relates the conqueror's assassination and his distribution of his lands among his survivors.

Even without these interpolations, the Cambridge manuscript may not have resolved all of the confusion over the "original" *Roman de toute chevalerie* had it survived in its complete state, but Brian Foster's lament for its linguistic superiority over the other copies still gives pause:

> From the point of view of language there is no doubt that [MS O. 9. 34] is by far the best text ... [it] is a careful and reasonably early MS., but on the other hand it is so incomplete in comparison with [Paris, Bibliothèque Nationale MS 24364] and [Durham, Durham Cathedral Library MS C.IV.27V,] that we must with great reluctance dismiss it as the basis of a literary text.[7]

As this book argues, each of these manuscripts has much to teach us about the reception of the *Roman de toute chevalerie* in a particular time and place, as they were recognized by medieval readers, if not by modern scholars, as the "Roman de toute chevalerie." Given that Thomas composed the first comprehensive, vernacular romance of Alexander's life and the legends that it accumulated on either side of the Channel, the experience for his readership would have been markedly different for those accustomed to the *Pseudo-Callisthenes* family of texts and French Alexander romances. For at least a century in England, the most popular of these Latin texts (the Valerius *Epitome*, the *Epistola Alexandri*, and the *Collatio cum Dindimo*) had been collated and bound into singular codices, yet they remained distinct, individual texts therein. Their readers would have thus worked through achronological, disjointed stages: approaching first the biography of Alexander from the Nectanabus episode to his poisoning in Babylon (the Valerius *Epitome*), they would have then perused ancillary texts on the marvellous flora and fauna that populate India (the *Epistola Alexandri*) and Alexander's debate with an ascetic Indian philosopher (the *Collatio cum Dindimo*). In similar fashion, audiences and readers of French Alexander romances would have known them in serial fashion over the twelfth century until Alexandre de Paris's compilation of the *Roman d'Alexandre*. In the *Roman de toute chevalerie*, however, one sequentially encounters a complete biography, from the beginning to the end of Alexander's reign and empire, and can thus trace the progress of his formative years, his greatest military achievement in the conquest of Persia, his easternmost campaigns in the exploration of India, and the moment at which cracks in the foundation of the Macedonian Empire first appear.

The producers of the Trinity College manuscript evidently sought to use Thomas's text as a vehicle by which to incorporate material from the very French romances that he had avoided and thereby offer an even more expansive narrative of Alexander, and it was this last aspect of Thomas's narrative that especially attracted their attention. While the tragic ethos of the conqueror's legend had been founded on the act of treason committed against the youth ruler as he enjoys the height of his power, Thomas, especially for a clerical writer aware of various literary traditions in Alexander's reception, does not follow the neat Continental French romance account of Alexander's death and his survivors' universal mourning. Rather, he reminds his audience, as had the *Parva recapitulatio*-redactor and Ralph Gubiun before him, that Alexander's death had grave political consequences for his empire and his subjects. This is apparent not only in the actual moment of Alexander's death, when Thomas will recall his fellow monastic and clerical writers' interest in the Macedonian civil wars, but also in the prophecies regarding Alexander's death, the supernatural episodes that Thomas appropriates from the Valerius *Epitome* and the *Epistola Alexandri ad Aristotelem.* In the first such prophecy, Thomas recounts Alexander's exploration of an Ethiopian volcano, reputedly the site of divination. Making his sacrifice and posing his question, the king receives the first in a series of disheartening oracles, after making sacrifices to the gods and thanking them:

"Ke joe, Alisandre, ke tut doi justiser,
Les hommes terriens e les regnes consiller,
Kar sur tut le mond m'avez fet eshaucer,
Si com vous estes deus pussant e dreiturer,
Dites moi si joe doi en Grece repairer
E veer ma mere e mun maistre ke joe ai cher,
E trouer mes sorurs e mes amis baiser,
E eshaucer Macedonie e ses leis adrecer,
E richeir mes parens, mes compaignons aider,
Ke de mes enemis me pusse a dreit venger."
Une voiz lui dit: "Reis, ne t'estuet iceo prier!
De tut ceo ne te volent li deus pas otrier."
Tristes devint li reis, si se prist a esmaer. (fol. 30r)

"that I, Alexander, ruler of the world and presider over the peoples and kingdoms of the earth, have been elevated above all the world. Since you are a powerful and just god, tell me if I will be allowed to return to Greece and see my dear mother and master and find my sisters in my arms again and kiss them, and glorify Macedon and codify its laws, make my family wealthy and help my friends, and be able to exact vengeance on my enemies." A voice said to him, "King, your prayer is futile! The gods do not wish to grant you any of these things." The king was saddened and dismayed.

Situated within a lengthy catalogue of wondrous beasts and peoples in exotic lands (the legacy of the so-called *Epistola Alexandri ad Aristotelem*) and Alexander's holy war against Gog and Magog, this scene is altogether deflating. As he will continue to do throughout the final quarter of his poem, Thomas emphasizes the ultimate failure of Alexander's enterprise and the conqueror's morose awareness of this fact.

His protagonist's despair over the oracle in Ethiopia soon escalates in the well-known episode of the prophecies of the trees of the sun and moon in India. Originally included in the *Epistola Alexandri*,[8] these trees and the priest who presides over them foretell the circumstances of Alexander's death in Babylon, and in Thomas's telling, when Alexander hears of the trees from an itinerant, elderly man, he displays a temper rarely seen in the *Roman de toute chevalerie*:

"Veillard, vos i mentez!
Cestes controveures, si jeo vif, comparez.
Mi baron, tel eschar cum oez venger devez!
Jeo, Alisandre, qui sui sur toz roys coronez
E del chef de l'occident empereres clamez,
Quant ore sui par tels escharniz e gabez." (7050–5)[9]

"You are lying, old man! By my life, you will pay for these falsehoods. My barons, you must avenge me for this taunt you have heard! I, Alexander, crowned above all other kings and proclaimed emperor to the ends of the West, am now mocked and taunted by these words!"

Still, Alexander seeks to hear what the trees foresee for him and so again becomes privy to the redundant report that he will conquer Asia but fail to return to Macedon and see his family. This time, however, that report forces Alexander to adopt a new strategy.

As he and his barons weep over a prophecy in which they cannot help but believe, Alexander immediately senses the dangers of rumours and emotional outbursts so deep into enemy territory. First he attempts to quell the public outcry over the prophecies:

"Barons, ne plorez!
Tut me couient suffrir quant issinc est comandez.
Communement vus pri ke cest consail celez;
A homme nel diez ne jammes n'en parlez.
Granz honurs vus dorrai e richesces asez,
E frai en vos voleirs e quant ke volez.
Si nul de vus le dit, cher ert comparez." (fol. 31r)

"Barons, do not cry! It befits me to suffer all the things thus commanded. I ask all of you together that this proclamation be kept secret – never speak of it to men or gods. I will bestow upon you great honours and riches plenty, and I will fulfil all your desires, whatever you wish. However, if any of you speak of this, you will pay for it dearly."

However, when Alexander himself gathers more information from the trees about his death, he attempts to remain publicly stoic, to deny the accuracy of such predictions, and to intimidate his men:

"Il vus est ben suez
Joe sui par tut le mond dutez e cremuz,
E pur ma grant puissance sui joe pur deu creuz
E nient pur homme mortel en terre tenuz.
S'il sevent le consail ke ore est avenuz,
Viaz ert le mond vers moi commeuz
E çoe k'avum conquis poet tost estre perduz.
Pur çoe command a tuz k'il soit ben teuz.
Ne dites a nullui içoe k'avez veuz.
Ne sai si çoe est veirs, mes tost serreit creuz.
Si Deu veut, ben poet estre ke soie deceuz
Par engin de l'eveske pur tolir mes vertuz.
Mut par est fous ki creit les diz de cesty feuz." (fol. 31v)

"You well know that I am renowned and feared throughout the whole world, and on account of my great power I am believed a god and not considered a mortal of earth. If any know the proclamation just foretold of me, the world will quickly rise up against me, and what I have conquered could be lost entirely. Therefore I command everyone to keep silent; do not tell anyone what you have seen. I do not know if this prophecy is true, but it will be immediately believed. If God wishes, then I am simply being deceived by a trick of this priest in order to deprive me of my strength. He is a crazy man who believes the words of this fool."

In the *Epistola Alexandri ad Aristotelem*, the source for this scene, Alexander merely keeps the prophecy of his impending death to himself, so as not to bring danger upon his men, and orders the officers nearest him to remain silent about the whole affair.[10] For Thomas, the oracle of the trees of the sun and moon becomes a communal experience. For the first time, the Macedonian army and its leader face significant opposition, not on the battlefield but from a seemingly divine presence. The terminus imposed (or at least threatened) on their success, their empire, and Alexander's life has a profound emotional effect, particularly in that, as the last in a series of prophecies, the words of these trees accord with what many readers would have known to be the actual circumstances of Alexander's death.

As Thomas continues with his description of wondrous beasts and the Candace episode, an ominous sense of futility lingers in the text, and the prophecies of death and destruction that Alexander hears in the East serve within the poem as the collective counterpart to the prophecies and prognostications from his childhood. His biological father Nectanabus had twice predicted to Olympias that Alexander would conquer lands to the limits of the eastern world, and upon Alexander's birth, his supposed father Philip, knowing both that this future king was not his son and would never return to Macedon, had proclaimed it folly to let the child live ("e folie ly semble qu'il tant vist ou dure").[11] When Alexander hears in Africa and India that he will never see home again and soon die young in Babylon, Thomas's readers, the beneficiaries of a comprehensive Alexander narrative, can recall these words of his fathers, yet they can also see how such prophecies and the poem as a whole connect Alexander's demise to his scandalous family.

Rejecting the typical ending of Alexander legends – both Latin and French narratives ended with laments and eulogies for the fallen conqueror – demanded that Thomas acknowledge the historical context of the Macedonian Empire. His primary Latin source, the Valerius *Epitome*, records Alexander's death in its typically understated manner: "quo illo hausto mox lectulo datur, intellexitque, se moriturum. Ordinatis itaque rebus dispositisque principibus ac ducibus suis, prout sibi libuit, spiritum emisit" (after Alexander drank the poison, he was carried to his bed, and he saw that he would die. After he had arranged his affairs and provided for his nobles and officers according to his wishes, he breathed his last).[12] As I have discussed elsewhere, Anglo-Latin scribes supplemented this conclusion with a variety of epitaphs, some suggestive of the irony of a man celebrated for his deeds of arms being slain by a drink and others condemning the butchery of his reign.[13] Thomas undoubtedly held his protagonist in high regard, but he did not include in his work any concluding paeon on Alexander's virtues or lament for the fatal glass of wine delivered by Antipater. He instead mingles pity with condemnation in blaming the collapse of the Macedonian Empire on Alexander's barons, the instigators of a civil war fought for control of Alexander's lands. Thomas thus shows no interest in the understated neatness of the conqueror's final arrangements in the Valerius *Epitome* but leaves his audience with a parting reminder that Alexander was unable to curb the ambitions of his barons and so failed to secure for his lands and subjects a peaceful transition of authority.

So begins the first death scene of the Trinity College manuscript with Thomas's account of Alexander's last moments, in which he delivers a lengthy speech, at once reflective and prophetic and surviving only in this copy:

> Alisandre prent la cupe si en beit bonement.
> Com grant doel dun tel hom quant sa mort i prent!
> Li beiveres fut ague e si chet trenchantment
> Tut li ret le ventrail a poi kil ne fent.
> Li reis gette la cupe e dist oiant sa gent:
> Tut icil ki maiment poent estre dolent
> Ensurketut ma mere e mi autre parent
> Kar coe ke ai beu est ma mort verement.
> Ne pus longes vivere les anguisses en sent.
> Antipater m'ad mort par son felon present.
> Gardez ke nul n'en beive a tuz le defent.
> Oscis mad come traitre e tut felonessement.
> Ne quid ke mes moerge reis par tel entuschement
> Dont tel mal vienge aprof men escient
> La dolur en est grant e fort le vengement.
> Li munde le sentira deskal chef del occident. (fol. 39r)

> Alexander took the cup and drank gladly from it. What great sorrow that so noble a man found his death in doing so! The drink gave him a sharp pain, and he felt as if it had cut him. It tore his whole stomach, so that he could barely live. The king threw the cup down and called out to his men, "All of those who love me can grieve, especially my mother and my other family members, because what I have just consumed spells my certain death. I can no longer live, and I feel the anguish of death. Antipater has killed me with his criminal present. Make sure that no one else drinks it, for it will kill everyone. [Antipater], you have killed me like a traitor, in an entirely criminal fashion. I think that no king's death through poisoning will cause such evil as mine. The grief will be great, and the vengeance fierce. The world will feel it unto the ends of the West."

As the concerns expressed in this passage transition from the grief of his loved ones to his certain death to the ramifications of that death for his survivors, Alexander's speech crescendos in its emotional intensity and political scope. He worries not only for the private tragedy soon to be suffered by his family but for the public, political tragedy awaiting his empire as well. He does not articulate the latter in terms of anarchy, or of officers unable to cope with the administrative duties of ruling an empire or to avoid the temptations of power, but foresees the coming tragedy of Macedon in two threats to its stability, "dolur" and "vengement," a progression from grief to a violent desire for revenge. His ominous words even suggest that Macedon alone will not suffer but that the entire world (fittingly towards his west, encompassing the lands that he did not reach in life) will feel the effects of his death and the subsequent actions of those whom he will leave behind.

In the Trinity College manuscript, Alexander's fear over the violence that will overcome his successors is textually and visually confirmed over several folios. Immediately after his prophecy above, he collapses from the fatal poison, and his men argue over the burial of his corpse. Following the tradition established by the *Pseudo-Callisthenes*, Thomas relates that three groups seek possession of the body: the Babylonians wish for it to remain in Alexander's new capital, the Macedonians wish to bring it home, and the Persians wish to retain Alexander's body, as he had served as their Great King since his defeat of Darius. The image of this debate depicts the three parties, presumably with the Macedonians in the middle, in a traditional medieval arrangement of survivors around a corpse, as discussed below. As they impose their authority by pointing at the corpse and thus laying claim to it, the Macedonians reject the implorations of the other two parties, their subjects who clearly appeal to their foreign conquerors in a submissive manner. Such an arrangement resolves the disagreement for the viewer and suggests the Macedonians' attempt, at least, to maintain political authority in enemy territory. The actual resolution comes, however, from a divine source, as the oracle of Jupiter in the Valerius *Epitome* becomes the voice of God in Thomas's telling (and the face of God on fol. 39r) issuing a directive to bury the corpse in Alexandria.

Although the matter is resolved, the instability among Alexander's survivors is soon apparent once again. Just as he predicted, grief first overtakes his men, and at the conqueror's tomb "grant doel li soen menerent / Batirent lur palmes lur cheveuz detirerent / Lur riche garnemenz danguisse decirerent" (his men began to grieve considerably, and in their anguish they clapped their palms and tore their hair, and they ripped apart their fine garments [fol. 39r]).[14] Although only three

Figure 4.1 The grief over Alexander's death (Cambridge, Trinity College MS. O.9.34, fol. 39v). Reproduced with permission of the Master and Fellows of Trinity College, Cambridge.

lines long, the scene attracted the interest of the illustrator of the Cambridge manuscript enough to include a portrayal of the "grant doel."

The artist conveys in this scene two significant themes, the primary one of the grief of Alexander's survivors and the secondary one of the growing divide among them. Still, he merely foreshadows this animosity by spatially arranging the barons at three points of the bier, the head, foot, and centre, just as he did in the debate over Alexander's burial on the preceding folio. They remain unified by their grief, emphasized by the men at centre looking towards their peers to their left and right. At the same time, the artist makes it clear that this is no ordinary burial scene suggestive of any calm resolution or, in modern parlance, a sense of closure. The Trinity College, MS O. 9. 34 burial scene exudes the violent, physical reaction of pulling hair and rending garments towards Alexander's death and serves as a harbinger for the disorder that concludes Thomas's narrative. Together, this drawing and the words below it regarding the outbreak of civil war indicate that although Alexander attempts to secure political order after his death by dividing his wealth among his men, he cannot prevent this outpouring of grief and the subsequent turmoil among his fractured baronage. The representation of despair, with men not only disfiguring their bodies and garments but weeping and covering their eyes as well, may suggest an omen of forthcoming political violence, but it also reflects the typical ethos of Alexander romance, as the conqueror is shockingly murdered, his men lament, and the reader is reminded how extraordinary Alexander was in his brief career.[15]

As Alexander foretold, however, this brief moment of grieving would be followed by a prolonged period of strife, described just below the image in the continuation of Thomas's narrative of how the conqueror's survivors took up arms against each other and fought for control over the Macedonian Empire:

> Apres lensevelir li ducs se desevrerent
> En lur propres terres e en lur citez allerent
> E les chivalers par les regnes manderent.
> Icil ke poeient e puis sen assemblerent
> Efforcerent lur murs e lur citez fremerent
> E garnirent lur turs de guerre saturnerent.
> Communement par tut le mond se mellerent
> Li povere e li chetif cest estrif comparerent
> E la mort Alisandre mut cher achaterent
> E icil des regnes ke plus la desirerent
> Premers se repentirent por le mal ke troverent:
> En servage cheirent en peur ke nen erent. (fol. 39v)

After burying Alexander, the leaders separated and went to their respective lands and cities, and they summoned their knights throughout the kingdoms. Those who were the most powerful and who then gathered together fortified their walls and secured their cities, protected their towers, and turned their minds to war. They fought each other throughout the entire world; the poor and the enfeebled paid for this strife, and they paid dearly for the death of Alexander. And those in the kingdoms who most desired the death of Alexander repented for the first time because of the evil they encountered, and they fell into servitude worse than that in which they had been.

Thomas then qualifies this "mal" and "servage" in a curious concluding passage:

> Grant merveille est de gent ki encontre reson tirent.
> Changent en curages e en lor quer desirent
> Noveautez e changes dont sei meimes enpirent.
> Tant com Alisandre vesqui, li baron lenhairent
> Detraistent par paroles e plusurs mals bastirent
> E felonessement par poisun le trairent
> Ou sist a son manger granz maus as regnes firent.
> Cil ki au consail furent onques nen ioirent
> En tel aventure e en tel paine cheirent
> Dont il e tut lur eir pus en repentirent.
> Plus de quinze reaumes tel dolur en soffrirent
> Eeissille en furent; la soe mort mal virent.
> La gent en fut destruite e des terres fuirent.
> Povere e cheitif lur herite guerpirent
> Li reis e li princes lur vies en perdirent
> Pur la mort Alisandre qu'il a tort mordrirent. (fol. 39v)

> What a wonder that these people acted against reason! They changed their intentions, and in their hearts they desired the novelties and changes that they initiated themselves. While Alexander was living, his barons hated him and slandered him and formed plots against him, before they traitorously poisoned him at the dinner table. This was a great misfortune for his empire. The culprits gained no advantage from this act, for they and their descendants alike were subjected to great pain and punishment. More than fifteen kingdoms suffered tremendous grief and exile because of this murder. They paid dearly for his death. By the death of Alexander, so unjustly killed, his people were killed and took to flight, the poor and the enfeebled lost their inheritance, and the king and his nobles lost their lives.

Not only do these lines pass judgment on the treachery committed against Alexander and the fighting among his successors, but they also call attention (again) to the widespread public suffering owing to both. Just as Alexander feared, the world beyond his army and his enemies, the world of such innocents as the "povere e cheitif," is implicated in the violence sweeping across his divided empire, and in what amounts to a moral commentary, Thomas condemns not merely the conspirators against Alexander but all of the barons.

The producers of the Cambridge manuscript may have simply wished to present as full an account of Alexander and his barons as possible, a compendium of the conqueror and his empire, but the result is confusing on the page. Following Alexander's death in the Anglo-Norman narrative and the passage above, which concludes Thomas's narrative, Alexander allocates his lands in the interpolations from Alexandre de Paris's *Roman d'Alexandre*. Twelve of the eighteen drawings in this addendum to the first series of concluding images depict Alexander crowning each of his twelve successors, the *douze peres* (the addendum's first five drawings repeat Alexander's poisoning and dying moments from the French *Roman d'Alexandre*) and act as a textual-visual footnote to the *Roman de toute chevalerie*. Near the end of his poem, Thomas writes that Alexander divides his holdings among his successors, but his text does not specify which successor received which province. That information is rather found in the French *Roman d'Alexandre*, and the additional text and drawings in the codex thus serve a practical purpose for the scribe of the manuscript by explicating a scene over which Thomas did not linger. Still, there is a thematic discontinuity between the original, Anglo-Norman text and the Continental addition, for the latter simply concludes with Alexander's portioning of his lands among twelve successors, their public, unanimous mourning for the poisoned conqueror, and their appointment of Ptolemy as their leader. In Alexandre de Paris's telling, the story of Alexander becomes so admirable that in life and death the conqueror is the paradigm for "li rois qui son roiaume veut par droit governer / Et li prince et li duc qui terre ont a garder / Et cil qui par proëce veulent riens conquester" (kings who want to govern their kingdoms justly, princes and dukes who protect the land, and those who wish to conquer any land valiantly).[16] From folios 39v–44v, the Cambridge manuscript concludes by following laisses 5–37 of branch four of this French romance (Alexander's division of his lands among his *douze peres*), laisses 39–40 (Emenidus's lament that the death of the conqueror will plunge the entire world into sorrow), laisses 50–1 (a procession of mourners passing by Alexander's corpse and the preparations for his burial), laisses 38 (a second lament from Emenidus), and finally laisse 53 (a volatile outburst by Perdiccas on the cruelty of Fortune). The conclusion of this interpolation is thus composed of a traditional commentary on Fortune and a prolonged articulation of the sorrow and praise due in equal measure to the fallen ruler.

In the first drawing of what appears visually on the folio as a third ending to the manuscript, Alexander appoints Ptolemy to his new position of leadership, as the other beneficiaries stand about them.

Figure 4.2 Alexander addresses his successors (Cambridge, Trinity College MS O.9.34, fol. 43r). Reproduced with permission of the Master and Fellows of Trinity College, Cambridge.

As the dying king appoints his eleven successors, now crowned and wearing the symbols of their newly granted authority, they stand once again in three divided groups, the gaze of these barons become kings has turned from their leader towards each other. Then, in the final drawing ("Comment Al se lessad morir"), Alexander has fallen back dead, and his successors stand divided at the head and the foot of the bed.

The men mourn and show clear signs of despair and confusion (the wringing of hands and uncertain glances), and while some look down at Alexander's corpse others look over again at their onetime peers,

Figure 4.3 The death of Alexander (Cambridge, Trinity College MS O.9.34, fol. 43r). Reproduced with permission of the Master and Fellows of Trinity College, Cambridge.

now competitors, and the scene conveys grief and perhaps even uncertainty over the future of the empire.

The arrangement of the Trinity College burial scenes, with Alexander's corpse flanked by two equal groups of survivors, evolves from a long history of depicting the burial of the Virgin in various media.[17] Attendants who stand on either side of the Virgin traditionally show – not unlike Alexander's successors in the Trinity College manuscript – grief, fear, and uncertainty while standing beside her body and facing each other, and the producers of the Cambridge copy of the *Roman de toute chevalerie* thus had a convenient model for depicting Alexander's corpse and his men's reaction to his death. It is striking, however, that they use these pictorial exemplars, just as they do the French interpolations, to obfuscate Thomas's narrative of civil war. The Trinity College manuscript's final folios, spanning Alexander's division of his lands among the *douze peres* and their grief and confusion over his body, make it exceedingly difficult to recall Thomas's final passage on folio 39r, in which he rebukes the barons for their hatred of Alexander, their civil war, and the ensuing public massacre for which they must be held responsible.

The dissonance between Thomas's conclusion and the final words and images of a manuscript of his romance is equally evident in Bibliothèque Nationale MS 24364, a copy of the *Roman de toute chevalerie* that was made for a baronial or knightly audience under Edward I (as discussed in the next chapter). Although the Paris manuscript was likely produced in London, its language is not Anglo-Norman but Continental French adapted by a French copyist, and the same can be said of the manuscript's illuminations.[18] Over the final three folios and their four drawings Alexander divides his empire, but then his men simply mourn his passing and prepare an extravagant burial for him. The barons in the Paris drawings look both downward towards Alexander and across his body towards each other, and in their physical gestures of holding their hands together against their chests suggest both a sense of reverence for their king and sadness over his death. The final two folios of the Paris manuscript, in which the text concludes the French interpolations and returns to Thomas's original ending, are adorned by three images, which convey, respectively, mourning (some of the barons pull their hair and look away), confusion (standing again in three groups around the corpse, the barons raise their arms outward and upward and look in different directions), the divine directive to bury Alexander in Alexandria (the face of God looks down at the corpse and separates the barons into two groups), and, finally, grief again (the barons tear their hair, look down at the corpse, and support their faces with their hands). The last stanza of the Paris manuscript, however, is Thomas's highly critical final passage on the devastation wrought by this war, while the last image, with the caption "Le doel sur la tombe Alisandre," shows neither resentment among the barons nor the hint of impending war.

The barons remain in a state of grief, and yet there is the suggestion of (from left to right) confusion, particularly in the absent-minded stare of the far-left figure, the continuing physical expression of lament in the middle figures who tear their garments and hair, and quiet reflection in the far-right figure, with his sorrowful face supported by his hand. For

Figure 4.4 Alexander's men grieve at his tomb (Paris, Bibliothèque Nationale MS 24364, fol. 87r). Reproduced with permission of the Bibliothèque Nationale de France.

these barons, despite the stanza above the drawing, Alexander's death elicits shock and sadness, hesitation, and uncertainty regarding the future of the empire, rather than the instantaneous desire to dismember it in fighting for the largest share. Thomas may have wished to remind his audiences of the disastrous ending to Alexander's empire, but the producers of the manuscripts of his work wished, it seems, to whitewash to various degrees (at least the Paris copy ends with Thomas's own words) this conclusion. By the time the earliest copy of the *Roman de toute chevalerie*, the Trinity College manuscript, was produced, in fact, Alexander's reception was undergoing another of its many transformations, and Thomas's caution in presenting the conqueror as an exemplary ruler was an increasingly antiquated view.

Contexts of the Trinity College *Roman de toute chevalerie*

Produced at least half a century after Thomas's poem, the Cambridge copy suggests that there remained an interest in Alexander's life and exploits among England's vernacular readership, whether they were attracted to the battles and adventures that characterize much of the *Roman de toute chevalerie* or the manner in which Alexander's barons take up arms against each other at the end of the narrative and undermine the empire built by their ruler. When he wrote the *Roman de toute chevalerie*, Thomas responded largely to the Valerius *Epitome*, the Latin text that served as the foundation for much of vernacular Alexander romance in western Europe, and provided the first vernacular Alexander narrative in England, following a re-examination, in Anglo-Latin, of classical histories of the Macedonian Empire in previous decades. While the one glorified Alexander's career, the other condemned his ambition and that of his successors. By the mid-thirteenth century, however, Anglo-Latin accounts of the conqueror and his successors had altered their tone considerably, owing to the increasingly available Christian and Jewish anecdotes, discussed below, that glossed over his vices and transgressions. In chronicles of the time, the successors were often cited not so much for their behaviour after Alexander's death as for their role in the larger construct of history, as the Macedonian Empire gave way to various dynasties before the age of Roman dominion. Both the forgiving attitude towards Alexander and the sparser treatment of his successors' civil war are apparent in the historical writing at St Albans, home to the prodigious scriptorium long speculated to have produced the Trinity College manuscript.

Although Ralph Gubiun had helped a century earlier to recover and disseminate the most vociferous of Alexander's ancient Roman critics in his *St Albans Compilation*, later generations of historians at the monastery expunged this criticism of its more egregious charges and suggest the increasing influence of Judaeo-Christian anecdotes of quite a different tone. In the *Flores historiarum*, Roger of Wendover conceives of Alexander's career in little more than four succinct stages: his succession to the Macedonian throne and first battle with the Persians, his conquest of Persia, the Indian expedition, and his death and the division of his empire.[19] However, this text, continued by Matthew Paris as the *Chronica majora*, has received scant attention for its portrayal of Macedon, and its basic sources for Macedonian history, although they have much to tell us of Alexander's evolving thirteenth-century reception, have gone misidentified and misunderstood. H.R. Luard, the editor of Matthew's composite chronicle for the Rolls Series, cites them as Ado of Vienne and Hugh of St Victor, whose world chronicle and allegory on 1 Maccabees have, respectively, little or nothing to do with Roger Wendover's original text or Matthew's continuation.[20]

In fact, Roger arranged an amalgamated text of Orosius and Justin, two of the same source-texts that Gubiun consulted for his earlier Alexander compilation. Rather than merely interpolating the several folios' worth of details on Macedonian history that fill the *St Albans Compilation*, Roger reveals an interest only in the clash of two empires, Macedon and Persia, and their two rulers, Alexander and Darius, and much of his account of Alexander addresses military matters (e.g., the conqueror's raising of an army upon taking the throne, Darius's numerical superiority and tactical advantages, and Alexander's successive, shocking victories on the battlefield). However, at this point, Roger strays from the tone of both Justin and Orosius, whose criticism of Alexander's temper, paranoia, and corruptible nature had informed the *St Albans Compilation*. This marks a radical decision for a historian relying on Roman accounts of Macedon, and it surely helps to account for Matthew's later portrait of Alexander as a noble and heroic conqueror.

Roger's Alexander displays exemplary behaviour throughout the *Flores*, which is all the more surprising considering that this chronicle focuses on the war with Persia, which Roman authors had argued was the catalyst for his corruption and seduction by eastern notions of royalty. In Roger's text, when the Macedonians overrun the Persian camps after their victory at Issus, they find treasure and the abandoned royal family:

> In castris Persarum multum auri et ceterarum opum inventum est, et intra castrorum captivos capta est Darii mater, et uxor, soror quoque, et duae Darii filiae, quarum redemptionem oblata Darius etiam regni sui dimidia parte non obtinuit. Illas tamen Alexander haberi apud se ut reginas praecepit, filiabusque non sordidius matrimonium, sed dignitate patris, sperare iussit.[21]

> In the Persian camp they found a great deal of gold and other riches, and among the captives were Darius's mother, wife, sister, and two daughters, whom he tried to buy back, but failed, offering for each a half of his kingdom. However, Alexander commanded that they be treated as queens

among the Macedonians, and he told Darius's daughters to expect not a baser marriage but one befitting the dignity of their father.

This is a composite passage of interpolations from both Orosius and Justin – the former accounts for the statements up to Darius's failed attempts to bargain for his family, and the latter provides the concluding sentence – yet when Roger takes up Justin's narrative, he also edits the Roman writer's criticism, which had been preserved in the *St Albans Compilation*. The similarities between the *Flores historiarum* and this compendium are italicized below, while the source-author's name in brackets represents the marginal citations to the latter in Cambridge, Corpus Christi College MS 219:

[Orosius] *In castris persarum multum auri ceterarumque opum repertum. Inter captivos castrorum mater et uxor eademque soror et filie due darii fuere.* [Pop]... *easque haberi ut reginas precepit filias quoque non sordidius dignitate patris sperare matrimonium iussit.* Post hec opes Darii divitiarumque apparatum contemplat admiratione tantarum rerum capitur. Tunc primum luxuriosa convivia et magnificentiam plurimum sectari.[22]

[Orosius] *In the Persian camp they found a great deal of gold and other riches, and among the captives in the camps were Darius's mother, wife, sister, and two daughters.* [Pompeius Trogus, i.e., Justin] ... [Alexander] *commanded that they be treated as queens, and he told Darius's daughters to expect a marriage no baser than the dignity of their father.* Afterwards he contemplated the display of Darius's wealth and riches, and he was seized with admiration for such great things. Then he first began to strive for luxurious banquets and frequent shows of affectation.

Roger oddly has no concern for Alexander's degradations as he marches eastward, and he maintains a generic account of the conqueror, based not on personality but on the tally of his victories. His Alexander sheds no tears for the murdered Darius, but he does bury him honourably in a manner suitable for a king, and he moves swiftly on to India and the eastern ocean at the ends of the earth. Then, in an egregious understatement of history, Roger concludes Alexander's campaigns and his life as such:

Subactis denique omnibus Orientis gentibus usque ad flumen Indum et Occeanum, statuit remeare retrorsum. Verum cum Darium regem annis tantum quinque supervixisset, et a Babilonia reversus fuisset, suorum insidiis, in eadem urbe, in ipso aetatis et victoriarum suarum flore, vitam venero finivit, vitae videlicit suae anno tricesimo secundo, regni vero sui duodecimo.[23]

When he had at last conquered all of the races of the Orient as far as the Indus river and the Ocean, he decided to retrace his steps. Only five years after he had defeated the Great King Darius and set forth from Babylon, he was killed by treachery in that same city. Poison ended his days in the flower of his life and his victories alike – he was thirty-two years old at the time and in the twelfth year of his reign.

The economical narrative of the *Flores* does not address the violent ramifications of Alexander's death by disentangling the years of convoluted Macedonian civil wars that occupy two of the *St Albans Compilation*'s five books. Roger abridges that particular chapter of history as well, and even though Alexander's "empire was transferred to or dispersed among many,"[24] the chronicler's interest lay in whittling the Macedonian era of history in Justin and Orosius down to a survey of Alexander's career and the establishment of his successors' kingdoms, so that history reads as a genealogy, or a line of kings emanating from the famed conqueror. Roger thus presents a straightforward and factual account of Alexander's career: he conquered Persia and the entire East, and then he returned to Babylon, where he was poisoned by his own men and divided his global empire. Roger certainly does not transform the *St Albans Compilation* into romance with tales of Nectanabus or Alexander's fabulous exploits (that would be done by Thomas Walsingham in the fourteenth century),[25] but he expunges from Gubuin's work its most damning accounts of the Macedonian Empire and several generations of its leaders.[26]

In the generations after Roger Wendover, however, and by the time of the production of the Cambridge manuscript, monastic chroniclers re-evaluated Alexander's legacy as an idealized warrior-king for thirteenth-century Christendom. Two reasons account for this shift in Alexander's reception. As the sweeping monastic histories of the twelfth century evolved into sparser chronicles in the thirteenth century (a trend apparent in Roger's account of Alexander),[27] writers sought merely to contextualize the Macedonian Empire within Antiquity rather than to interpolate the philosophically minded Roman historians, who tended to view Alexander's career as one of increasing egomania and corruption by Persian decadence. In chronicles, the vital information was not the state of mind of the conqueror and his family and successors but the basic historical facts regarding their victories, defeats, and deaths. Moreover, the Judaeo-Christian anecdotes that spread through much of Europe via Norman Sicily and Italy became a popular point of reference for his career in chronicles and genealogical rolls, particularly as Peter Comestor's *Historia scholastica*, Peter of Poitier's *Genealogiae historiarum*, and scholastic commentaries (vehicles of Jewish episodes, including Alexander's visit to Jerusalem and enclosure of Gog and Magog, as well as pseudo-Aristotelian treatises on his rule) became widely available in monastic libraries over the thirteenth and fourteenth centuries. Through these apocryphal episodes, many of which had been interpolated into the *Historia de preliis* tradition and vernacular romances as well, these texts encouraged the proliferation of a heroic Alexander rather than the morally corrupt tyrant recovered from classical authorities in the twelfth century.

Roger's successor Matthew Paris, for example, influenced by these newly circulating anecdotes, goes well beyond the editing of potentially slanderous material from his sources to what amounts to rewriting the history and reception of Alexander in his *Chronica majora*. In Cambridge, Corpus Christi College MS 26, a holograph copy of the *Chronica*, Matthew (despite his criticism of kingship and his own sovereign)[28] glorifies Alexander in both the text and the drawings that accompany it.[29] In particular, he relies on the episode of Alexander's war against Gog and Magog that had long circulated in Jewish and Christian histories, beginning with his citation of a supposedly late Roman prophecy that upon the arrival of the Antichrist, evil will beset Christendom in the form of infamous races: "et tunc exsurgent ab Aquilone spurcissimae gentes quas Alexander inclusit, Gog et Magog" (in that time will rise up from the East the foulest races of Gog and Magog, whom Alexander enclosed).[30] A variation of this legend conflates Gog and Magog with the "Ten Tribes" of Jewish exiles whom Alexander was said to have enclosed near the Caspian Sea in fulfilment of God's will, and it is the descendants of this collective enemy that Matthew sees in the encroaching Tartars who threaten Christian Europe:

> Creduntur isti Tartari, quorum memoria est detestabilis, fuisse de decem tribubus, qui abierunt, relicta lege Mosaica, post vitulos aureos; quos etiam Alexander Macedo primo conatus est includere in praeruptis montibus Caspiorum molaribus bituminatis. Quod opus cum videret humanos

labores excedere, invocavit auxilium Dei Israel; et coierunt cacumina montium adinvicem, et factus est locus inaccessibilis et immeabilis. Super quem locum dicit Josephus "Quanta faciet Deus pro fideli, qui tantum fecit pro infideli?"[31]

These Tartars, whom I find abominable to call to mind, are believed to have come from the Ten Tribes, who broke away from Moses and his law after the incident of the golden calf, and whom Alexander of Macedon first tried to enclose in the crags of the Caspian Mountains with blocks of bitumen. When he saw that this task exceeded human strength, he called upon the God of Israel for assistance, and the mountaintops joined together in turn, and the place was rendered inaccessible and impassable. Josephus [Flavius] asked of this, "How much will God do for a man who put his faith in Him, if He did so much for an infidel?"

Matthew thus presents Alexander as a warrior-king appointed by God and one whose power remains relevant to thirteenth-century threats,[32] and he even goes so far as to present the conqueror as a "Christlike model ruler," whom he draws holding the *orbis terrarum* and trampling underfoot beasts reminiscent of Psalms 90 (91).[33]

Influenced by the thirteenth-century re-evaluation of Alexander's applicability as a model ruler and rejection of the portrayal of his tyrannical behaviour, Matthew crafts a version of the conqueror that aligns with the brand of kingship seen in both the *Roman de toute chevalerie* and in contemporary *chansons de geste*, a genre whose continuing popularity evidently caught his attention. It has been recently suggested that in his portrayal of the baronial uprising against Henry III in 1258, he appropriated the tropes of the *chansons* to examine "the right of feudal barons to employ rebellion as a political tool in order to modify royal behaviour and/or royal policy," and although sympathetic to the barons' cause in resisting misguided rule, he nonetheless concedes the immutable authority of the crown.[34] Neither Matthew nor his predecessor Roger had, however, characterized Alexander as a king whose actions justified any resistance among his baronage, much less the crime of regicide committed in Babylon. Rather, their presentation of Alexander – Roger had expunged his worst qualities and Matthew elevates him to a fighter against evil and defender of Christian Europe – suggests that he was not only capable of uniting his barons to support his eastern campaigns but also of maintaining peace and order within his empire. Thomas of Kent's concern with the fate of the impoverished and the general devastation of the conqueror's empire amidst the civil war after his death may very well have resonated, then, with Matthew and his fellow historians. Despite their pro-baronial stance in the thirteenth century, chroniclers at St Albans possessed the same moral outrage over rebellion and civil war as Thomas expresses at the end of his romance.[35] In a section of his *Flores historiarum* entitled "De uariis poenarum generibus, quibus affligebantur Christiani" (On the various types of punishments with which Christians were afflicted), Roger Wendover paints, for example, a bleak picture of a land decimated by civil war but attests to the shared responsibility of the two parties for this dire situation.[36] John is a violent avenger-king whose brutality the chronicler deplores,[37] but the barons are responsible for their own nefarious acts witnessed across England, a stance echoed by a poem entitled "Plange plorans" interpolated into the chronicle of another St Albans historian nearer the end of the thirteenth century, William de Rishanger, and one that expresses support for the barons but sorrow for the devastation of England.[38]

The themes of strong kingship and baronial cooperation with the crown may also have helped Thomas's Alexander romance appeal to a mid-thirteenth-century secular audience, judging by the texts popular at the time, such as the *chansons de geste* of the Charlemagne cycle surviving in manuscripts contemporaneous, or nearly so, with the Cambridge copy. The *Chanson d'Aspremont* (seven thirteenth-century copies),[39] *Otinel* (a mid-century copy),[40] and *La Destructioun de Rome* (a late-century copy) recount battles of Charlemagne's knights and Saracens,[41] *Le Pelerinage de Charlemagne* (one copy) tells of his journey with the *douze peres* to Constantinople,[42] *Gormont et Isembart* (one early-century copy) features the Muslim convert Isembart and the Saracen king Gormont attacking France,[43] where they are slain by Louis, and the *Chancun de Guillaume* (a mid-century copy) tells of William, Vivien, and Gui's campaign against Saracens.[44] With the evolution of Insular romances and heroes and the genesis of English identity in the genre in the late thirteenth century, the defence of Christian Europe against Saracen armies would become an increasingly popular topos,[45] but the fascination with the religious conflict between the Muslim East and the Christian West is already apparent in these Continental *chansons de geste* circulating throughout the century. By narrating Alexander's campaigns against a variety of enemies in the Levant, the Middle East, and central Asia, Thomas of Kent ensured the ongoing appeal of his romance for a readership drawn to tales of European rulers either resisting Saracen armies on the homefront or invading Muslim lands in the Crusades. Moreover, like the figures of these *chansons de geste*, Alexander is a valiant and just ruler, eager both to fight alongside and reward his magnates in the invasion of Persia and beyond. Particularly in the Trinity College copy, the oldest to include the ancillary expedition of the *Fuerre de Gadres* (when Alexander's barons strike out on their own) and to relate so carefully which lands each baron receives from his dying king, the attraction to this narrative of the Macedonian feudal army is understandable for a thirteenth-century audience.

There is good evidence for a corresponding, feudal appeal in Arthurian literature of the time as well. Under John and Henry III, the baronial readership of Arthurian narratives, dissatisfied with their own monarch, purportedly became "more susceptible ... to the image of a king with the characteristics of King Arthur: noble, just, courtly, chivalrous, and looking to the advice of his barons."[46] This same attitude may account for the evolution of Arthurian romance under Henry III, as Arthur's knights question his authority and assert their independent agendas,[47] part of a general thirteenth-century trend in emphasizing the secondary and tertiary individuals fighting for Arthur's empire, members of "the collective" distinct from "the individual enterprise" of their king.[48] For whomever the Trinity College *Roman de toute chevalerie* was intended, a similar feudal interest may be inferred by the episodes that the scribe includes in the manuscript, the *Fuerre de Gadres* episode and the allocation of lands to the barons in Alexander's last moments.[49] Over the thirteenth and fourteenth centuries, baronial audiences were increasingly drawn to Alexander romances in both French (evidenced by the Paris manuscript of the *Roman de toute chevalerie*) and Middle English, and the inclusion of the *Fuerre de Gadres* and the careful explication of what the barons win from Alexander for their service suggests what the next extant manuscript of Thomas's romance would confirm, namely that Henry III and Edward I's magnates were drawn to the Alexander legend, with its eastern campaigns and complementary relationship between the king and his baronage.

Here, too, exists a corollary in the baronial, or ancestral romances, as well the Continental *chansons de geste* evidently popular in Anglo-Norman manuscripts during the first half of the thirteenth century. *Boeve de Haumtone* and *Gui de Warewic*, which survive in two and five mid-thirteenth manuscripts, respectively,[50] continue the same style of *chanson de geste*-inspired travel narrative as did Thomas, and the martial adventures of Alexander and his feudal army may have equally resonated with the readership of unexpectedly successful protagonists, or "self-made men," narratives, including the Continental Arthurian romance of *Fergus* (surviving in two mid-thirteenth-century copies),[51] the Anglo-Norman *Fouke Fitz Warin* (a near contemporary of the Trinity College manuscript of the *Roman de toute chevalerie*), and the *Histoire de Guillaume le Maréchal*. While the *Histoire* presents William as "the moral opposition" to John's disastrous rule,[52] it reflects on the rebellions against Henry II as a calamity for the nobility and aristocracy – a stance that contrasts with Thomas's concern not for the magnates but for the helpless commoners of the Macedonian Empire after Alexander's death – and references the *Fuerre de Gadres*, the same text interpolated for the readership of the Trinity College *Roman de toute chevalerie*, and identifies Alexander with heroic virtue.[53] *Fouke Fitz Waryn* offers, on the other hand, baronial criticism of bad rule, and rather than distance its hero from the king, it celebrates his willingness to stand against John and fight for baronial rights. In so doing, the poem examines the breakdown of chivalry in its own manner, with its narrative inspired by John's corruption, poor kingship, and breaking of oaths to his magnates, alongside adventures abroad and wondrous beasts and dragons, the sort of exoticism that made the Alexander legend so appealing.[54] When John no longer maintains his feudal contract with his barons, the protagonist of the romance goes on the offensive to recover the lands unlawfully taken from him by his king, and yet his quest is not merely self-serving. He becomes, as recently assessed, a hero of the baronial cause against unreliable kingship: "disinherited, wrongfully outlawed, and pursued by a corrupt monarch, [he] manages nevertheless to reestablish moral order in feudal society through his victory over an unjust lord and king."[55]

John's loss of Aquitaine, Poitou, Anjou, and Normandy, the First Barons' War, "a feudal conflict between a demanding and unreliable overlord and a volatile group of his tenants-in-chief,"[56] and renewed baronial uprising against Henry III in the 1250s and 1260s provide possible political and literary contexts for the Trinity College copy of the *Roman de toute chevalerie* – and indeed for the portrayal of kingship in Anglo-Norman literature – no matter whether it was made by a monastic or secular workshop. In the years just after this manuscript was produced, the oldest surviving copy of the Anglo-Norman *Brut*, which concludes with Henry III's death in 1272 and dates to the last years of the thirteenth century or the first years of the fourteenth, sheds further light on the literary portrayal of the feudal relationship in the years between the Cambridge and Paris copies of the *Roman de toute chevalerie*.

Likely written for a baronial readership and supportive of their cause in an era when animosity towards John and his successors led to a declining interest in Arthurian narratives,[57] this version recounts the barons' wars against John and Henry III but concludes in optimistic fashion with the reconciliation between the two factions and "the peace [that] was proclaimed throughout all England."[58] Julia Marvin's invaluable scholarship on the Anglo-Norman *Brut* suggests, however, that this mention of peace is neither a convincing nor an efficacious resolution for the long-standing tumult of the thirteenth century. This version of the *Brut* clearly places the blame of the century's royal-baronial conflict on a perception of the misguided kingship, even tyranny, of John and Henry III. Together the kings' behaviour and resulting necessity of baronial opposition convey the chronicle's primary themes of "the bad consequences of the abuse of royal power, especially when the king puts his own personal will above law or oath," the devastation of civil war, and the value of dialogue and respect between the king and his baronage.[59] In its appreciation for the public suffering induced by war between the two, the *Brut* recalls Thomas of Kent's concluding lament for the "poor and enfeebled," yet, like Thomas, the author of the Anglo-Norman *Brut* also emphasizes how good rule can benefit a kingdom, both on a larger geo-political scale and for the subjects at home.

For the latter, as Marvin argues, the presence of Arthur in the chronicle offers "an ideal king for an audience sick at the thought of civil war,"[60] and he offers a paradigm by which to measure Edward I like, I believe, the Paris manuscript discussed in the next chapter. Not only as a conqueror abroad, a bringer of domestic peace for his subjects, and a just ruler for his baronage, but as a leader of what amounts to a holy war and "a religious obligation ... against the [Roman] emperor and his pagan allies, who want to destroy Christianity," Arthur becomes a forerunner and exemplum for Edward, and when the barons eagerly heed Arthur's call to arms, the chronicle represents the ideal of John's generation as well:

> This moment is unlike anything else in the entire text, and it clinches the contemporary connection. The struggle against strong and numerous pagan forces, in which the soldiers bind themselves by oath, is no longer explicitly directed towards the enforcement of Arthur's legal claim, but rather towards the glorification of the one true faith. It has become a crusade, and King Arthur a crusader, like Edward I and doubtless some of the prose *Brut*'s first readers.[61]

To be sure, in the years between the production of the Trinity College and the Paris copies of the *Roman de toute chevalerie*, the characterization of Arthur, and occasionally Alexander, and their imperialist agenda was occasionally called into question.[62] The early-thirteenth-century *Waldef*, extant in a thirteenth- or fourteenth-century manuscript,[63] not only criticizes Arthur as an ambitious emperor, particularly after his conquest of the Romans,[64] but also criticizes the Alexander legend and perhaps even the Staufen emperors of the time, collectively the target of much animosity from the ruling houses of Atlantic Europe through the character of Guiac.[65] Like Alexander, Guiac seeks to expand his imperium beyond the Mediterranean into the earthly paradise, and like Alexander he receives warnings on the dangers of pride.[66] Although the ancient conqueror is also a paradigm for feats of arms in *Waldef*, in the aftermath of the battle that leads to Guiac's coronation, the poet even observes that such carnage and destruction had not been seen since the days of Alexander, who "caused so much bloodshed."[67] Similarly, *Gui de Warewic*, whose continuing popularity is undeniable, given the fifteen thirteenth- and fourteenth-century manuscripts in which it survives,[68] places "an important stress on the injustices perpetuated under imperial rule."[69] Anglo-Norman versions of Continental romances from this period are also telling, including the *Prose Lancelot*, Chrétien's *Percival*, *Perlesvaus* from the Arthurian tradition, *Octavian et Dagobert*, reminiscent of classical settings in the manner of the *Roman de toute chevalerie*, and *Partonopeus de Blois*, another eastern-themed work involving both the Empress of Constantinople and the Danes.[70] While *Octavian* evokes the names of Octavian/Caesar Augustus and the Ottonian emperors, its protagonist is less a cruel tyrant than an unconfident ruler prone to heeding bad counsel and allowing himself to be deceived by those around him.[71] Chrétien's *Percival*, on the other hand, offers a damning caricature of Arthur as "a distant, defenseless, cuckolded king"[72] reflective of the "world ill regulated by its customs, chronically prone to crisis, and repeatedly destabilized in the absence of effective upholders of its institutions" in Chrétien's later Arthurian romances.[73]

As for the *Roman de toute chevalerie*, even as it celebrates Alexander and (until the very end) his baronage, it offers an ominous reminder of imperial failure. The poem's heroic warrior-king, his mighty feudal army, and their campaigns against eastern enemies are all threatened by the act of treachery in Babylon: in the aftermath of this tragedy, the barons, having already bickered over where to bury their fallen emperor, yield to greed and ambition and incite a civil war that undoes their military efforts over the previous twelve years. In so undercutting the previously glorified bellicosity of Alexander's career, Thomas's romance does not neglect how the conqueror's empire came to an end, when a once unified feudal society fell victim to the throes of civil war. For Thomas, his complaint of a troubled empire extends beyond the king, the baronage, and the knighthood – the triumvirate of *chevalerie* – to encompass the common citizens, the poor and enfeebled, of Alexander's lands. The *Roman de toute chevalerie* is thus not in the end an exclusive text when it comes to political anxiety. All of the peoples from Macedon to India were invested in Alexander's continuing reign and welcome him as a ruler, and his death ensures their collective fate of civil war.

Although it is tempting to read the manuscript as a reflection of a harmonious baronial-royal enterprise, which it undoubtedly is for the majority of the narrative, on the eve of the Second Barons' War, "a movement which was designed to give justice to everyone,"[74] its dismal ending is hard to overlook. One disgruntled, treacherous baron has Alexander poisoned, and the rest cannot avoid a self-destructive civil war. As in Matthew Paris's assessment, the barons have the right to assert themselves, to fight, and to receive their due compensation, but the fact of strong kingship remains. Alexander is never less than fair and just towards the men who fight for him (and even for the men who once fought against him), but his barons simply cannot rule themselves after his death. It is an unavoidable conclusion to Thomas's narrative that the scribe and artist of the Trinity College manuscript do not gloss over, and it lends a certain royalist reading to the codex, that barons need to be ruled by an authoritative king. Yet he need also be a good king, and that qualifier would be as imperative for the feudal readership, those who fought first to expand Plantagenet sovereignty under Edward I and then to suppress it under Edward II, of the copy of the *Roman de toute chevalerie* in the Bibliothèque Nationale.

Chapter Five

Paris, Bibliothèque Nationale MS 24364: Alexander, Chivalry, and the Wars of Edward I

By the thirteenth century, Alexander had become an increasingly recognizable icon of a brave, virtuous king, figured for the Plantagenet kings in a variety of locations. From at least 1230 until 1252, Henry III commissioned in his royal palaces at Clarendon and Nottingham "Alexander chambers" with murals of the Macedonian conqueror that were perhaps modelled on romances,[1] as suggested by the recent identification of the *Pseudo-Turpin Chronicle* as the inspiration for the narrative of Roland amid images of the Crusades in the royal chapel at Claverley.[2] With his campaigns in the Levant and visit to the Holy City, Alexander undoubtedly evoked the crusading ethos for thirteenth-century readers and viewers, including Henry in his chambers,[3] but under Edward I Alexander portraiture informed a larger discussion of good kingship. Supplementing his earlier scholarship on the Painted Chamber at Westminster, Paul Binski has recently argued that the two bands of murals drawn from 1 Maccabees are composed of two types of figures, men of virtue to be imitated, including Alexander, and men of vice who warn of "wicked governance and its consequences."[4] Yet Alexander was not only a paragon of wise rule and chivalry for Edward; he became, too, a model of conquest and imperialism.

The genesis of the latter may very well lie in the pseudo-Aristotelian *Secretum secretorum*, a purported book of the philosopher's lessons for the young Alexander seen by medieval readers as a model for appropriating and applying divinely ordained power.[5] Increasingly popular both on its own merits and as a model for other political manuals in Plantagenet England, the *Secretum secretorum* became a predominant record of Alexander's exemplary kingship for royal audiences. The first Latin translation, undertaken by Roger Bacon, was perhaps even intended for Henry or Edward.[6] Once educated under the tutelage of Aristotle, Alexander, according to Roger, honed his extraordinary power and authority and

> Convaluit ... in sanitatis observacione per observanciam sui sani consilii et imitacione precepti. Et ideo subjugavit sibi civitates, et triumphans adquisivit sibi cuncta regna, et tocius mundi solus tenuit monarchiam, et in omnem terram exivit fama sua, et per omnia mundi climata omnes gentes et diverse naciones subiciebantur suo imperio et precepto, Arabes atque Perses neque fuit gens aliqua que auderet ei resistere in facto vel dicto.[7]

> grew strong ... in minding his well-being through heeding [Aristotle's] sound counsel and following its precepts. On account of this, he subjugated cities to his rule, triumphantly sought out all kingdoms for himself, held sole control of the entire world, and his reputation travelled to every land; every race and diverse nation in every climate of the world was subjugated under his authority and command, and neither the Arabs nor the Persians nor any other race dared resist him in deed or speech.

This translation of the *Secretum secretorum* began to promote the teaching of Aristotle (or writings presumed to be his) and the revelation of secrets whose "tremendous power [...] allowed Alexander to conquer the world" and "would be useful in the present-day struggle against Islam as well as in the upcoming battle with Antichrist."[8] Alexander was equally useful for inspiring foreign campaigns to expand the boundaries of Plantagenet authority, and, as they did with Arthur, poets and chroniclers especially compared Edward with the Macedonian conqueror near the end of the thirteenth century,[9] when "the exercise of a presumed overlordship changed to conquest" in Scotland and Wales.[10]

Edward himself had spent considerable energy cultivating a chivalric sensibility in his court, and judging by the literary reactions of the early fourteenth century, his efforts paid posthumous dividends. The prince whom Robert of Gloucester had lauded as a "hardi kniȝt & god"[11] for his heroics in the Second Barons' War was received by the period just before the Paris manuscript as a second Richard the Lion-heart, a figure of his own romance, and the benefactor of Arthurian idealism, all of which aided his "ambition ... to create an imperial, British-wide kingship."[12] With such a political vision supported by recollections of the heroes of English historical romance, Edward appears in the years contemporaneous with the Paris manuscript of the *Roman de toute chevalerie* (1307–12) as their equals in death. Still, this admiration now had a provisional clause. While in the thirteenth century Edward could simply serve as a "novus ... Ricardus" and a prince who recalled the former king's chivalrous approach to warfare ("bella per Eaduuardi similis et probitate Ricardi"),[13] he did not lack for conflicts with his barons, particularly in the 1290s, when "political unity ... could not be maintained under the pressures of war finance and military logistics."[14] In Peter Langtoft's telling, despite frequent comparisons with Arthur and his standard of kingly excellence, Edward failed to live up to this exemplum in at least one respect by not allocating to the baronage what he conquered with their assistance. If Edward "of the land of Scotland had shared and given," Peter writes:

> To his English barons, by just quantities,
> The land over there would have been in his power,
> And his men heritors of it for ever.[15]

By 1307, however, just before the production of the Paris manuscript, elegists mingled their admiration with anxiety over the future of the throne, and criticism of Edward I was deflected onto his son. A French poem from Edward II's reign laments, for example, that with his father's body buried ("ore si gist soun cors en tere"), the new century is already in decline ("si va le siècle en decline").[16] This piece survives in Cambridge, University Library MS G. I. 1, a ca. 1307 copy of the *Short English Metrical Chronicle* with a unique ending among the surviving manuscripts, but its editor omits the Anglo-Norman lines and their English translation that conclude an addendum to the chronicle: "Ke de enfaunt fey rey ... Dunke vet la tere a hunte ... And of a child maked king. / þanne is þe londe vndirling."[17]

This sentiment pessimistically addresses the nascent reign of Edward II in a political transition in which, in Michael Prestwich's words, the new king "had alienated most of the support which he inherited from his father, and his misuse of patronage had meant that he had not built up any worthwhile backing of his own."[18] If this alienation reflected the stance of the knights and barons identified in the Paris copy of Thomas's romance (men, as discussed below, accustomed to serving a warrior-king in Edward I) then this copy of the *Roman de toute chevalerie* is further seen as a book that recalls Edward I and his feudal army in a less than hopeful time. According to John of London, the author of the

Commendatio lamentabilis, a prose elegy written upon Edward I's death, the barons simply lamented their king as a "vir bellator ab adholescentia sua egregius" (an outstanding fighting man since his youth), while the knights framed their sorrow in terms of historical imperialism:

Olim cum Alexandro rege Macedonum reges Persarum et Medorum devicimus, et provincias orientales subegimus, nunc in fine temporum cum magno rege Edwardo contra illustrem regem Franciae Philippum guerram decennalem suscepimus; Vasconiam in dolo praepossessam recuperavimus vi et armis, Walliam hostili caede comparavimus, Scotiam truncates ejus tyrannis in ore gladii invasimus.[19]

Once upon a time with Alexander, King of the Macedonians, we conquered the kings of the Persians and the Medes, and we subjugated eastern lands. Now more recently with the great King Edward we have undertaken a ten-year war against the famed Philip, King of France. By strength and arms we recovered Gascony, which they previously possessed by deceit, we disposed of Wales by slaughtering the enemy, and we invaded Scotland by cutting off its tyrants with the tips of our swords.

Another elegy for Edward contemporaneous with the Paris manuscript declares:

if Alexander the Great, king of the Greeks, ruled in the equity of justice, in the power of warring down his enemies, and in energy and wisdom of mind, as the books written about him make clear, we may say with justice that this most illustrious and holy king [Edward] ruled as Alexander did with respect to these three things.[20]

This passage clearly privileges Alexander's intellectual qualities, reminiscent of the popularity of the *Secretum secretorum* discussed above. As the student of Aristotle and a king associated with learning and scientific exploration, he rules with wisdom and an appreciation for justice, which by their placement in the list of Alexander's best qualities seem to outshine his *virtus*, or fighting spirit. However, in the late thirteenth and early fourteenth centuries, if Edward was to recall Alexander, he had to rely on this third quality, martial authority, more than the others. Anglo-Norman and Middle English variations on an elegy for the king in London, British Library MS Harley 2253, for example, respectively praise him for his role in the Crusade of 1271–2 and, more effusively, as an "an important knight within Christendom as a whole."[21] In an age when Alexander was regarded by romance writers and historians alike as defending Western civilization against such forces of evil as Gog and Magog, the association of a crusading king and the conqueror was high praise indeed.

The *Vita Edwardi Secundi*, written contemporaneously up to 1326, confirms that this sort of praise could not apply to Edward's son and successor:

> Oh! If our King Edward had borne himself as well at the outset of his reign, and not accepted the counsels of wicked men, not one of his predecessors would have been more renowned than he ... If he had followed the advice of the barons, he would have humbled the Scots with ease. Oh! If he had practised the use of arms, he would have exceeded the prowess of King Richard.[22]

As this passage suggests, a lack of respect for Edward II's fighting spirit was hardly the sole cause for anxiety among his barons and their knights in 1308–12. Many of the barons who quarrelled with the king during these years had argued with his father over heavy taxation in the 1290s (income that Edward sought to fund the wars in which the individuals identified in the Paris manuscript fought),[23] but the baronial opposition against the new king took on an increasingly antagonistic tone, one even suggestive of the kingdom's decay and impending collapse.

At the centre of the controversy over Edward's kingship in 1308–12 lay the perceived misguided counsel of Piers Gaveston and Edward's favouritism towards this one voice among his baronial ranks.[24] The issues with Gaveston and baronial authority in Edward's reign are readily apparent in political documents contemporaneous with the Paris manuscript. In Edward's coronation oath, for example, with its controversial addendum that "had clearly been intended ... to ensure that in any future struggle the King would be held to observe the magnates' decision,"[25] was a contentious clause in the years during which the Paris manuscript was produced. On the one hand, it suggests a notion of social consciousness, in that it directed Edward to "uphold and defend the laws and righteous customs" of "the community of the realm."[26] As Roy Martin Haines argues, this addendum to the coronation oath was applied to Edward's sovereignty already in 1308, in the so-called Homage et servent declaration of Parliament: "to preserve the [coronation] oath ... should the king fail to right a wrong and to remove something harmful to the people, as well as to the prejudice of the Crown, there must be constraint."[27] This declaration also acknowledges the necessity of caring for Edward's subjects, for it concludes with the hope "that, since [the king] is bound by his coronation oath to keep the laws that the people shall choose, he will accept and execute the award of the people."[28] Yet these documents, as well as the Boulogne Agreement of 1308, wherein the barons pledge "to redress the oppressions" committed against the people of England and to amend "the honour of God, our lord and king, and all of his people,"[29] were intended as well to oust Piers Gaveston from his royal privilege and increasing authority over his fellow barons.[30]

In the Ordinances of 1311, with their insistence that "through evil and deceptive counsel our lord the king and all his subjects are dishonoured in all lands," the threat of Gaveston's influence and Edward's misguided kingship is tantamount to the dissolution of the kingdom:

> the crown is in many respects reduced and dismembered, and his lands of Gascony, Ireland and Scotland on the point of being lost if God does not give an improvement, and his kingdom of England on the point of rebelling because of oppressions, prises and molestations.[31]

The barons behind the Boulogne Agreement and Ordinances had supported Edward I's reign and were thus involved in a high-stakes game of baronial checking of monarchical sovereignty that had been waged since the 1290s.[32] These were the barons of the very generation of those whose coats of arms appear in the Paris manuscript; they fought for both Edward I and II, and they fought to establish then maintain the kingdom mentioned in the passage above.

The Paris Manuscript: Patronage and Readership

These individuals were also interested in the Alexander legend, judging by their affiliation with Paris, Bibliothèque Nationale MS 24364, the second surviving manuscript of the *Roman de toute chevalerie* and the only copy that provides a clear historical context for its production. Unlike the Cambridge and Durham manuscripts, codices of unknown provenance and debatable reasons for production, the Paris manuscript reveals on its frontispiece an identifiable patron, a knight who served under Edward I, and it has been dated to 1308–12,[33] the tumultuous beginning to the young Edward II's reign, owing to confrontations with the baronage and the Piers Gaveston scandal. The Paris copy also represents the first complete, surviving manuscript of Thomas's poem, with its eighty-seven folios of neatly written text in double columns and 311 illustrations, the work of two artists.[34] While the first seven folios provide Thomas's version of Alexander's childhood and the early days of his reign, fols 8r–30v feature the same *Fuerre de Gadres* interpolation as found in the other manuscripts of the *Roman de toute chevalerie*, and after Thomas's narrative of the Persian and Indian campaigns, the manuscript includes the other common interpolation from Alexandre de Paris's *Roman d'Alexandre*, that regarding the division of Alexander's lands (fols 79v–86v).

As for the patronage of the manuscript, clues abound from fols 1r–48r, in which appear approximately twenty-five coats of arms of barons and knights who served under Edwards I and II and were summoned to Parliament during 1308–12. The first seven of these coats of arms appear together on the manuscript's first folio: those of Sir William de Huntingfield (†1312/13), Lord William la Zouche (†1353), an unidentified man named Herteclew, Lord Warin le Latimer (†1349), Sir John d'Engaigne (†1322), Lord Thomas le Latimer (†1334), and Lord Richard Basset (†1314).[35] The last evidently came from the most distinguished of the baronial families identified in the manuscript, as the Bassets received the barony of Great Weldon in 1122,[36] while Richard himself received the title Lord Basset by parliamentary writ in 1298–9.[37] Thomas le Latimer, too, became a baron by writ in 1299, a title inherited by his son Warin, and William la Zouche received his barony by writ in 1308. William de Huntingfield, a fifth-generation knight, provides links to two of the individuals identified on this folio, as his sister married Richard Bassett, and he was the nephew of John d'Engaigne,[38] believed to be the patron of the manuscript on account of the frequency with which his coat of arms appears in its illustrations.[39] Although these men had fought for Edward I in Scotland, Wales, and Gascony (and would later fight for his son),[40] John d'Engaigne stands out among the others in the literary presentation of arms in the late thirteenth century. As a veteran of the king's Scottish wars, he is listed on both the Falkirk Rolls of Arms (1298)[41] and the roll of arms for the Siege of Carlaverock (1300), in which his banner is described as "a handsome one / of red, crusilly, with a dancette of gold."[42] Having served Edward I in his Scottish wars and signed a letter to Boniface VIII to support his king's claims to Scotland,

John was summoned to Parliament from 1299 to 1321, well into the reign of Edward II, and died in 1322.[43]

We cannot know how these individuals felt regarding the aforementioned controversies of the early years of Edward II's reign or what stance they took against Piers Gaveston, but important facts of John's life are evident. He signed a 1301 letter to Boniface VIII claiming Edward I's ancient claim to Scotland,[44] he fought for Edward I's imperial agenda, and his coat of arms appears in the romance presentation of those who served at Caerverelock. Judging by the Paris manuscript, he also took an interest in the Alexander story. Each of these details must influence the reception of his copy of the *Roman de toute chevalerie*, but so, too, must the political milieu in which it was produced. Thomas of Kent's version of Alexander romance is atypical, as discussed in the previous chapters. It would be all too convenient to surmise that the *Roman de toute chevalerie* attracted John on account of its battles and scenes of gallantry. Of course these aspects of Thomas's poem must have proven quite appealing, but John did not own a copy of a French Alexander romance, which would have fulfilled his desires for heroics and the celebration of an ancient warrior-king to the utmost. His manuscript, although it translates an Anglo-Norman romance to Continental French, is still ultimately that produced by Thomas in the late twelfth century, a romance of failure. Alexander dies, his barons fight among themselves, the great Macedonian Empire is torn asunder, and the people therein suffer unduly. Only the first is characteristic of all Alexander narratives, and it is at least plausible that in a period when Edward II's barons "made a series of spasmodic responses" to the faults of their king before the "systemized" opposition reflected in the Ordinances above,[45] armed themselves to enforce their own agenda, and referenced the oppression of Edward's subjects,[46] John d'Engaigne would have recognized the vulnerable political balance suggested by the poem – the need for a strong king supported by his baronage – beyond the splendour of Alexander's battlefield exploits.

The scribe and artists of the Paris copy did not introduce significant alterations to Thomas of Kent's original narrative for John's copy (as had the producers of Cambridge, Trinity College MS O. 9. 34, and as would those of Durham, Durham Cathedral Library MS C. IV. 27B), yet Thomas's portrayal of Alexander as an exemplary warrior-king resonates in a particular manner in this copy of the *Roman de toute chevalerie*, given the readership for whom it was produced. John's interest in the text is in large part understandable. As suggested by the explicit ("Ici finist la romanz de tute chevalerie") in this manuscript, Thomas's poem survived in the early fourteenth century as a record, perhaps even a manual, of chivalry. At the same time, the poem celebrates then condemns the Macedonian barons' relationship with Alexander, a relationship that begins with the king heaping treasure on his nobles to inspire their loyalty for his campaigns abroad and ends with criticism of their treachery and failure to maintain Alexander's empire. For John, then, the manuscript presents in text and image battle scenes familiar to men like himself, but for the knights and barons identified by the coats of arms around his own, the manuscript features a largely idealized union between the crown and the feudal army in a time of tense relations between the two in England. The most notable characteristic of the Paris manuscript, its translation of Thomas's Anglo-Norman into Continental French, further reflects its knightly-baronial audience.[47] From the second half of the thirteenth century onward, English readers, particularly aristocratic and royal patrons, regarded Anglo-Norman as inferior to the language spoken and written on the Continent, but these patrons maintained an equal interest in the literature of both tongues.[48] During this time, in the reign of Henry III, French served as "the language of his baronial elites,"[49] and in the century of the Paris manuscript, Anglo-Norman was to be dismissed as "a medium whose pastness was emphasized by the fact that the centers of French linguistic authority and vigor lay ... on the continent."[50] While "the exaltation in French of native English heroes in a romance context" was patronized by barons in the thirteenth century,[51] the fourteenth century remained a decidedly French age of books in England, judging by the surviving inventories of aristocratic and royal collectors.[52]

Even as Edward I cultivated an interest in ancient warriors and heroes alongside such domestic ones as Arthur and Richard the Lion-heart,[53] Alexander remained a unique literary figure in fourteenth-century England. Thomas had been successful in establishing an Alexander romance for Insular audiences, but by the time of the Paris manuscript French Alexander romances undeniably dominated his legend in the Middle Ages, and in England, romances were soon to shift to Middle English, as discussed in chapter 7. As a knight of the early fourteenth century, John d'Engaigne still looked, however, to an Anglo-Norman Alexander created for his Anglo-Norman forbears – again reminiscent of the Richard the Lion-heart who "conformed to the familiar feudal concept of a 'warrior-king'" in Thomas of Kent's age[54] – despite the Continental French of his manuscript. If he had desired a truly French Alexander, that established by Albéric's Alexander romance and which evolved into Alexandre de Paris's compilation in the twelfth century, he would have had plenty of contemporary options, attested by the prolific number of manuscripts of the *Roman d'Alexandre* and other French Alexander romances. He deliberately chose the *Roman de toute chevalerie*, I believe, and any number of reasons may plausibly explain his reasoning. In terms of Insular romance, Thomas's Alexander may simply have seemed on par with Richard the Lion-heart through their supernatural births, wars against eastern infidels, and shocking deaths at a young age, or Arthur, with whom he had long been read in comparison.[55] Yet the story that Thomas composed about Alexander, his barons and knights, and his ultimately failed empire could just as well have held a particular attraction for John d'Engaigne, a man who fought for Edward I to expand his imperial vision but, in the years to which the Paris manuscript is dated, witnessed the difficult transition to a new reign and the threat of losing the lands that he had helped the previous king to win.

Thomas of Kent's Feudal Narrative

Thomas's poem emphasizes the feudal dynamic to such an extent that the scribes of its manuscripts could have identified it as the "Roman de toute baronie" as justifiably as the "Roman de toute chevalerie," yet his narrative does not necessarily present an idealized feudal relationship. Rather, across Thomas's romance there is a tension between the conqueror (driven by ambition and his belief that his eastern campaign is one against evil) and his barons (driven by desire for material reward and generally cautious in their eastward expedition) that is ultimately resolved just before Alexander's death. For a baronial readership, such as that identified in the Paris manuscript, the Alexander narrative may have been appealing, then, not simply for its battles and adventures but also for the prolonged, negotiable relationship between a king and his baronage that Thomas depicts. From the moment that Alexander matures into a powerful figure in his father Philip's court, the public, cooperative relationship between the throne and the baronage and the knighthood dictates the Macedonian political scene and the new ruler's chances of success in the East. Immediately after Alexander fulfils the prophecy that only a future king could tame the man-eating horse

Bucephalus, for example, Philip establishes his presumed son as his heir-apparent in a lavish ceremony:

> Phelippe tint lespee li roy dreiturers …
> Bucifal ly dona qui fu fort e cursiers.
> Cent vallez fut li rois pur samer chevaliers
> Qui tuit ont bones armes e bien coranz destrers.
> Sufferent en bataille les granz esturs pleners.
> Cist serviront lenfant pur dons e pur luers.
> Mult par fu grant la feste e li riches mangers.
> Qant napes surent traites sen partent esquiers.
> Li rois fait aporter chargie dor cent somers
> A Alisandre les done par mules par destres
> A chevalers novels as mestres boteilliers
> Mareshcaus e ceus e a ces despensers
> A ces jugleors e fols platoners. (fol. 4r)

> Philip, the rightful king, held [Alexander's] sword … and presented him with Bucephalus, a strong and swift horse. For love of his son, Philip dubbed one hundred worthy knights, all of whom had handsome arms and good, swift steeds. In battle they would suffer many a great assault, and they would serve his son in exchange for gifts and praise. The feast was exceedingly grand, and the foods were scrumptious, and when the tablecloths were removed, these riders left. The king had led forth a hundred packhorses loaded with gold, and he gave them to Alexander and then gave as many mules as steeds to the new knights, the head cupbearers, the farriers, the treasurers, the jugglers, the jesters, and the beggars.

The scene is notable not simply for its pomp but for the fact that Philip handpicks an entire generation, Alexander, a new knighthood, and a retinue of supporters, to succeed him, and, through money and gifts he secures for his successor a cadre of young knights who, for continued material rewards, will fight for his cause. Yet the presence of Philip and especially Antipater, who will one day orchestrate Alexander's assassination in Babylon, suggests the foreboding turmoil that lurks beneath the extravagance and hopefulness of the scene. Philip may have accepted Alexander as his son and dubbed him his heir, but their relationship will soon face its greatest test, the confrontation over Philip's plans to divorce Olympias and marry Cleopatra. This moment of celebrating Alexander as Philip's heir has no source in the Valerius *Epitome,* and Thomas creates an episode with a certain irony, in that Philip publicly grants power to a young man who is neither his son nor his supporter, and while Alexander will expand the limits of Philip's empire, in so doing he will effectively nullify the memory of his predecessor, a father figure whom he violently opposes even after this scene. Within Thomas's narrative, the celebration of Alexander being named Philip's heir and the hundred knights as his champions of the next generation of the Macedonian Empire represents a hopeful moment, despite the bad blood between Philip and Alexander and the ultimate treachery of Antipater.

After this public recognition of Alexander as his father's heir apparent, he still requires the loyalty of his father's barons and knights, as his nascent sense of authority is reliant upon quick and decisive military victories. Following the intrigue and pomp of the court life that Thomas portrays in the early part of his romance, centred upon Nectanabus, Olympias, and Philip, he casts Alexander in a series of elaborate battle scenes, another facet of the poem that would likely have appealed to an early-fourteenth-century feudal audience. Like the heroes of ancestral, historical romances favoured by barons in the twelfth and thirteenth centuries,[56] Alexander proves himself a leader equally focused on empire and glory, and he surely seemed for John d'Engaigne the warrior-king idealized by French poets two centuries earlier as a ruler who staked his legacy on bravery, sound leadership, and largesse towards his supporters. Even as a prince intent on quelling a nascent rebellion against his father, Alexander senses that his men fight an uninspired battle and takes immediate command:

Veit li reis Alisandre les soens asparpeillez
Treis feiz sone sun corn e sis ad raliez
Kar unc en bataille ne fu esmaiez.
Abaisse sun espie ad rei sest esleissez
Lescu li ad fendu e losberc desmaillez,
E prent le mort a terre de lui sest venger. (fol. 6r)

Alexander saw his men scattered, and three times he sounded his horn to recall them, for he had never been dismayed in battle. He lowered his lance and charged towards the [enemy] king. He struck him through the middle of the shield, broke his chain-mail, knocked him to the ground dead, and thus achieved his vengeance.

Fighting under such a prince, Alexander's barons and knights enjoy countless opportunities to establish their fame, to interject their opinions and advice, and to serve Alexander's imperial agenda in a communal fashion, rather than obliging the whims of a tyrant. Thomas thus celebrates the heroics of the men who establish, both in their strategizing and martial valour, Alexander's sovereignty over Persia and a new Macedonian empire, and the invasion of Persia, the victory that would solidify Alexander's reputation and authority in Asia, becomes a joint royal-baronial enterprise – quite possibly the most appealing aspect of the poem for a feudal audience under Edwards I and II.

The baronage, both Macedonian and foreign, remains largely devoted to Alexander, even though various political leaders across the Greek-speaking world to India dare to oppose him. Ultimately this support results from Alexander's brand of authority over his barons. When he takes the throne after Philip's assassination, for example, Alexander publicly proves that he rules through alternating generosity and intimidation. His first act of regal benevolence is to distribute Philip's treasure among the baronage ("le tresor Phelippun ad il dunc defferme / A tuz lad largement despendu e done" [fol. 7r]), but he does not limit his largesse to his magnates ("li conte li baron e li conte aloss" [fol. 7r]) who pay him homage. The common subjects of Alexander's kingdom are not excluded from the adventure and wealth ahead, as Thomas relates that "ni ad dunc si si povre qui qe ne fut enbreve" (none was so poor that he was not included [fol. 7r]) in Alexander's ranks, and there is the implication, not for the only time in the poem, that the new king leads a union of all capable Macedonian fighters into Asia.

Moreover, on the eve of the Persian campaign, he delivers a rousing speech on the necessity of defending liberty and battling tyranny that reinforces this union of king, magnates, and citizen soldiers:

Il ad tort vers moi bien voil qui le sachez
Kar rentes e treu volt aveir de mes fiez.
Ne me semble raison quil seit paiez
Kar de mes ancessors fut a tort otriez
E ceo qui est a tort ou pris ou purchacez
Nen est dreit ne raison coe est sovent jugez ...
A tut vostre poeir pur mei vus efforciez
Car pur vostre franchise od mei guerreiez
E pur coe est raison qui vus la desrainez. (fol. 33v)

> [Darius] wrongs me, I want you to know, because he wishes to have rents and tributes from my fiefdoms. It does not seem right to me that he receive this income, because my ancestors were defeated by force, and it does not seem right or reasonable that one demand what has been taken or bought by force ... Arm yourself for me with all your might, for you fight alongside me for your liberty, and it is right that you defend it.

The combination of monetary reward and nationalism clearly fires the support of Alexander's barons, who realize that the tribute demanded by the Persians can fund the Macedonian army and that of "li bacheler li preuz li enseignez" (the valiant and heady youth [fol. 33v]). However, for the nobles concerned more with money than adventure, there is little choice but to follow Alexander. As Alexander explains to them upon his coronation, rejecting him as king means bringing a declaration of war and an outburst of anger against the baronage ("e sil i at nul home kil voille son mandement contredire / Si seit fors del pais en sa guerre en syre" [fol. 7r]), a similar threat to that uttered towards the barons of Tyre (in an episode notorious for demonstrating the conqueror's fury), when Alexander promises to strip them of their lands and fiefdoms if they do not join his army with their knights. Still, the men ultimately succumb to Alexander's threats and call to freedom fighting and empire building, and so long as he rewards them for doing so, his barons remain devoted to him.

Even the barons of Persia and India yield to Alexander's noble magnanimity, partly because his style of leadership does not depart from that of the rulers whom he defeats. When debating the defence against Alexander's impending invasion, for example, Darius and his barons voice their opinions in a strikingly democratic fashion. Genuinely distressed, Darius cries out, "conseillez mei baron qui estes mi parent" (advise me, barons who are my kin [fol. 38v]), indicative of a bond that Alexander cannot yet forge with his barons through financial reward and occasional threats. No fewer than four barons, including the king's own brother, offer extensive advice, all of which informs Darius's decision to mobilize his army against the invading Macedonians. The only comparable scene of equal representation occurs in Athens, when the city's senators likewise debate how to handle Alexander's threats (fol. 37v). Here, however, Thomas would have found a model for this public debate in the Valerius *Epitome*.[57] For the Persians, and for the Indians, too, when Porus deliberates with his barons during Alexander's easternmost campaign, kingship may rely more on the display of extravagance than battlefield valour, but there remains an undeniable respect between the kings and their barons. For Alexander and his Macedonians, kingship demands its particular brand of extravagance in the form of payment to and treasure sharing with the barons, a policy that supports his vision of grandeur (including the fight against Gog and Magog in his eastern campaign) and the heroic reputation gained by his men in battle. Unlike the Roman Alexander recovered earlier in the twelfth century, Thomas's version of the conqueror is not tempted by eastern wealth, for his concerns are imperial and ideological. Establishing the largest possible Macedonian empire against human and monstrous enemies remains his objective throughout the *Roman de toute chevalerie* and echoes Nectanabus's original prophecy for the child who would expand the limits of the Macedonian *imperium* into the East.

Yet an ideological disparity between the crown and the baronage reveals itself as the army marches on India. The Macedonian barons fear the well-funded Indian army and argue that a larger, better equipped force is needed to overcome Porus. As one Tiberius of Rome expresses his fear, Alexander's barons, knights, and mercenaries are currently paid, but "tresqe hom na aveir damis est poevre assez" (as soon as a man has nothing, he is just as poor when it comes to friends [fol. 45v]). With this implication that loyalty is a quality for sale, he advises that Alexander heavily tax his subjects in Europe, use half of the income to continue paying the baronage and the remainder to bribe Porus's allies to turn against him. Yet Alexander prefers the counsel of another baron, Salome (notably Persian rather than Macedonian), who defends his leader's sense of noble honour:

> tut vus serviront come a lur seignur.
> En Perse se mettrunt en travaille en irrur.
> Par vostre proesce par force ensement vigur
> E par travalerie de vostre grant valur
> Conquerrez les Yndiens e les citez entur. (fol. 46r)

> everyone follows and serves you leader as a leader. In Persia you put yourself in mortal danger. By your prowess, strength, and vigour, and the knightly manner of your great valour, you will conquer India and the kingdoms around it.

Alexander's men will always be financially rewarded; he began his reign by bestowing Philip's treasure upon them, and when the Indian barons transfer their loyalty to him near the end of the Macedonian campaigns, he rewards his international baronage in similar manner, when "est emperere sur trestuz reclame / Si ad Europe e Asie en lige poeste" (he was proclaimed emperor over all, and Europe and Asia were both under his power [fol. 76r]). Reward is also fundamental to resolving the tension between the king and the baronage in the severest threat to their harmonious relationship during the Indian campaign. As this campaign becomes one of exploration rather than conquest, Alexander relies on the pride and fighting spirit to which the Persian baron Salome appeals in the passage above, while the Macedonian barons, far from home and wary of pursuing their transcontinental march, feel a certain dread over surpassing the normal limitations that they believe the gods to have placed on mortal men.

Having seen more of Africa and Asia than they dreamed possible, and knowing that their leader insists on seeing more, the barons' fear escalates when a tremendous storm blows upon them, and they quickly interpret it as a sign of divine wrath:

> Coe est a mult bon dreit ke nus avom turmient!
> Nus errom encontre deu e contre son talent.
> Ses secrez encerchom e fesum malement
> E coe volum enquerre par nostre hardement
> Ke deus a mortel home ne granta nient. (fol. 59v)

> It is for a very just reason that we are tormented! We err against God and his wishes, and we do evil in seeking his secrets and being led by our desire to dare to investigate what God does not wish to grant at all to mortal man.

Although Alexander initially tries to alleviate his men's fear by lecturing them on the brutalities of winter in some parts of the world, the storm and its snowfall ultimately frighten him as well. Alexander respects the power of the gods, but not because he feels that investigating the mysteries of nature is tantamount to blasphemy. Nor does he respond to Ptolemy's cry that "a powerful god" harries the army ("cil est deus sovereins qui tieuss darz nos lance" [fol. 60r]). For Alexander, the power to control atmospheric conditions is one that he lacks and thus admires, but it does not deter him. In fact, the momentary fear over divine authority only incites his desire to know and conquer more of the world. While his barons believe that with Asia and Africa in submission to Alexander, only western Europe remains ("ore ni ad a dire si sol occident non" [fol. 60v]), he soon finds a means of achieving as close to divine authority as he can realize: not believing that he is a god or promoting the rumour nonetheless (one of his destructive vanities in Roman histories), but fighting for a divine cause.

The opportunity to translate his invasion of Asia into a holy war comes from an unusual source, one of the monsters whom the Macedonians frequently encounter in the East. The one-eyed, monopod, neckless, and black-skinned creature frightens Alexander's men not so much with its appearance, after all of the wonders that they have encountered, as with the temerity with which it addresses the king. "Quantke avez … fet" (Whatsoever you have done), he challenges Alexander, "ne prise mie un boton / Quant navez veu lorguillus rei felon / Ke meint ultre la mer sa vers aquilon" (is worthless, for you have never seen the proud, criminal king who remains across the sea, towards the north [fol. 60v]). He goes on to describe Gog and Magog and similar races of humanoid monsters in Grendel-like terms as those of Nimrod who built the tower of Babel. Combating widely known, diabolical forces, especially those perceived as threats to the Christian West, afforded Alexander a literary persona akin to that of Richard the Lion-heart, whose defamation at the hands of monastic and clerical historians was being replaced by chivalric romance and who became an English icon of kingship and crusading while scribes continued to produce the manuscripts of the *Roman de toute chevalerie*.[58] At the same time, the campaigns against Gog and Magog and those who would undermine the civilized world allowed Thomas to definitively distinguish the agenda of his protagonist and the barons. While the latter require considerable encouragement, given that material gain is not a motivating factor so long as they remain fearful of the gods, for Alexander, to fight such mysterious forces is to follow the guiding principles of both moral rectitude and high adventure. In his mind, exploration and an unexpected holy war constitute a single, unified objective, and the opportunity awaiting his army in the recesses of Asia represents a stand against the evil that threatens his civilized world and a new responsibility to govern his increasingly international empire. As Suzanne Conklin Akbari writes of the narratives of Alexander's eastern campaigns, they portray a ruler who "having established the borders of the known world through conquest, [now] also must bear the burden of maintaining the order of his territory within."[59] Whether or not Alexander's passion to defend the civilized world is genuine, he presents the new enemy in compelling terms. The conquest of Asia is futile without defeating evil, according to his political argument, and he defines the suddenly high stakes of his campaign as having two potential outcomes, either Macedonian victory or global suffering ("tut le mond ent ert a prof contraliez" [fol. 64r]).

The Macedonians may have feared punishment for discovering too many divine mysteries, but the emboldened monster who tells of Gog and Magog relates that these peoples are not mere sinners but spiritual and geographical outcasts from God. Alexander hardly needs any more motivation to accept this unexpected challenge, and once the preparations for battle are underway, the barons respond again to the promise of reward. They do not share their leader's enthusiasm for fighting the supposed forces of evil or engaging in a holy war in the East, but, just as with the Persian and Indian campaigns, they recognize that, whatever the justification for Alexander, he sees Gog and Magog as necessitating a new theatre of combat. He gives his barons lavish gifts of gold and estates according to rank, promotes knights to counts and barons, and as the men pitch camp and prepare their arms, Thomas portrays an army that epitomizes the ideal of a feudal relationship for his medieval readers. Even the Macedonian coats of arms feature the Plantagenet lions rampant. From the perspective of the barons and knights, the Macedonian army becomes glorious not in Alexander's determination to keep evil at bay from the civilized world but in his determination to create an atmosphere of financial gain and upward mobility. The barons and knights fight for Alexander because he rewards them for doing so (and has since his coronation), even when they are reluctant to continue his campaigns. And their reluctance is considerable in this section of the *Roman de toute chevalerie.*

Alexander continues in reminding his men that their odyssey into the farthest reaches of Africa and Asia requires a communal sacrifice to save the civilized community. If his army fails, Alexander warns them:

> Tut li homme del monde ne lur freient puis lesser
> Ne nes porreient puis de nos terres chacer.
> Puis navereit li monde as bones genz mester
> Car nul ne si porreit encontre eus aider
> Mult purreient idunc li poeples damager. (fol. 64v)

No man in the world will be able to defeat [Gog and Magog and other evil races] after they are left alone, and no one will be able to chase them from our lands afterwards. Never again will good people have sovereignty in the world, for no one will be able to help them against these forces.

In subsequent passages, Thomas modifies the basic narrative of the Gog and Magog episode. Recognizing that he and his army cannot conquer the evil peoples (in this telling, there are twenty-four), Alexander prays for divine assistance and is ultimately able to enclose his enemies behind iron gates sealed with bitumen. The key distinction, however, in the version of the story in the *Roman de toute chevalerie* is that God does not perform the action of enclosure for Alexander but inspires him to come with a military strategy to drive Gog and Magog into a vulnerable position, and the conqueror himself oversees the enclosure. This moment, like the campaign, requires continuous fighting and strategizing, and Thomas relates that the Macedonians spent sixteen months battling the twenty-four groups of outcasts. Piety thus plays less of a role here than in those versions discussed in chapter 1 (especially in the most popular Latin source-text, Peter Comestor's *Historia scholastica*), and for Thomas the Macedonian victory rather results, it seems, from the militant, chivalrous lifestyle, the lifestyle of sacrificing physical safety to win glory and renown. In what serves as the coda to Alexander's battles against evil in the East, Thomas does not mention the role of divine intervention and again recalls the fighting spirit of his protagonist:

Coment poet Alisandre conquerre tant honour
Encontre itanz reis e tant emperour
Tant ducs e tant prince e tant riche almazor,
Kil ne suffrist batailles e meint dur estur? (fols 66rv)

How would Alexander have been able to conquer so honourably such kings and emperors, such dukes and princes and wealthy emirs, if he had not suffered battles and so many assaults?

Here, on the boundary between their accomplishments in Persia and their final campaign in India and between human and decidedly more challenging non-human foes, Alexander and his barons are able to reflect on the empire now inclusive of three continents and their deeds stretching back to Philip's appointment of his son and his baronage as the future of Macedon and to stand united in their objective. The barons no longer express their fears and anxieties over Alexander's agenda as they march into India, but here, amid the marvels they encounter, they find new cause for anxiety. After the trees of the sun and the moon foretell Alexander's death, the conqueror and his army enjoy one final victory in the series of battles against Porus, and Thomas reflects once more on their accomplishments across Europe, Africa, and Asia. A line later the Candace episode begins, and then Alexander and his men march to Babylon, where he drinks the poison prepared by Antipater and his survivors yield to the grief and violence discussed in the previous chapter. Having assuaged his men's doubts over the campaign into the East and led them to victories over what he considers forces of evil and then the Indian king Porus, Alexander bequeaths to them, in the end, an empire that they cannot sustain.

Questions of Kingship and the Paris *Roman de toute chevalerie*

Alexander's ability to secure his barons' loyalty through reward and his own bravery suggests a relationship that the manuscript's patron would have appreciated. For John d'Engaigne and his fellow knights, serving Edward I's cause in Scotland was not simply a matter of material gain, as Michael Prestwich has shown that in the years of John's participation in Edward I's campaigns, barons still provided knights to the king out of feudal obligation, and many knights simply paid their own expenses.[60] Of John and the feudal barons and barons by writ with whom he is associated on the first folio of the Paris manuscript there are few certainties, although some details are considerably helpful in surmising his interest in the *Roman de toute chevalerie*. For John, where and when he fought for Edward I in Scotland, his role as signatory to the letter to Boniface VIII to claim Edward's sovereignty over Scotland, and the literary celebration of his arms and deeds are biographical details that reasonably explain why he would be drawn to the Alexander legend. However, his patronage of this manuscript, produced during Edward II's tumultuous first years on the throne and rendering an Anglo-Norman romance into Continental French rather than featuring a copy of a competing French Alexander romance, raises some intriguing issues about John's reception of the Alexander legend and, more generally, the political contexts of the legend in thirteenth-century England.

The years leading up to the Paris copy of Thomas's romance certainly witnessed conflicting reactions among English writers towards Plantagenet kingship, and baronial rebellion against their kings from John to Edward III inspired a lively tradition of sacred and secular political literature that evaluated the impact of irresponsible and unjust kingship and civil war on all social classes while displaying sympathy towards and bias for the baronial cause.[61] In the years following the Cambridge manuscript, the 1264 Battle of Lewes, in which the barons captured both Henry III and his son Edward, inspired a corpuscula of Latin poems. The result, in David Matthews's words, was "a world in which members of the English royal dynasty are consistently and bitterly criticised," Simon de Montfort became a literary hero of chivalric virtue, and good rule (and, in the minds of the barons, the failure of the Plantagenet kings to exercise it) was a common theme for generations.[62] Political songs from the era tend to address this theme through a reflection on previous and current broken, royal promises and the deliberate conflation of historical examples of bad kingship. "The Song of Lewes," recalls, for example, John's failure to uphold the Magna Carta through Henry III's own inability to adhere to the Provisions of Oxford,[63] and the fourteenth-century "On the King's Breaking His Confirmation of Magna Charta," whose author comments simultaneously on Edward II's breaking of the 1311 Ordinances and again on Henry and the Provisions of Oxford to warn his audience that grandfather and grandson alike are untrustworthy kings and to inspire them with the memory of a time when "a group of barons successfully rebelled and then forced the king to give up some of his powers to them."[64]

As discussed above, upon Edward I's death in 1307 elegies for the fallen warrior-king served as elegies for the future of his kingdom as well, owing to the lack of confidence in his son. Around 1312, the oldest surviving version of the "Prophecy of the Six Kings" proclaims the "exceptional public grief" after the death of this Dragon of "three habitations," England, Scotland, and Wales, and two years later the feared loss of Edward's attempted empire became a reality.[65] At least two of the barons identified in the Paris manuscript's first folio, Thomas le Latimer and Richard Bassett,[66] were taken prisoner at Bannockburn, Edward II's disastrous loss in the war against Scotland. Contextualized as such – immediately following Edward I's death and produced during the debates and occasional armed threats between Edward II and his baronage – the Paris manuscript of the *Roman de toute chevalerie* reads as a eulogy for what John d'Engaigne's generation had accomplished. It is admittedly convenient, and perhaps obvious, to argue that John saw in the exploits of Alexander and his army a loftier, more successful version of what he had achieved within Edward I's army. Whether because of the dashing young prince eager for battle, reminiscent of Edward's exploits in the Crusade of the 1270s, or the campaign against a formidable foe to the East (Persia/Levant/France), John may have recognized at the very least a reflection of what Edward I had undertaken from the 1270s onward, akin to the chivalric celebration of the *Song of Caervelerock* and the romances of Arthur and Richard the Lion-heart. The latter two were motivated by the crusading spirit and the killing of Saracens, themes so crucial to the success of Anglo-Norman *chansons de geste* and the romantic notion of English heroes abroad.[67] Edward did not realize his vision of leading western Europe on an extended crusade,[68] but he had spent two years fighting in the Levant before his campaigns against the Welsh and Scots, and within late-thirteenth and early-fourteenth-century literature his victories were clearly lauded. We can only assume that John took a certain pride in his role in them.

Still, having witnessed the troubles of Edward II's first years on the throne and perhaps foreseeing more on the horizon, John's outlook for England's future was surely altered during the years when he took an apparent interest in the Alexander legend. He may even have acknowledged this and offered his own subtle protest against the future of his nation by the placement of his coat of arms. On several occasions, John's arms are drawn on Alexander's primary foes, Darius of Persia and Porus of India. As a veteran of Edward's Scottish campaigns, John could presumably have had his arms affiliated with Alexander's barons and knights, and if he felt particularly emboldened by commissioning an Alexander romance, he could, of course, have ordered his association with the conqueror himself. Yet he did neither and affiliated himself instead with the two men who challenge Alexander's supremacy and ultimately lose. By the end of the manuscript, a good deal of malaise and disappointment lingers. The Macedonians may have bested their enemies abroad, but they lost all that they had acquired, and both sides, Macedonian and foreign, lay in disorder. In turn, Edward I may have clashed with the baronage and fought on various fronts in Scotland, Wales, and France, but by 1307 that mattered far less than it had in John's fighting days of the 1290s. A new king meant that the fights with the baronage would begin all over again, and the battlefield exploits would not be celebrated, as they had been in the days of Caervelerock and Falkirk, but lamented, as those at Bannockburn would soon learn. With the death of Alexander, the death of Edward I, and the ill-fated beginning of Edward II's reign, the dream of imitating the Macedonians had become futile for John, his fellow knights, and their barons.

Although other writers and scribes, including that of the next surviving manuscript of the *Roman de toute chevalerie* (Durham Cathedral Library MS C.IV.27B), were soon to underscore the transience of Alexander's rule and the limitations of his authority; his reputation as an exemplary ruler remained largely undiminished. Edward I had long considered Alexander as an exemplary king, as evidenced by the conqueror's portrait in the Painted Chamber at Westminster, and after his death, he would be the subject of elegiac comparisons with the ancient warrior-king. Thomas's romance provided the men who fought for Edward the same notion of Alexander. As discussed above, the *Roman de toute chevalerie* flavours the conqueror's invasion of the far reaches of Asia with the rhetoric of a holy war against the enemies of the civilized world, particularly Gog and Magog, widely associated in the thirteenth and fourteenth centuries with the confrontation between Christian Europe and the pagan East. For the next generation of readers of the *Roman de toute chevalerie,* Alexander's role as God's agent against such evil forces would be emphasized as one of the main topoi of the romance, even as for men like John d'Engaigne and his peers, the fantasy of serving a king worthy of Arthurian-Alexandrine comparisons became unattainable. As Thorlac Turville-Petre notes, within a decade of the Paris manuscript, the barons rose up in armed rebellion against Edward II, and the revised Middle English *Brut,* now continued into the 1320s, lamented "þe shame and despite þat þe gentil ordre of knyghthode there hade at that bataile" of Bannockburn.[69]

Chapter Six

Moralizing Alexander in Durham Cathedral Library MS C.IV.27B

Whereas the *Roman de toute chevalerie* recounts the anxieties inherent in the power struggles among Alexander and his royal family and warns against the potential of royal-baronial animosity to undermine a kingdom and the well-being of its subjects, many fourteenth-century writers and scribes cast Alexander as a symbol of failed and futile kingship. In a century that witnessed the deposition and possible murder of Edward II, the ebb and flow of his son's military-political successes and failures, outbreaks of the Black Death, the death of Edward the Black Prince, and the deposition and possible murder of Richard II in its final year, Alexander came to be defined by the suddenness of his death and the quick dissolution of his empire as much as, if not more than, his battlefield exploits and adventures. The Macedonians lacked the imperial longevity of the Romans and failed for the most part to provide medieval writers in western Europe with myths of founding fathers, as had the Matter of Troy, and the inherent warnings of Alexander and his successors' inability to maintain their mutual authority over the classical world would leave a deep impression on fourteenth-century writers.[1]

Such was the reception of the conqueror both appropriated and exaggerated by the producers of Durham Cathedral Library MS C.IV.27B in the mid-fourteenth century. Although no reliable clues as to the manuscript's scriptorium or patron survive, it does suggest at least two reading agendas. The first six of the manuscript's 201 folios feature a list of rubrics that correspond to the picture captions in the Cambridge and Paris manuscripts, and as Keith Busby notes, the chapter titles in the Durham codex that cover a battle are identified by blue rubrics, and Alexander's campaigns are labelled as "bella" throughout the narrative, signs of readership reflective of chronicles and histories and supported by occasional marginal annotations from historical texts.[2] In fact, these annotations reveal a telling range of sacred and secular and classical and medieval texts. Most are written on the folios relating the first phase of Alexander's career, the invasion of Persia, in which two passages from Josephus's *Antiquitates Judaicae* on Alexander's interaction with the leaders of Jerusalem frame several details on the battles between the Macedonian and Persians from Orosius.[3] After Alexander's victory and subsequent campaign into the East, however, marginal annotations taken from Peter Comestor's commentary on the Book of Daniel (fol. 188v), the Valerius *Epitome* (fol. 189r), a brief note that Alexander gave his ring to Perdiccas ("Et dedit annulum suum Perdicce," fol. 190r), and a passage from Curtius Rufus's *Res gestae Alexandri Magni* (fol. 195v) all focus on his death in Babylon and reveal the reader's secondary interest in the narrative.[4] These notes engage generally with the common fourteenth-century moralities on Alexander's death (e.g., he was killed by treachery at the height of his career, and his earthly sovereignty was checked by a divine power) and specifically with the interpolations found only in the Durham copy of the *Roman de toute chevalerie.* Collectively they suggest a reader interested in bolstering Thomas's Anglo-Norman narrative with traditional historical authorities available in Latin (Josephus and Orosius) and in moralizing Alexander's death with texts that emphasize the limits of his mortal power (Peter Comestor), the notion, inherited from the *Pseudo-Callisthenes,* that the man undefeated by a world of armies was felled by a glass of wine (the Valerius *Epitome*), and the multitude of historical kings murdered by traitors (Curtius Rufus). That these annotations are written in an anglicana hand raises the possibility that the mid-fourteenth-century patron of the manuscript did not add them himself and that the book remained of interest later in the century and perhaps into the next.

No record of ownership survives before 1726, when Thomas Rud first described the codex in Durham Cathedral Library,[5] but the manuscript is safely assigned "to ownership in a clerical establishment of some kind where a reader had access to copies of the Latin histories."[6] The texts consulted for the marginal annotations certainly required access to a library well stocked with the usual Alexander narratives (and one unusual one, if the passage from Curtius Rufus was copied directly from the Roman history, a rare text in England), and Brian Foster proposes that Richard of Bury ordered the manuscript from St Albans.[7]

As Lord of the Privy Seal from 1329 to 1333, Richard received and purchased several books from the prodigious scriptorium, but he returned many upon being named the Bishop of Durham,[8] an office which he held from 1334 to 1345. During this time, a book collector of Richard's stature may very well have obtained the *Roman de toute chevalerie*, yet no evidence links the Durham manuscript either to him or the scriptorium at St Albans, and the best inferences to be drawn from the book's history have to do with its language, its arrangement, and the numerous texts introduced into the narrative by its scribe. At any rate, the reliance on Josephus and Orosius as canonical authorities had long been commonplace. Each appears, for example, on Durham Cathedral Library MS B.IV.24, a twelfth-century book-list of texts available at the monastery, along with the works of Virgil, Ovid, and several classical poets and contemporary chronicles,[9] suggestive of the readership of a "secular, aristocratic mode of life" in Durham at the time.[10] While Orosius's history was moved near the end of the fourteenth century to the Spendiment – a storage room adjacent to the cloister and one reserved for books that had fallen out of fashion – the *Antiquitates Judaicae* remained among the "modern" books in the cloister itself, and its continued use may account for the interest in Alexander's visit to Jerusalem, interpolated in the Durham copy alone among the surviving copies of the *Roman de toute chevalerie*.[11]

That an Anglo-Norman text was preserved in the age of Middle English Alexander romance is not surprising. Even into Richard II's reign, Anglo-Norman remained "the language of the court, of chivalry, [and] entertainment," and French Alexander romances as models of chivalry still captured the imagination of Edward IV in the following century.[12] This is not to say that the Durham copy was intended for a royal patron, but the *Roman de toute chevalerie* certainly belongs to the continued Insular interest in Anglo-Norman and Continental French romances. Like the Paris manuscript, it is a product of a century that saw language increasingly affiliated with social class in England,[13] but the Durham copy stands closer to the last decades of widespread French composition within Insular literature.[14] Despite the linguistic and social bond associating these two fourteenth-century complete manuscripts of Thomas of Kent's romance, a key distinction remains: the Paris copy and perhaps the fragment of the *Roman de toute chevalerie* in Oxford, Bodleian Library, MS Lat. Misc. B. 17 adapted Thomas's work into Continental French, while the scribe of the Durham manuscript presumably worked from an exemplar of the romance in its original dialect. This manuscript retains, in a manner of speaking, the original "Englishness" of Thomas's romance at a time when Insular writers were delivering Alexander romances to a new, anglophone audience and Continental French Alexander romances continued to thrive, spurred on by the dominance of the Parisian dialect.[15] Moreover, the Latin marginal annotations in the Durham manuscript point to an educated and engaged reader, similar to that suggested in Oxford, Bodleian Library MS Rawlinson D 329, a fourteenth-copy of the Anglo-Norman *Brut* with Latin and English annotations.[16]

Besides the annotations, the Durham *Roman de toute chevalerie* also features various interpolations, including the episodes from the *Roman d'Alexandre* of Alexandre de Paris common to the other copies of Thomas's poem (the *Fuerre de Gadres* interpolation and passages concerning Alexander's dying moments, division of his lands, and the laments of his successors) and passages on Alexander's visit to Jerusalem, a lesson on mortality taught by a stranger explicating the so-called Wonderstone, and Alexander's lament on treachery as the cause of regicide, all unique to the Durham copy of Thomas's romance.[17] This manuscript should not be dismissed, however, as a repository for whatever Alexander material the scribe had at his disposal. The interpolations and marginal notes collectively pass moral judgment on the conqueror's reign as one founded on the self-serving agenda of conquest that, with its sudden end, is destined to serve the moralizing, Christian review of classical history. As such, the Durham manuscript underscores beyond the other copies of the *Roman de toute chevalerie* the limitations of Alexander's authority imposed by divine proclamations and prophecies, what Suzanne Conklin Akbari identifies as the "danger and inevitable destruction" facing the conqueror in the east, north, and south, where he finds discouraging omens, and the west, towards which he never ventures.[18] Together, the interpolations and marginal annotations thus present a clear exemplum of the limitations of all kings, a reading of history that has its own tradition in Durham. Janet Burton argues that historical texts in the monasteries of northern England were esteemed for their didactic value for contemporary readers, and of the three largest manuscripts of the *Roman de toute chevalerie*, the Durham copy undoubtedly presents the story of Alexander as a moral lesson.[19] It thus hints at a readership interested in histories and romances of Alexander and a scribe who chose his additional sources selectively and arranged them to produce a composite narrative of Alexander reflective of fourteenth-century trends in his reception.

The Interpolations

1) Alexander's Visit to Jerusalem

Alexander's interaction with the Jews and visit to Jerusalem, the first interpolation in the Durham manuscript, is the most circulated of the four in medieval texts and codices. Although the interpolator cites Josephus Flavius as his source (and the scribe/reader of the manuscript includes marginal references to this text), this episode was widely available in the brief Alexander narrative in Peter Comestor's twelfth-century *Historia scholastica,* which relied on Josephus and the I^2 recension of the *Historia de preliis,* as well as the *Antiquitates Judaicae* itself, known in England since the Conquest through the Latin translation of Cassiodorus.[20] Thomas of Kent had originally cited Josephus as one of his canonical, historical authorities, and the Paris manuscript includes what is likely his original mention of Alexander's contact with the Jews, an episode in which Alexander writes to the leaders of Jerusalem as their sovereign and demands tribute and supplies for his army, and when they refuse, citing their vow not to take up arms against Darius, Alexander vows revenge in turn. In the Durham manuscript, the interpolation relating Alexander's interaction with the Jews occurs after this heated exchange, but when he arrives in Jerusalem in this continuation of the episode, unique to this copy, Alexander participates in an unexpected scene of reciprocity. While Jaddus, the high priest of Jerusalem, reveals that God told him to admit the Macedonian into the city, Alexander immediately bows to his host, much to the confusion of his soldiers. As an explanation he quickly announces his own dream vision, in which Jaddus promised him victory in Persia and a message of divine assistance:

E pur ceo quil m'ad iesqes encea aidez
E tenu covenant e de rien faillez
A laide de dieux ai ieo Dayre outreiez
Par qi ieo espoire fournir mes volentez
De toutes autres choses qe jeo ai enpensez. (fol. 118r)

Because this man who has just come to help me kept his promise – and did not at all fail to do so – that with God's help I would conquer Darius, I thus hope through him to accomplish my desires in everything else that I am about to attempt.

Anticipating victory through this vision, Alexander assuages the fears of the priests, who interpret for him the prophecy of Daniel, supposedly revealing that the Macedonian was destined to conquer Persia. For their role in boosting their guest's confidence in his future success, the Jews receive the right to live peacefully in Babylon and the restoration of their ancestral laws.

In the Paris copy of the *Roman de toute chevalerie*, the interpolation of the *Fuerre de Gadres* diverts attention from the Jerusalem episode. In both this and the Durham manuscript, as Alexander besieges Tyre, he sends out messengers who

As citez denviron tant dit e tant prie
E vers les orgoillus firerement manace
Qe toz venent al curt ly riche e ly prise.
En totes les terres not nul si envoise
Ne vienge al curt a ly ou il est al sie
Fors de Jerusalem dont li roys est ire. (fol. 26v)

To the surrounding cities he so spoke and implored and so fiercely threatened the proud that the wealthy and the nobles all came to [Alexander's] court. In all the lands was not found a man so emboldened that he would come to the court where [Alexander] was seated outside of Jerusalem, which had drawn the king's ire.

It seems here that Thomas intended some portion of the narrative from a Latin translation of Josephus, possibly to demonstrate further Alexander's volatile temper. In the Durham manuscript, his message to Jerusalem does precisely that, and his subsequent assault on Tyre, a veritable icon of Alexander's emotional instability, only exaggerates his temperamental character. Yet before he completes this assault, both manuscripts shift the focus of the narrative from the conqueror to that of his barons in its longest interpolation, the *Fuerre de Gadres* episode from the French *Roman d'Alexandre*. As Emmanuèle Baumgartner argues, while this episode emphasizes the vital fraternal bond within the Macedonian army and brings to light the worthy pagan Gadifer (who would appear in another fourteenth-century Alexander romance, *Perceforest*), the story also "foregrounds the ostentatious pursuit of a futile kind of glory, while poorly concealing the heroes' desire to enrich themselves and ceaselessly acquire other possessions."[21]

Whether or not the scribe of the Durham manuscript recognized this sense of futility, the outcome of the episode – a general's death and Alexander's retribution against noble enemies – accords with much of what the codex offers. Darius, too, is a worthy adversary, and his death in the next major section of the manuscript (over forty folios recounting Alexander's conquest of Persia) serves a moralizing purpose for both the reader, in encountering the sudden downfall of a powerful emperor and Alexander's predecessor, and for Alexander himself, who weeps and tears his hair upon his rival's death (fol. 115r). Moreover, in this section Thomas underscores his hero's magnanimity towards Darius's survivors. After executing his rival's murderers and distributing the Persian treasure to his own soldiers, Alexander treats Darius's family nobly ("monstre grant franchise") and "done lur richesces e aime sanz feintise" (gave them riches and loved them genuinely [fol. 116v]), reflective of the paternal relationship between the Persian king and his foreign successor.[22] Yet the Persians, and to a lesser degree the Indians, remain allied to Alexander; these are the peoples, after all, who ultimately welcome him as their ruler, join his baronage and help govern his empire, and mourn his passing. Those who oppose Alexander in the earlier sections (the king Nicholas, anonymous armies throughout the Near East, the Tyrians, and the Athenians) do not enjoy such intimacy with him, nor do they desire it.

Based on Alexander's first menacing contact with the Jews, it would seem that they belong on this list as well, yet their relationship changes significantly in the second part of the interpolated Jerusalem episode. The continuation of this episode maintains the thirteenth-century fashion of presenting Alexander as a king ordained by God, yet the narrative as a whole casts doubt on the conqueror's true intentions. His dream vision instils in Alexander hope for divine assistance in his campaigns, but Jaddus and the priests cleverly exploit that hope by explicating the prophecy in Daniel:

> Le livre Daniel out devant lui portez
> Ou il trouent escrit qe par un en Grece neez
> Le powoir de Perse serra aventiez.
> Quant lui rois lad oie sen est reconfortez
> Il entent qe de lui fu ceo prophetez. (fols 118rv)

The book of Daniel, wherein it was written that the strength of Persia would be cast down by one born in Greece, was brought before [Alexander]. When the king heard the prophecy, he was comforted, because he understood that it referred to him.

If, one supposes, Alexander were not the intended conqueror of the prophecy, he might return to his earlier antagonistic stance against the Jews. As it is, the interpretation of Daniel acts as a convenient public staging for Alexander's benefit. Still, it has an impact on his confidence in his campaign into Asia, if not yet his spiritual faith, and as has recently been argued, the Jerusalem episode signifies his first encounter with monotheism, and the fact that Alexander recognizes the Jewish God as his protector attests to his nascent humility in the narrative.[23]

A couple of decades before the Durham manuscript, a convenient example of baser motivations for Alexander's excitement over the prophecy of Daniel being explicated in Jerusalem makes for a telling comparison with the Anglo-Norman romance. In the Oxford scholar Nicholas Trevet's *Historia ab origine mundi*, based on Roman, Jewish, and ecclesiastical works,[24] within the span of a folio occur the two well-known episodes of Alexander's visits to Jerusalem and to the temple of Jupiter Ammon in Egypt. The point of the first follows tradition, namely to establish his alliance with the Jews and to convince Alexander of his future success in Persia, yet set alongside the story of the temple of Ammon (taken from the *Philippic Histories*) the visit to Jerusalem and Alexander's public shows of authority there lacks the sincerity of the version in the Durham manuscript. If the visit to Jerusalem offers a purported prophecy from the Jewish God, then the story of Alexander at the temple of Ammon presents a wholly fabricated prophecy in Trevet's history:

> Igitur Alexander cupiens originem diuinitatis adquirere simul et matrem infamia liberare per premissos subornat antistites quid sibi responderi uellet. Ingredientem templum statim antistites ut Hammonis filium salutant. Ille letus dei adoptione hoc se patre censeri iubet … Tertia interrogatione poscenti uictoriam omnium bellorum possessionemque terrarum dari respondetur. Comitibus quoque suis responsum, ut Alexandrum pro deo, non pro rege colerent. Hinc illi aucta insolentia mirusque animo increuit tumor exempta comitate quam et Graecorum litteris et Macedonum institutis didicerat.[25]

Alexander, wishing to be associated with a divine origin and to absolve his mother from slander, coerced through his messengers the priests [of the oracle] into saying what he wished to hear from them. The priests immediately saluted him as the son of Ammon when he entered the temple, and Alexander, happy that he had been adopted by the god, ordered that he be considered his son ... When Alexander had asked them his third question, they responded that he had been granted victory in all of his wars and possession of the world. There was a response from the oracle for his companions as well, and the priests ordered them to accept Alexander as a god, not as a king. Afterwards Alexander's insolence increased, and a wondrous swell of pride grew in his mind, and he neglected the affability that he had learned in Greek literature and through Macedonian customs.

This moment is naturally a turning point in Alexander's career and his assimilation with eastern political culture. Swayed by his desire to be considered a god, he strays not only from modest and imperturbable behaviour but even from his nationality and upbringing. Following the account of his visit to Jerusalem, however, this second "prophecy" becomes an even more distressing scene of Alexander's degradation. This second story, an act of vanity and political stumping (promoting a divine lineage to attain the office of pharaoh), pointedly undercuts the first, a supposedly sacrosanct moment of Alexander's preeminent role in providential history. In the temple of Ammon, Alexander shows his vainglory and pride, increasingly destructive to the point that he promotes his own divinity, all of which stands in stark contrast to the expected behaviour of a ruler chosen to do God's bidding for the Jews.

For the Durham manuscript's interpolator, however, the Jerusalem episode culminates in a celebration of Alexander's suddenly heartfelt kindness towards the Jews:

Puis après lui rois fasoit ordiner
Qe Jerusalem poesse demorer
En pees e quieté tot temps a durer.
Qe furent nafrez fesoit i saner,
Et les alassez fit il remounter;
Et lors devers Inde se fit remuer ...
Dieu lui doint sa grace de bien espleiter! (fol. 118v)

Afterwards the king gave the order that Jerusalem remain in peace and quiet for all time. He ordered that the wounded be tended there, and the weak be put on horses, and then he set out for India ... May God grant him the grace to succeed!

Such kindness, and the interpolator's prayer for Alexander's continued success, corresponds to Thomas's original treatment of the conqueror as one who, despite being the child of sorcery, becomes an exemplary leader with a demonstrable piety towards the gods, and who, despite his occasional fits of anger, treats his enemies compassionately and is ultimately mourned by them in Babylon. The interpolator of the Durham manuscript seemingly recognizes these facets of Alexander's character in the *Roman de toute chevalerie*, and while he clearly wishes to address both the conqueror's relationship with the gods and the reception of his death in Babylon, he does not necessarily maintain Thomas's ultimate admiration for his hero's reign.

2) The Wonderstone

Thirty folios later, Alexander has a second realization of divine authority in what amounts to a companion scene for his visit to Jerusalem. Amid the section of the manuscript concerning the wonders of the East, Alexander enters the so-called earthly paradise, ultimately based on a twelfth-century Latin text entitled the *Iter ad Paradisum*.[26] As in the Latin narrative, his intention is to collect tribute from the leader of the mysterious land, but an equally enigmatic figure greets him with a riddle instead. In recognizing Alexander's previous conquests and current intentions in the earthly paradise, the stranger presents "tribute" in the form of a small stone that outweighs any amount of gold, silver, or precious metal. Only when covered in dirt does the ball balance the scale against the other objects, which the man explains as a metaphor for Alexander's reign: as long as he lives, no one will match or surpass his authority, but when dead and buried Alexander will be no more venerable than any other corpse, and he will soon be forgotten. The moral of the demonstration is predictable enough, but Alexander's reaction is decidedly not:

Et dit le grant dieu qe trestot crea
Est sire de cele terre ou il Adam forma.
Cele terre n'est pas moy ne iames ne serra
Mes cil q'en Macedoigne en songe me conseilla
E me promist conquerre trestot quant qil y a.
Le powoir de Perse a moy baillera.
Fiablement mon host ileqes amenera
Pur qi amur les Jewes nul des miens greva

Einz les desportai e assez honura
Ordeine qe mielz est e ceo qe lui plerra
De mort e de vie e quant qe mavendra. (fols 149rv)

And he said, "The great God who created everything is lord of this land, where he created Adam. This land does not belong to me, nor will it ever, but to the One who advised me in a dream in Macedon and promised that I would conquer everywhere I travelled and that He would give me the strength of Persia and safely lead my army there. For love of him the Jews were not aggrieved by my men, but I spared them and honoured them well. May he command whatever is for the best and whatever pleases him regarding my death, my life, and whatever befalls me.

This interpolation significantly alters the original purpose of the reference to the earthly paradise in the *Roman de toute chevalerie*, present in the Cambridge and Paris copies, wherein Alexander proposes to his barons a trip to the land "ou dieu forma Adam nostre priere ancien" (where God created our ancestor Adam [fol. 148r]). A few lines later, however, he has an inexplicable change of heart and apparently having found little of value in the paradise decides to return to India instead.

While all of the manuscripts of Thomas's poem pinpoint the locations at which his progress into Asia and Africa is stopped, emphasize the prophecies of his death, and relate the one person to deceive Alexander before Antipater (Candace, the queen who entraps a disguised Alexander in her bedroom), they also insist on his frustrations and sorrow in such moments. Only the Durham manuscript, with its portrayal of Alexander's trust in the Judaeo-Christian God during the visit to Jerusalem and recognition of divine sovereignty over the earthly paradise, features the extended narrative of the voyage and demonstrates the conqueror's willingness to respect and even acquiesce to a higher power. If God grants Alexander so many other lands, it seems, then he is content to realize that he cannot, and should not, occupy Jerusalem and the earthly paradise. Rather than merely filling out a narrative for a pre-existing reference to one of Alexander's minor excursions, the interpolation in the Durham manuscript offers an opportunity both to comment on his reign in the relative terms of fleeting empires and to emphasize again his acquiescence to a Christian scheme of divine authority over all mortals, no matter how exalted.

He does not renounce his pride and belligerent lifestyle, as does the Alexander in the Latin *Iter ad paradisum* and the Strassbourg copy of

Lamprecht's romance based on it,[27] but he does recognize and respect the monotheistic authority greater than himself. The scene thus represents an act of humility on Alexander's part but hardly an adoption of new moral values or a new agenda in his march eastward.[28] In comparison with Continental versions of the episode, however, Alexander's humility in the Durham manuscript is striking. Versions of the "Wonderstone" episode appear in the mid-thirteenth-century *Prise de Defur* and the *Voyage d'Alexandre au paradis terrestre* often appended to it in the *Roman d'Alexandre* manuscript tradition, as well as in an early-thirteenth-century prose compilation entitled the *Faits des Romains*. In all three of these texts, Aristotle, not a Jewish elder, interprets for Alexander the symbolism of a jewel engraved with the image of an eye (the *Faits*), an actual human eye (the *Prise de Defur*), and an apple (the *Voyage*). In the first, Aristotle merely explains to his former pupil that when Alexander's eyes are open (i.e., when he is alive) he figuratively outweighs the world, but not when his eyes are covered (i.e., when he is dead).[29] In the *Prise de Defur*, his interpretation also addresses Alexander's behaviour, as he explains that the uncovered eye is heavier than the lands conquered by Alexander but considerably lighter when covered, signifying that the human eye covets all that it sees in life but nothing in death and that when he secures victory over one people, he will seek many more.[30] Finally, in the *Voyage*, Aristotle's explication becomes emotive and distraught. Here, he interprets the eye in similar terms as he does in the *Prise de Defur*, but he also understands it as a sign that Alexander's death is approaching and encourages the conqueror to value virtuous behaviour over greed.[31] His outburst has a profound effect on those within earshot, and Alexander stoically accepts his fate,[32] all of which recalls the Macedonians' reaction to the trees of the sun and the moon that likewise foretell the conqueror's death in Babylon.[33] Each of these Continental versions depart from the *Iter ad paradisum* in a crucial respect. While in the Latin account, the Jewish sage Papas warns Alexander about the dangers of ambition, the conqueror heeds his advice and from his deathbed instructs his survivors to do the same.[34] In the *Faits*, the *Prise de Defur*, and the *Voyages*, he simply continues his march to Babylon after hearing Aristotle explain the significance of the eye or apple. Alexander may not disavow his ambition in the Durham *Roman de toute chevalerie* either, but his recognition of a higher power that has overseen his victories and his acceptance of his own limitations in this text comparatively demonstrate a self-awareness and maturity not seen in the Continental versions.

The scribe/reader of the Durham copy also recognizes the importance of Alexander's concession to divine authority. Quoting a line from Peter Comestor's version of Jerome's commentary on Daniel discussed in the previous chapter, the same interpretation explained to Alexander during his visit to Jerusalem, the marginal annotator writes, "hanc potestantem a se non habuit Alexander sed fuit virga furoris Domini in filios pestilentes" (Alexander had this power not on his own, but because he was an offshoot of the Lord's anger against noxious races [fol. 188v]). Again, the context for this line concerns Daniel's vision of beasts, the third of which is a leopard (representing Alexander) with four heads (representing his four most powerful successors):

> Tertia bestia quasi pardus, et habebat alas avis, et quatuor capita erant in ea, et potestas data est ei; hoc est regnum Graecorum, quod comparatur pardo, qui saltu ruit in mortem propter impetum Alexandri. Et varii colores, diversa sub eo regna significant. Alas habuit, quia nihil velocius victoria Alexandri; quatuor capita ejus quatuor sunt Alexandri successores. Nec hanc potestatem habuit a se Alexander, sed fuit virga furoris Domini in filios pestilentes.[35]

> The third beast looked like a leopard, and it had the wings of a bird and four heads, and power was granted to it. This represents the kingdom of the Greeks, which is comparable to a leopard, in that in leaping it rushes to its death, as seen in Alexander's impulsive attack. It has various colours, each signifying a different kingdom. It has wings, because nothing was so quick as Alexander's victory. Its four heads represent Alexander's four successors. Alexander had this power not on account of himself, but because he was an offshoot of the Lord's anger against noxious races.

The marginal citation from Peter Comestor clearly argues that Alexander's success was attributable not to his own merits but to the will of God, a theological reading underscored by the annotator's comment on the next folio, taken from the Valerius *Epitome*: "Et quem totus orbis ferro superare not potuit uino et ueneno exstinctus occubuit" (And he whom the entire world could not overcome with the sword was overcome by poisoned wine and lay dead [fol. 189r]). Together, the two lines in the Durham manuscript imply that its reader took particular interest in Alexander's mortal limitations and his confrontation with divine power (not surprising, given the moralizing interpolations in this copy of the *Roman de toute chevalerie*) and made careful note of the moments in the text that attested to these limitations.

Here again, a contemporary chronicler provides valuable context for a romance view of Alexander's legacy and relationship with monotheism. Ranulf Higden of St Werburgh's Abbey in Chester arranged an impressive number of texts on the Macedonian Empire in his universal history, the *Polychronicon*, to provide a lengthy narrative of Alexander, his predecessors, and successors. He relied mainly on Justin's epitome of the *Philippic Histories* but supplemented this Roman narrative with several minor romance and historical sources.[36] The result is an expected pastiche of a narrative, but one that clearly emphasizes the futility of Alexander's career in its final sections. Higden's intentions are evident in an intriguingly unique version of Alexander's correspondence with the ascetic Indian philosopher Dindimus. While this epistolary debate between a materialistic warrior and an abstemious pacifist had circulated in England for several centuries, Higden presents a very curious resolution to the two parties' disagreement. By the conclusion of their correspondence, Alexander finds himself charmed by the simple and tranquil lifestyle of his critic, and in his last letter to Dindimus, the conqueror writes the most personal and emotive admission found in any Alexander narrative of medieval England:

> Tu de Deo veniens in quieto vivis loco; ego inter formidines vivo; custodies meos timeo; magis amicos quam hostes formido; nec ipsis carere nec aliis me credere valeo. De die gentes fatigo, de nocte fatigatus timeo. Si occidero quos formido tristor. Si rursum lenis fuero contemnor. Et si tecum in convallibus vivere voluero, id mihi non licebit.[37]

> You are a man of God, and you live in a peaceful place. I live amid dread, and I fear those who protect me, and I shudder at my friends more than my enemies, but I am able neither to be without them nor to entrust myself to them. By day I exhaust other people, and by night I am exhausted by fear. If I kill those whom I fear, then I am sorrowful; if I am lenient again, then I will be despised; and if I wished to live with you in your valley, then I would not be permitted.

Alexander not only foresees his end, but even as the mighty world conqueror he is also justifiably afraid and as unsure of what actions to take as he is certain of his death. His letter conveys, too, a chilling self-awareness, the realization that he has literally run out of space and time to conquer and that the one place to which he so desires to travel, Dindimus's utopian valley (similar to the Durham manuscript's account of the earthly paradise), is forbidden to him. There is in this unique letter an undeniable irony appropriate for Higden's views on Alexander; driven by ambition to conquer all of the known world, the Macedonian rather poignantly realizes that not only is he denied entrance into an eastern locale for which he desperately yearns but also that, because of his impending death, his days of campaigning and conquering are over.

As he draws his history of Alexander to a close, Higden repeatedly underscores the mortality of the conqueror and the transience of what he has built on earth. In his last chapter on Alexander, Higden interpolates passages from the *Philippic Histories*, Peter Comestor's *Historia scholastica*, Vincent of Beauvais's *Speculum historiale*, and Josephus's *Antiquitates Judaicae* to address both portents and traditional narratives of Alexander's death, beginning with the oracular responses of the trees of the sun and the moon. As in other texts, the trees warn the conqueror that he will die by poisoning in Babylon in the following year,[38] but as Higden continues, he writes in his own voice, not as an interpolator:

> Cum Alexander totum Orientem subjugasset, in redeundo versus patriam propriam legati Occidentis, scilicet Africae, Hispaniae, Italiae, venerunt Babyloniam, ut ejus ditioni se subjicerent. Ille autem sperans ex hoc monarcham orbis se futurum, prae nimio gaudio oblitus responsi arborum solis et lunae, Babyloniam intravit praedictis nunciis locuturus.[39]

> After Alexander had conquered all of the Orient and was in the process of returning to his homeland, legates from the West, namely Africa, Spain, and Italy, came to Babylon to submit themselves to his authority. Alexander, hoping that from this submission he would become king of the world and overcome with joy, forgot the responses of the trees of the sun and moon, and he entered Babylon to speak to the aforementioned legates.

The temptation of a global empire, Alexander's objective since departing for Persia as a twenty-year-old king, simply outweighs the earlier instance of self-doubt expressed to Dindimus and dread that would at least be expected from the responses of the trees of the sun and the moon. One day full of hope for global monarchy and the next day dead, Alexander is relegated to the "others" of the fifth age of world history (from the Babylonian Captivity to the birth of Christ), those whose reigns and influence must be read as distant points of reference within Greek, Roman, and British history.[40]

3) Alexander's Concerns for His Empire

Similar resignation is evident in the Durham manuscript's third interpolation. Here, on his deathbed in Babylon, Alexander recognizes that his poisoned wine is fatal and delivers a stoic address both to comfort his survivors and warn them about the responsibilities of kingship. As his men weep, Alexander calls out:

> Et ore si ieo doi mes iorneez conter
> Fors qe poy des anz ieo ni poes noter
> Et si mes victoires commence a noumbrer
> Qe fortune me vot de grace destine
> Longement ay vesqui ceo puis ieo tesmoigner. (fol. 195r)

> And now if I have to count my days, I am only able to reckon a few years, and if I begin to tally the victories granted me by the grace of Fortune, then I have lived a long time – I can attest to this.

Taking such comfort in a career seemingly defined by its victories rather than its sudden end, Alexander only reveals distress over the manner of his death. He realizes that he is "nen suy le primer / Des roys qe sunt mortz par enpoisoner / Ou par traison de lur prive conseiller" (neither the first nor the last of kings killed by poison or by the treachery of their closest counsellor [fol. 195r]), and he reflects on his own (nominal) father, Philip. This particular king, he recalls, felt more secure on the battlefield than in his own hall, because in the first he was accompanied by his proud soldiers, but in the second, he was prey to his dearest, and most treacherous, friends. So it is that Philip and now Alexander join other kings murdered by their own men, kings whose ranks outnumber, as the latter conqueror warns his survivors, those killed in war (fol. 195r). Within the *Roman de toute chevalerie*, this anxiety over regicide is particularly justified. The dying conqueror's biological father Nectanabus was treacherously killed by Alexander's own hands, and Alexander won control of the Persian Empire not by personally defeating Darius but by alighting upon his dying rival, murdered by traitors within his own ranks. Once again, the Durham manuscript undercuts the emotions elicited by Alexander's individual death. In this version, there is nothing so unique about Alexander's death. It may indeed be cause for tears and vengeance among the Macedonians, but in the larger scheme of history, he simply adds to the long list of kings treacherously murdered. Nor is this attitude only expressed as the scribe's third-person commentary on his protagonist, which would deflate the dramatic effect of the scene. Alexander's own recognition that he will become a proverbial face among the crowd of kings continues his acquiescence to forces beyond his control, seen already in the interpolated passages of his visits to Jerusalem and the earthly paradise and in such prophecies as those offered by the trees of the sun and the moon.

The marginal note on this passage (fol. 195v) ultimately comes from Curtius Rufus's *Historia Alexandri Magni*, although an intermediary source-text is possible: "aliorum quoque regum exitus si reputaveritis, plures a suis quam ab hostibus interemptos numerabitis" (if you consider the deaths of other kings as well, you'll reckon that several of them were killed by their own men rather than their enemies).[41] The context for the line is a near fatal wound that Alexander suffers in India, one that leaves him bedridden for seven days. His officers plead with him to end his campaigns and return home to Macedon, and he counters with an impassioned speech on the opportunity to win eternal glory by conquering unknown lands and relies on the prescient argument that traitors in his own ranks represent more of a danger than the enemies ahead in India. Although both the annotator and the author of the interpolation (if not Thomas himself) seemingly have Alexander's speech in Curtius Rufus in mind – the Anglo-Norman lines on Philip being safer in battle than at home with his queen parallel the speech in the Latin history – Alexander's words in Curtius Rufus are spoken not in response to the poisoned drink he consumes in Babylon but to his men's desire to leave India. The annotator seems, then, to call attention to the source-text for the speech in the main narrative, perhaps believing that Curtius Rufus provided the basis for the Anglo-Norman speech or perhaps simply understanding the commonalty of the two scenes.

4) The Statements of the Philosophers

The sentiments on the limitations of Alexander's authority and his mortality conveyed by both the interpolator and the reader-annotator culminate in the final unique passage in the Durham manuscript, which is the most explicitly moralizing of the four. Commonly referred to as the statements of the philosophers at Alexander's tomb, the lines describe the lament (the verb on fol. 196r is "compleignant") of thirty-two philosophers who visit the conqueror's extraordinary golden sarcophagus and utter a series of sententious observations: yesterday Alexander had heaps of gold for treasure, today his tomb serves as his treasure; he ordered others but now they order him (presumably regarding his burial); he ravaged the earth but now earth covers him; he had powerful friends and enemies but now they are all his equal in mortality; he led a great army but now they bear his coffin; he intimidated with his wrath but now no one fears him; the world was too small for his ambition but now a shallow plot suffices him; and his vaulted chambers were too confined for him but today "le summet de sa sale" (the roof of his room) presses upon his nose (fols 196rv).

The observations of the philosophers are interpolated, as the manuscript cites, from Peter Alfonsi's twelfth-century *Disciplina clericalis* but circulated widely in England.[42] However, like these earlier interpolations, the passage plays a larger role in the folios around it. The text immediately preceding the philosopher's statements recounts how Alexander was buried extravagantly in Alexandria:

Pur ceo qe ne duit ester a nul temps obliez
Mes qe tote gentz qe par la sunt passez
Puissint remembrer du roy renomez
Le meillur guerreur qe fu de mere neez
Et qe unques en bataille hostes ad guiez. (fol. 196r)

So that he would not be forgotten in any time but remembered by everyone who passed by his tomb as a renowned king and the best warrior born of woman who ever led his army into battle.

As if to reassure the reader of Alexander's mortal rather than divine nature (the born of woman remark pointedly fails to mention Nectanabus and his sorcery), these lines preserve Alexander from oblivion and establish for him a memorial appropriate for a hero of romance.

Eight thousand lines into the *Roman de toute chevalerie*, the text describes a massive tomb for the conqueror in an exotic land, yet the specific location (the "Quarsus" in Alexandria) suggests that the tomb be envisioned as a landmark or destination for the manuscript's readership. The subsequent words of the philosophers, however, assess the sarcophagus in starkly temporal terms. They realize that in an instant Alexander and his deeds have been confined to the past, and the tomb becomes a hollow memorial, despite the intention of the conqueror's survivors, for what amounts to just another corpse. After the philosophers' statements, the scribe even supports their assessment: "Ore est acompliz qe fu pronosticez / Par la petite pierre qe li fu mandez / De Paradis terrestre, cum devant est contez" (Now is fulfilled the prophecy of the little stone that he was given in the earthly paradise, as told above [fol. 196v]). At the very least, this commentary proves that the passage as a whole was intended to complement the Wonderstone episode, and the scribe of the Durham manuscript imposes a moralizing reminder of mortality and temporality on the poem that he copied, for while the last folios of the codex are missing, what remains (interpolated from the French *Roman d'Alexandre)* addresses the emotional reaction of Alexander's successors to his passing. Rather than immediately turning to the origins of their civil war, this copy presents the philosophers' judgment as a commentary on the mortal limits of all kings before exploring the sorrow of Alexander's officers. This reaction among the barons, one that ushers the readers towards a tragic resolution of Alexander and his empire, tellingly rearranges the text that concludes Paris, Bibliothèque Nationale MS 24364 (the discord among the conqueror's survivors) and the repeated scenes of Alexander's death and partitioning of his lands and the animosity among the barons in Cambridge, Trinity College MS O.9.34. Moreover, the Durham manuscript's interpolation of Alexander's own awareness that he is but one of many kings who die in undesirable circumstances and the reminders of his mortality in the Wonderstone and the philosophers at the tomb episodes provide the reader with an alternative reception of the poem, and Alexander's career therein need not be remembered only for its tragedy or political discord but for its futility instead.

In imposing such a devalued conception of Alexander on its reader, the Durham manuscript faithfully represents the moralizing trends in the conqueror's fourteenth-century reception, when narratives of his career became increasingly dismembered, retold piecemeal, and applied to various types of exempla for various purposes.[43] The *Alphabet of Tales*, a Latin compendium of exempla arranged by a Dominican friar in the early fourteenth century and translated into English in the fifteenth, features, for example, anecdotes regarding Alexander's fleeting empire. He is compared to a tree that requires many years to grow but can be felled in a moment,[44] and he receives the Wonderstone (interpolated, as discussed above, into the Durham manuscript of the *Roman de toute chevalerie*) as a symbol of mortality, in that it outweighs any earthly substance unless covered in dirt.[45] Similarly, one of the most famous scenes of Alexander romance, his attempt to fly via a griffin-led chariot, became such a familiar identifier for him over the fourteenth century that it appeared as both a legible icon in English churches and as an illustration in codices that made no mention of it. The scene was also carved on several misericords, a popularity that demonstrates a twofold appropriation, so that not only was the most enduring of the fantastic images of the conqueror instantly recognizable as Alexander for its viewers, but in a Christian setting, it was read allegorically as a figure of human transgression and the fall.[46] In this view, the influence of which is apparent in the Durham manuscript, Alexander devoted his brief life to an ill-advised legacy built on campaigns and an unwavering desire to reach unexplored and sometimes unattainable lands.

The Contexts of Fourteenth-Century Kingship

A similar tendency to contextualize Alexander within the ranks of classical rulers and national heroes is evident in the fourteenth-century courtly appropriation of his romance legacy, one presenting novel ways to imagine the conqueror and the limits of his political exemplum, particularly as his conquests had long outshone for many audiences the dismal end of the Macedonian Empire. Such an emphasis on Alexander's death and its ramifications especially suits the last quarter of the fourteenth century, a time that witnessed the deaths of Edward the Black Prince and Edward III in quick succession and concluded with the deposition and possible murder of Richard II. The Durham manuscript may predate these events, but it is not necessarily removed from the social and political anxieties of mid-fourteenth-century England. As a critical assessment of kingship, this copy may both fulfil the anxieties of the Paris manuscript, namely that Edward II's reign was bound for disaster, and reflect the dynamic period of Edward III's own reign in the middle of the century, from the complaints of the baronage and the commoners against his continuous wars to his "remarkable political recovery" of the 1340s and 1350s based on a string of military victories and his inevitable decline after the Treaty of Brétigny in 1360 into the 1370s.[47] In fact, the Durham manuscript was produced amid Edward's long-standing engagement with the Alexander legend.[48] As the Prince of Wales, he received from Walter de Milemete in the late 1320s two versions of the *Secretum secretorum*, the same pseudo-Aristotelian guidebook to emulating Alexander known to his grandfather and great-grandfather,[49] and in his regency he maintained a collection of Arthurian, Trojan, and Nine Worthies romances and,[50] again like his grandfather and great-grandfather, had at least one decorative item celebrating Alexander's deeds in images.[51] Yet in the early 1330s, Edward received another manual of kingship, William of Pagula's *Speculum regis Edwardi III*, that "presents an image of a divided, unhappy England, the poor people oppressed and, but for the lack of a leader, prepared to revolt," owing to the king's reliance on purveyance, the confiscation of others' goods for royal use.[52] William's agenda was to warn his king not to adhere to what Ralph Hanna identifies as the "Alexandrine tyranny" reflected in his burdensome treatment of his subjects and nation.[53] As does the scribe of the Durham manuscript, William includes the sentiments of the philosophers who gather at Alexander's tomb to dismiss the vanity of his accomplishments. The anecdote insists on the mortality of all men and encourages "frequent consideration of the uncertain brevity of life."[54]

Like the Cambridge and Paris manuscripts, the Durham copy of the *Roman de toute chevalerie* may very well represent the uncertain political environment in England in its time, and as such it suggests a good deal about Alexander's role in other contemporary theories of kingship. In W.M. Ormrod's view, fourteenth-century political literature assessed kingship by the "stark contrast between 'good kings' and 'bad kings'" and "a strong emphasis on the historical and mythological past and the assessment of each ruler by direct comparison with his predecessors … [and] a great deal of emphasis placed on heroic deeds of arms."[55] The last, what he qualifies as "militant monarchy"[56] in the courtly or popular imagination, is naturally the most evident in the Durham manuscript, as in many romances or *chansons de geste*, and many nobles and aristocrats in England on the European Continent were the benefactors of comparisons with Alexander.[57] The question in the Durham manuscript of "good" or "bad" kingship is not, however, so easily resolved. As a ruler in this copy of the *Roman de toute chevalerie*, Alexander is just, magnanimous, inspiring on the battlefield, and altogether successful in the game of empire-building, yet the interpolations and marginal annotations draw undeniable attention to his murder, the collapse of his empire after his death, and the limits of his authority, attention that threatens to negate the first half of the manuscript, with its campaigns in the main narrative and military history culled from Orosius in the margins. How the reader remembers the text upon finishing the manuscript surely goes a long way in determining the reception of this version of

Thomas's poem, and while Alexander's battlefield success presents the heroic conqueror expected by fourteenth-century aristocratic readers (e.g., those of the Paris manuscript), the subsequent emphasis on his failures and the inevitable decline of Macedonian dominion suggests the appropriation by the monastic or clerical author-scribe of Alexander as the most (in)famous exemplum of fleeting kingship in classical history.

This disparity between reader and author-scribe results in part from the increasingly moralistic stance against Alexander in the century, as outlined above, but it also attests to contemporary conceptions of historiography. As Jesse M. Gellrich argues, the fourteenth century "produced an unprecedented number of philosophical histories, works that approach the past as a record of 'universal' truths and 'exemplary' morals necessary in the present," as well as chronicles based on the Orosian scheme of divinely ordained history and the "hortatory history" of well-known figures and their exploits.[58] Here, too, is the Durham copy of the *Roman de toute chevalerie* reflective of its age, for the superficial reader, particularly one equipped with common preconceptions of Alexander, would easily identify the "exemplary" and "hortatory" aspects of the narrative, whether those promoting an admiration for Alexander the warrior-king or an awareness of the fragility of the man and his empire, both undone by ambition and animosity. As Alexander himself laments in the passage interpolated after he drinks poisoned wine, regicide by treachery may not be a universal truth in the annals of history, but death certainly is, and there are enough cases of treason against kings to recognize it as a universal threat. Finally, with its frequent reminders of God's authority over Alexander and the conqueror's inability to secure a lasting union for his successors after his death, the Durham manuscript subtly implies the Orosian framework of history. Alexander, according to divine prophecy, conquers Persia (representative of the Achaemenid Empire), he is convinced that God will oversee his victories according to his will – excluding the liminal spaces at the edge of civilization where Alexander finds only prophecies of his death and the region known as the earthly paradise – and when he dies and his survivors quarrel over where to bury him, a singular voice commands that "le voloir a Dieu" (the will of God) is to have him interred in Alexandria.[59] At last, after a career whose successes and limitations are dictated by a higher power, Alexander's dismembered empire will be absorbed over time into the Roman imperium. In the Durham manuscript, the causes for this transition of power lay equally in the divinely ordained scheme of history brought into relief by the scribe and annotator and the jealousy and discord that lead the only remaining human characters, Alexander's officers and barons, to yield to a self-destructive civil war, an outcome that Thomas of Kent had underscored in his composition of the romance two centuries earlier.

Thomas was seemingly interested in the anti-exemplary possibilities of the death and division at the end of his narrative, despite the value he placed on the exemplary episodes in the core of his narrative, Alexander's establishment of an empire through strategy and military supremacy. Two centuries later, the scribe of the Durham manuscript more demonstrably appropriated Alexander and Macedon as a disconcerting emperor and empire, and the reader of the codex could admire Alexander as a political and military visionary so long as he took care to recognize the limitations of the conqueror's sovereignty and to contextualize the Macedonian Empire as one in a series of classical powers. Not unlike the stories of Arthur and Troy, Alexander offered at once much to emulate and much to avoid, and the Durham manuscript surely takes advantage of this simultaneity. Like those stories, too, Alexander and his transitory empire were best understood in their historical context, both classical and contemporary. While the Matter of Troy provided the founding fathers of nationhood and the Matter of Britain the paradigm of Insular kingship, the Durham manuscript was intended to shed a moralizing light on Antiquity's most famed conqueror in a time when Alexander was frequently read as a symbol of transience, yet in a time as well when he was uniquely applicable to the sudden vicissitudes of English history.

While in composing the *Roman de toute chevalerie* Thomas had captured the tension within the Macedonian royal family and the internal threats to an empire soon to crumble under the baronage, the Durham manuscript certainly emphasizes the didacticism inherent in the poem's conclusion (death befalls all kings, and the grandeur of their empires quickly fades), but its general emphasis on Alexander's subordination to a higher power, encounters with prophecies and strangers insisting on his impending death, and the dismissal by the philosophers of his earthly achievements are peculiarly suited for its time of production. Clearly written and read by someone with an interest in historical comparisons, the Durham manuscript was produced between the two decades of terrifying outbreaks of the Black Death in England, the 1340s and 1360s, and after Edward II had "lowered the reputation of his country abroad and at home [and] was the means of bringing the monarchy into the most serious crisis that had faced it since 1066" (realizing the fears of the barons and knights behind the Paris copy of the *Roman de toute chevalerie*) and had paid a terrible price for it in 1327.[60] The spectre of the plague should not be considered a direct influence on the producers of the Durham manuscript, but in bringing thoughts of mortality to the forefront of chroniclers' minds and in threatening all echelons of society as a pestilence presumed "divine in origin and ... punishment for sin,"[61] the Black Death may have compounded the tendency towards fatalism in the last folios of the Durham manuscript, particularly coupled with the fate of Edward II in the generation before the codex. That a king could not only be deposed but also, according to Geoffrey le Baker's chronicle, be forced to wear a crown of hay, shaved with water from a ditch mingled with his own tears, tortured, and finally sodomized with a soldering iron, would surely undermine the sacrosanct conception of kingship for the scribe of the Durham manuscript and its readers, particularly those who later witnessed the similar fate suffered by Richard II in 1399.[62]

Moreover, the scribe of the Durham manuscript could contextualize the English throne in his own age following the model of secular, chivalric-inspired historiography. Jean le Bel, echoed by Jean Froissart, writes, for example, of "a commonly held view among the English – and it has often been seen in England since the days of King Arthur – that between two worthy English kings there has always been one of less wisdom and prowess."[63] The Macedonians were vulnerable to similar criticism. Surpassing the dreams of his oft-besotted father Philip to challenge Persia, Alexander dominated a vast expanse of the known world, only to leave it in the incapable hands of men ruled by ambition and delusions of grandeur. As the reader is reminded throughout the Durham manuscript, Alexander's sovereignty surpassed all of his contemporaries but still had severe limitations imposed on it, and his authority vanished with one drink of wine. Fourteenth-century readers of English royal history could see that between the glorified belligerence of his father and son, Edward II's reign ended in a whimper, with his emotional response at his deposition, when he "quite freely admitted that he had governed them and the land badly and with tears and on his knees he cried them mercy for this and asked them to pardon him."[64]

For English political history, the boundary between secular and monastic and clerical historians must be appreciated, but in the Durham copy of the *Roman de toute chevalerie* that boundary is curiously blurred. Much of the narrative appeals to a secular audience, but the manuscript, unlike the Paris copy, was in all probability written and annotated by a non-secular scribe and reader. The interpolation of the Wonderstone episode, the judgment of the philosophers, and the visit to Jerusalem, collectively mingle a sacred-secular agenda. This copy of Thomas's poem offers, for example, a reception of Alexander somewhere between the death of Edward the Black Prince in Chandos Herald's biography – in which the protagonist admits in dying that "for God, we are not lords here on earth; all will have to pass this ways [and] no man may scape,"[65] and an epitaph in which the corpse of Alexander tells the prince, "sum quod eris quod es ipse fui, derisor amarae / Mortis, dum licuit pace iuvante frui" (I am what you will become, and what you are I once was, a man scornful of bitter death while he was allowed to enjoy blissful peace)[66] – and the failures of Edward II's reign retold in the following century in the Middle English *Brut* as the result of the Prophecies of Merlin.[67]

Alexander in the *Roman de toute chevalerie*, the victim of prophecies in exotic lands since Thomas's original composition and now emphatically subject to divine authority in the Durham manuscript, reflects both views of history and the deeds of kings. With the manuscript's plethora of moralizing and prohibitive views of Alexander, its suggestion of the Orosian scheme of pre-Christian history, the conqueror's mortality, the ultimate authority of God, and, of course, treachery, it is not too far-fetched to read the Durham manuscript as a didactic and critical fourteenth-century historical allegory in the same vein as two of its contemporaries, *Wynnere and Wastoure* and *Richard the Redeless*, and *Mum and the Sothsegger* of a later generation.[68] It need not reflect the totality of the "economic upheaval, social conflict, and natural calamity [that] produced a pronounced streak of morbidity in the personality of the fourteenth century,"[69] but the changing reception of Alexander and the continued political upheavals in England surely inform the latest surviving manuscript of the *Roman de toute chevalerie*.

Chapter Seven

From Anglo-Norman to Middle English Alexander Romance

Between the productions of the Paris and Durham manuscripts of the *Roman de toute chevalerie*, Thomas of Kent's poem inspired the first Middle English Alexander romance, *Kyng Alisaunder*, which dates to the early fourteenth century, but the oldest record of which is a fragment of just over four hundred lines, the verses on folios 278–9 of Edinburgh, National Library of Scotland Adv. MS 19.2.1, the well-known Auchinleck manuscript. The Middle English poem also survives in the late-fourteenth-century Oxford, Bodley MS Laud Misc. 622 and slightly later London, Lincoln's Inn MS 150, as well as a fragment of a printed version from the 1520s.[1] None of these surviving copies features translations of the lengthy French interpolations that supplement the *Roman de toute chevalerie* in its thirteenth- and fourteenth-century manuscripts (the *Fuerre de Gadres* and the conqueror's deathbed allocation of his lands to his barons), and it is assumed that the Middle English poet had access to a text more closely resembling the "original" form of his Anglo-Norman source than survives today.[2] His decision to render his source into the English vernacular reflects the linguistic shift in England that had gained momentum since Henry III agreed to the Provisions of Oxford in 1258. As Geraldine Heng argues, the fact that Henry confirmed the Provisions in both French and English helped to establish the one as "the language of the baronial elites" who forced the king's hand and the other as "the language of the other social classes of [Henry's] realm."[3] It was a moment that propelled English towards some prestige,[4] aided, too, by the fear that Philip the Fair's victory over Edward I in the 1290s would ensure the linguistic dominance of French and the obliteration of English.[5] That Continental French was the language preferred in the Paris copy of the *Roman de toute chevalerie*, a codex affiliated with the very barons and knights who fought for Edward, likely points to the fashion of the language among "the great nobles [and] the history of an elite minority and insular colonization," but it also suggests the divergent audience for Alexander romances in the early years of the fourteenth century.[6]

In English, moreover, the Alexander legend attracted a range of audiences for the remainder of the century, apparent in the codices in which *Kyng Alisaunder* survives. The Bodleian manuscript is composed mostly of religious material (*The Vision of St Alexis*, a description of the Judgment Day, and a poem on the Advent) and items dealing with the Holy Land (travel notes on the pilgrimage thereto and the romance known as *The Siege of Jerusalem*) and recalls the reception of Alexander in the Paris *Roman de toute chevalerie* as a conqueror who is compatible with the crusading spirit and renowned for his defeat of enemies equally affiliated with Saracens and the forces of evil set against Christendom. Alexander was also received as a figure of the classical tradition and one to be compared against rulers of other legends. In Lincoln's Inn MS 150 (a holster book ca. 1400 from which the tales of marvels encountered in Alexander's campaign into India are excised), *Kyng Alisaunder* and *The Siege of Troy* represent the Matter of Rome and *Libeaus Desconus* and *Arthour and Merlin* that of Britain.[7] The last of these poems, in fact, is often attributed to the *Kyng Alisaunder*-poet, along with *Richard Coer de Lyon* and *The Seven Sages of Rome*, all of which appear in the earliest (yet now fragmentary) copy of the Middle English Alexander romance in the Auchinleck manuscript. This so-called *Kyng Alisaunder*-group has invited much debate, but the romances are affiliated by a number of common concerns and themes. Even *The Seven Sages of Rome*, which lacks the heroic protagonist and militaristic exploits of the other three texts, recalls various aspects of Alexander romance, as it situates its narrative in a classical setting (Rome), features a conniving empress (similar to the mothers of Richard and Alexander, as discussed below), an emperor worried that his gifted son will usurp him, and presents as its hero a clever boy who is well educated by philosophers.[8]

As for the three kings in the group, there is no question that contemporary authors and readers associated the stories of Alexander, Arthur, and Richard the Lion-heart.[9] In the opening lines to *Richard Coer de Lyon*, for example, the poet surveys the historical heroes of Antiquity, France, and England, now the subjects of romance:

Ffele romaunses men maken newe,
Off goode knyytes, stronge and trewe;

Off here dedys men rede romaunce,
Boþe in Engeland and in Ffraunce:
Off Rowelond, and off Olyuer,
And off euery Doseper;
Off Alisaundre, and Charlemayn;
Off kyng Arthour, and off Gawayn,
How þey were knyghtes goode and curteys;
Off Turpyn, and of Oger Daneys;
Off Troye men rede in ryme,
What werre þer was in olde tyme;
Off Ector, and off Achylles,
What folk þey slowe in þat pres.[10]

Strikingly, he references the ancient world in terms only of Troy and Alexander – the destruction of the one and the death of the other would resonate throughout history and would account for paradigms for chivalry throughout Europe – and surveys ancient and more recent heroes as all being worthy of having their tales told in the English tongue. Older narratives, that is, have to be translated from the "Frenssche bookys" foreign to "lewed" men,[11] an attitude echoed in the prologue to *Arthour and Merlin* that similarly comments on the prevalence of an Anglophone readership and the decline of those capable of reading French and Latin.[12]

It is also telling that early writers of Middle English romance considered Alexander a worthy protagonist for the new medium, alongside Richard and Arthur. Similar to Richard the Lion-heart, Alexander was a historical figure whose reception was complicated when "the act of translating [chronicles and histories] becomes an act of transforming" in romances,[13] and although not a domestic hero or king attached to baronial ancestry, as was Richard in romance, he quickly found favour among Anglo-Norman and Middle English romance audiences eager for tales of their own rulers.[14] The *Itinerarium peregrinorum* of the 1220s, for example, commends the two men for their character and valour,[15] and Alexander's victories in the Levant and the Middle East were compatible with crusading narratives and ensured his popularity among royalty and the gentry alike, as suggested by the inclusion of *Kyng Alisaunder* in the Auchinleck manuscript. One of the definitive revisions to the French *Prose Merlin* in *Of Arthour and Merlin* is the English poem's presentation of "Saracens" (in this case, pagan Danes) as Arthur's main enemy and the cause against which all of England can unite,[16] reminiscent of Alexander's efforts to unite the Macedonians against the Persians when he becomes king, and the B version of *Richard, Coër de Lyon* (the version surviving with *Kyng Alisaunder* in the Auchinleck manuscript) has been called both "the *chanson de geste* of Richard, the scourge of the Saracens"[17] and a "history" of the Third Crusade instilled with "virulent nationalism."[18] As Thorlac Turville-Petre notes of the Auchinleck manuscript, its "heroic figures come from the world over, but shoulder to shoulder with Alexander and Roland stand the knights of England," including those from the Arthurian tradition and pre-Conquest and Angevin England.[19]

All three narratives of Alexander, Arthur, and Richard the Lion-heart also reflect on the temporality and abrupt ends of their lives and, in the case of Alexander and Arthur, their empires as well, and all three feature protagonists with disreputable origins. Alexander is born of the sorcerer Nectanabus, Merlin of the devil, and Arthur of Merlin's enchantment (in a scene of disguise and seduction between Uther and Ygerne that recalls Nectanabus and Olympias), and Richard, in the later A version of *Richard, Coer de Lyon*, of a devilish mother, Cassodorien of Antioch.[20] Although *Of Arthour and Merlin* does not continue into the outbreak of civil war and the king's death, the fall of his empire had received ample attention in the thirteenth-century Continental *chansons de geste* and prose romances still popular in England in the early fourteenth century. *Richard, Coer de Lyon* offers, on the other hand, its own tale of treachery and familial intrigue, centred around his mother Cassodorien and his brother John. In an early scene in the romance, Cassodorien attends mass but cannot take the sacrament, and despite Henry's efforts to compel her to eat of the wafer, she escapes through the roof of the cathedral. Amid the confusion, she attempts to abduct John, an important detail that stigmatizes Richard's younger brother for the remainder of the poem. Henry, so heartbroken and ashamed that he never returns to the cathedral, names Richard his heir, but John lingers in the background, his antagonism seemingly determined by his mother's influence. While on Crusade much later in the poem, the report of treachery in England reaches Richard:

Off Yngelond hys broþir Jhon,
Þat was the fendes fflesch and bon,
Þorwȝ help off þe barouns some
Þe chaunceler þey hadde jnome,
And wolde wiþ maystry off hand

Be corowynd kyng in Yngeland
At Estyr-tide afftyrward.
Þenne answerde Kyng Richard:
"What deuyl," he sayde, "hou gos þis?
Telles Ihon of me no more pris?"[21]

John's attempted usurpation does not conclude the narrative, for the poem continues for another thousand lines, but his actions change the trajectory of his brother's story. Richard is able to secure a truce with the Paladin that allows Christian pilgrims to travel to Jerusalem, but as he makes his way back to England to suppress John's rebellion, he is felled by an arrow. The text of Karl Brunner's base text, Cambridge, Gonville and Caius MS 175, glosses over the event ("he was schot, allas, / In Castel Gaylard, þer he was"),[22] but another fifteenth-century version, that in London, College of Arms, MS Arundel 58, prolongs the death scene. Here, before he dies, Richard requests that he be buried next to his father, and in the poet's concluding remarks he celebrates his protagonist with an epitaph partly applicable, at least, to the pagan hero of *Kyng Alisaunder*: "Kyng Rycharde was a conquerour, / God gyue his soule moche honour."[23]

Finally, a variety of late-thirteenth- and early-fourteenth-century Middle English romances influenced by Anglo-Norman *chansons de geste* and romances rely on the pattern of an underdog hero cast into exile or setting off on adventures in foreign lands until he returns home to restore political, and typically personal, order (e.g., *Bevis of Hampton, Guy of Warwick, Havelok, Horn Childe and Maiden Rimnild, King Horn,* and *Libeaus Desconus*), and *Kyng Alisaunder* may have appealed to the same tastes that accounted for these texts' popularity. It may have appealed, too, to the contemporary interest in narratives of Christians fighting Muslims in the Mediterranean, such as those found in the *Otuel* romances and *Roland and Vernagu*. Like Otuel, some "Saracen" knights deserve Christian praise, as evidenced, of course, by the Latin West's application of Christian virtues to Alexander, the pagan conqueror from the Greek East. When the *Kyng Alisaunder*-poet departs from the *Roman de toute chevalerie* in favour of Walter of Châtillon's *Alexandreis*, he does so to expound on the deeds of two noble bodies of knights, Macedonian and Persian, whom he finds catalogued in the Latin epic:

Þis bataile distincted is
Jn þe Freinsshe, wel jwys.

Þerefore [J] habbe [hit] to coloure
Borowed of Latyn a nature,
Hou hiȝtten þe gentyl kniȝttes,
Hou hij contened hem in fiȝttes,
On Alisaunders half and Darries also. (2195–201)

This passage has drawn scholarly attention to the poet as a translator considering the merits of vernacular romance and Latin epic, but equally noteworthy is his celebration of the heroics of both Macedonian and Persian knights over the next two thousand lines. As the poet announces in his prefatory remarks, "oþere mannes lijf is oure shewer" (18) – a common sentiment in romances of the time[24] – and in his narrative, all characters, Macedonian or Persian, are potential models of virtue and vice.

Kyng Alisaunder: Portents of Temporality

Kyng Alisaunder neatly presents its story in four phases: Alexander's youth, his war against Persia, his eastern expedition, and his death in Babylon. In this survey of the protagonist's life, the poet underscores a range of anxieties regarding Alexander and his empire not unlike those discussed in the previous chapters. He certainly remains a chivalric figure, but his career also presents the distressing contradiction that for all of his glory, Alexander died ignominiously by treason and left behind a divided empire. The poet thereby situates Alexander not only within the construct of earthly *temporalia* but also within corruptible human behaviour, namely the desire for vengeance and ambition, seen in his treatment of Macedon before and after Alexander and in the vivid, lyrical interludes of seasonal change, for which *Kyng Alisaunder* is perhaps most known.[25] The Middle English version thus maintains both the *Roman de toute chevalerie*'s idealization of Alexander as a warrior-king and the reception of him as a figure evocative of cautious admiration and at times dismissive moralizing, common within the classical tradition. At the same time, the poet clearly found the topos of the protagonist who rises to glory from difficult circumstances just as important for the progression of his narrative. Rather than Thomas's confident young prince and king, devoted to his mother and capable of handling his barons to do his bidding, this Middle English Alexander appears in the earlier sections of the narrative as a man still maturing and struggling to assert his authority.

Perhaps his most politically validating act as leader of the Macedonians occurs in Tripoli, where he finds a statue of the Egyptian sorcerer Nectanabus, whom he knows to have been his father and who has been long suspected as such by others. In the Valerius *Epitome*, when Alexander hears that the statue was erected to honour Nectanabus, he willingly admits that he is his son,[26] and in Thomas of Kent's version Alexander continues to protect his mother and thus seeks to exonerate Olympias publicly from charges of adultery with Nectanabus and the regicide of Philip.[27] In *Kyng Alisaunder*, however, he wants only to console himself regarding his rumoured lineage and offers to reward the bishop for alleviating his anxiety over the "sklaunder ... þat J shulde ben biȝeten amys" (1551–3). Yet Alexander still responds emotionally to the proclamation for which he has paid:

> And after longe sacrifyeyng,
> [The bishop] com and seide to þe kyng
> Stillich, bitwene his lyppe,
> Þat his fader hiȝth kyng Philippe.
> Kyng Alisaunder vpon hym louȝ,
> And in herte was bliþe ynouȝ
> Þoo alþerfirst he vnderstood
> Þat he riȝth of kynges blood. (1561–8)

That the scene occurs privately rather than as a public announcement (to say nothing of the genuine happiness of a seemingly relieved, rather than scheming, Alexander) suggests that the young king seeks acceptance, as if he were attempting to prove himself worthy of his title and to move beyond the rumours and innuendo that have haunted him since his childhood.

So resonant had this slander against Alexander been in the Macedonian court that it nearly kept him from the throne. Philip, the poet tells us, had genuine reservations about naming the boy as his successor:

> Now is þe kyng wrooþ and grym,
> Who shulde be kyng after hym –
> His son Philippe, oiþer Alisaundre,
> Of whom he bereþ swiche sklaundre. (753–6)

Tellingly, only Alexander's half-brother Philip is identified as the king's son, while Alexander himself remains the son of Olympias and her lover, whether or not Philip-*père* believes the stories about Ammon consorting with his queen. After making sacrifices to the gods, he receives their proclamation that he should let both boys attempt to ride Bucephalus, the wild, man-eating horse, and whoever does so should be named the heir to the Macedonian throne. Even the divine voice remains ambiguous and refuses explicitly to name Alexander as the rightful successor, and only the actual competition of taming the horse settles the matter for Philip, his barons, and the audience. Equally striking is the placement of this scene. Philip's appeal to the gods to help choose a successor immediately follows Alexander's final interaction with his biological father Nectanabus. During their astronomy lesson, the traditional setting for the moment in both Latin and vernacular narratives, Alexander asks the sorcerer if he is truly his father, and Nectanabus admits at last that "sooþ is þe schlaunder" (740). Although he takes pity on his father, carries his corpse to Olympias, who likewise confesses the truth of her affair, and buries Nectanabus, the poet provides a dismissive epitaph: "sooþ it is, vpe al þing, / Of yuel lijf yuel endyng" (751–2). The sorcerer is dead, but the rumour that he is Alexander's true father persists until the conqueror has the priest in Tripoli declare him to be of "king's blood" (applicable, of course, to Nectanabus as well as Philip, but Alexander surely deduces the latter).

After hearing from the bishop that he is of royal blood, Alexander focuses his attention on leading his army away from Macedon into the Levant, the Middle East, and on to India, where he hears warnings of a different nature, those regarding his imminent demise. He becomes an assured conqueror, although he can never return home to Macedon, and it seems that he can never escape gossip and prophecies. The scene in Tripoli seems all the more a transitional moment in Alexander's reign, given the unique characterization of his family members in the Middle English poem. Whereas in the *Roman de toute chevalerie*, Philip is the aggressor, Olympias the victim, and Nectanabus skirts the boundary between both roles (an aggressor in his deception of the queen, but ultimately unable to prevent his son from murdering him), the *Kyng Alisaunder*-poet carefully alters the three characters in his treatment of his source-text so as to render each of Alexander's parents a villain worthy of punishment.

The *Pseudo-Callisthenes* and its recensions begin with a random series of events: in Egypt the pharaoh-sorcerer Nectanabus learns that an anonymous coalition of enemies will invade his lands, and after disguising himself he flees Egypt with no intended destination. He ends up in Macedon, where he sees Olympias and is compelled by her beauty to remain in the kingdom and seduce her. In *Kyng Alisaunder*'s unique version of this story, Philip leads twenty-nine other kings, spurred by envy of the Egyptians, against Nectanabus.[28] The change to the *Roman de toute chevalerie* is slight, but Philip's envy and decision to invade Egypt transforms *Kyng Alisaunder* into a revenge narrative. In response to Philip's attack, Nectanabus escapes not to wander haphazardly for safety, as he does in the Anglo-Norman account and in the Latin tradition. Rather, he deliberately chooses Macedon as his refuge, where he soon takes vengeance on the king by sleeping with his wife, tormenting Philip with dreams and portents of Alexander's divinity, and fathers the son who will be the object of innuendo for years in the Macedonian court. Caught in the middle of this intrigue between the two leaders is Olympias, who also seeks revenge against Philip for his rumoured divorce of her and search for a new bride, and she ultimately fulfils this desire by bearing Alexander, a child who will defend her from the animosity of the Macedonian court and whose existence will shame Philip and outshine his legacy.

Although this cycle begins and ends with Philip, it thus revolves around the desires of each of Alexander's three parents. Philip invades Egypt, formerly a successful nation whose pharaoh had never suffered defeat, out of envy and his desire to expand his realms; later, when Olympias and her son put the king increasingly ill at ease, the king will take his revenge by exiling her and seeking a new bride. Olympias, in turn, would never forgive her husband's disdain and desire to replace her, a plan that he considered well before the birth of Alexander. When Nectanabus comes to Macedon, therefore, he knows precisely how to seduce her with tales of a divine child who will offer the queen her utmost desire:

> He seide to hir, "gentil lemman,
> Jch habbe biyeten on þee a kyng
> Þat shal be Philippes maisterlyng.
> On erþe worþe non hym yliche –
> He shall conquere many kyng-riche." (398–402)

Clearly attracted to Olympias's dubious character and personal motivation in the *Roman de toute chevalerie*, the Middle English poet recasts her as a scheming, opportunistic queen. The glory that Nectanabus foretells above for Alexander is necessarily deferred until the boy comes of age. Although Alexander will protect his mother and compel his father to remain married to her before he ascends to the Macedonian throne, he can only begin to establish his reputation as a global conqueror after Philip's murder thrusts him into the spotlight.

In *Kyng Alisaunder*, Olympias plays an explicit role in this murder, beginning with a bedroom scene of collusion with the familiar figure of Pausanias, the nobleman who lusts after her and eventually slays Philip:

> So [Pausanias] yede and so he sent,
> Wiþ writtes and wiþ riche present,
> Þat he dude in bed stille
> By þe lefdy al his wille,
> And bitwene hem hadden yspeke
> Of Kyng Philippe to ben awreke.
> Wommans hert is wiþ þe werst
> She wil be wroken oiþer to-brest.
> By her boþer compasement,
> Þe kyng is wounded, verreyment,
> Dedly wounded þorouy þe nape,
> Þat he ne miyth þe deþ askape. (1335–46)

In the *Roman de toute chevalerie*, Olympias consents to submit to Pausanias's will only after he has killed Philip, but when the assassin then attempts to rape her and Alexander must intervene to save his mother, the queen again becomes the victim of a scheming man. She is not entirely inculpable, for she understands in her relationship with both Nectanabus and Pausanias how to achieve vengeance against Philip, but neither is she complicit in the regicide plot, as she is in *Kyng Alisaunder*. Her scheming with Pausanias leaves the impression that Olympias cannot wait for Nectanabus's prophecy of Alexander's glory to come to pass, and she takes matters into her own hands – effectively, of course, because Phillip's murder ensures that her son will be crowned king. While Alexander represents for Olympias a means of achieving dominance over her husband, Alexander in turn needs his mother, in Christine Chism's words, "to retro-engineer his own legitimacy."[29] He does all that he can to keep Olympias in court and married to Phillip, as he does in the *Roman de toute chevalerie*, until the moment when he succours his dying, adoptive father, mortally wounded by his wife's lover, and takes the throne.

As for Philip, he learns through a series of prophecies instigated by Nectanabus that the child will surpass him in authority to become the greatest of the Macedonian rulers but will enjoy an ephemeral glory that will end in tragedy.[30] In a dream that the *Kyng Alisaunder*-poet translates from the *Roman de toute chevalerie*, for example, Philip sees a bird fly onto his lap and lay an egg that rolls off onto the ground and breaks. A dragon that crawls from the egg and encircles the broken shell is quickly killed by the heat of the sun, a vision that the king's interpreter explains as such:

He seide, "O, sir kyng, saunfaile
Here is fallen gret merueyle.
By þis ilk litel dragon
Js bitokned þe quenes son.
Þe eye rounde shal signifie
Þat he shal habbe seignourye
Of þis rounde myddellerd,
Boþe of lewed and of lerd.
Ac he shal wende of londe fer,
To Grece and comen neuer ner.
He shal be poysond saunz retours
Of his owen traytoures.
Þat signifieþ þe dragonett
Ne may recouer to his recett." (591–604)

The knowledge of Alexander's future that Philip gains from such prophecies acts as a severe counterpoint in the narrative to Nectanabus's promises to Olympias of the boy's fame as a conqueror and the joy that Olympias finds in giving birth to such an esteemed future ruler. The prophecies and rumours about his queen's infidelity so haunt Philip that he decries the newborn Alexander as an "yvel fode" (666) who will cause harm for many men, a fear that will ultimately prove accurate for both enemies abroad and the Macedonians themselves.

Philip's fearful dreams, these portents surrounding Alexander's birth, and the *Kyng Alisaunder*-poet's frequent moralizing passages on earthly *temporalia* all help him to exaggerate Thomas's original interest in the prophecies surrounding the conqueror's demise in the last quarter or so of the narrative. Following the Latin legends and the *Roman de toute chevalerie*, Alexander's initial campaigns in the Levant and his conquest of Persia permit the audience to discredit the earlier prophecies of death and violence from his childhood, but his arrival in India sees the turning point of his success and emotional stability. When Alexander visits there the trees of the sun and the moon that foretell the circumstances of his death, for example, he must accept the fact that he will not return home ("ne comestou neuere in Grece londe" [6853]), but his men refuse to do likewise. They manifest their emotions with physical self-violence, just as they will upon his death, and they swoon, tear their hair out, wring their hands, weep, and bemoan their king's youth, strength, and largesse (6863–9). Alexander assuages them by assuring them that the prophecy represents the immutable will of the gods, but his stoicism is short-lived. In his second visit to the trees, they explain to him that he will die in Babylon through "envie and by tresouns," and he goes mad with grief, confining himself to his bed (6892–9), a reaction that now leaves his army in the position of having to come to terms with the devastating prophecies. They remind Alexander that they have followed him deep into enemy territory and faced all manner of foes and threats, and they convince him to come to his senses and not abandon them in such a vulnerable position (6900–13).[31] Their appeal is successful, but the soldiers are able to comfort their leader only temporally, for the episode of the trees of the sun and the moon recalls the narrative's broader concerns with the transgressions behind that death, namely envy and treason, already the cause of death for Alexander's two fathers, Nectanabus and Philip, and his primary foe, Darius, and soon to be the cause of his own death. For Alexander, death will come in a familiar guise, though it will not arrive as unexpectedly as it did for those before him. Unlike anyone else in the poem, Alexander receives the precise terminus of his life. It is April now, the trees report, but he will die on the following twenty-fourth of March, before the blossom of a new spring (6949–55). While Alexander and his men are devastated by this specific prophecy, the conqueror once again shows the contrast between the private and public reactions towards his impending death. Before his army, he leaves the sacred grove:

> his leue he took,
> For he woot his certeyn day.
> He wil fonde yif he may,
> Þeiy it be to hym yshape,
> On sum manere forto a-skape. (6967–71)

There exists, of course, no such escape, and as the poet began his narrative by asserting that the world is filled with care and sorrow, he now comments on the visit to the grove that one day there is laughter and the next weeping, one day health and the next sickness. "Noman that lyves," he concludes, "haþ borowe / From euene libbe forto amorowe" (6986–7).

Whereas Thomas establishes Nectanabus's premonition that his son will never return home from his campaigns, Philip's visions of Alexander's premature death abroad, and these trees of the sun and the moon, *Kyng Alisaunder* offers at once a fearful Alexander and a commentary on his career, particularly in his last moments in Babylon. Upon drinking the poison procured by Antipater, for example, Alexander has a troubling, prophetic vision of his own. As he recognizes the potency of the poison, he proclaims at the banquet table:

"Allas!" he seide, "Ich am neiy ded!
Drynk ne shal neuere efte more
Do to þis werlde so mychel sore
As þis drynk ha[þ y]do.
Allas! Allas! what me is [w]o
For my moder Olympias,
And for my suster, þat so fair was,
And for myne barouns, al þing aboue,
Þat Ich miyth in herte loue!
Hij ben lordeles – Ich am ded,
Þorouy a traitour fals and qued." (7853–63)

This outburst personalizes the generic anxiety over bloody vengeance in the *Roman de toute chevalerie* by revealing Alexander's concerns for those nearest him, both his surviving families and his baronage, who react to their dying king in violent fashion:

Þere men miytten reuþe ysen –
Many baroun his her to-teen,
Many fyst to-wrunge and hand,
Many riche robe to-rent,
Michel spray, mychel gradyng,
Michel weep, mychel waylyng,
Often bymened his prowesse,
His yingþe, and his hardynesse,
His gentrise, and his curteisie. (7872–80)

Not only does this scene repeat the army's reaction to the prophecy of the trees of the sun and the moon, but it also underscores their affection for their leader, for whom they provide an impromptu epitaph based on his prowess, youth, hardiness, nobility, and courtesy. For Alexander, however, this outpouring of physically self-destructive grief surely justifies his fears that his "lordeless" army and empire will soon find themselves in dire straits. The men remain united in their despair, but this collective sorrow is crippling and equally justifies their own fear (articulated in the sacred grove when Alexander likewise yielded to mourning over threatening prophecies) that when their king passes away, they will remain alone and vulnerable in a hostile land far from home.

It is at this moment that the poet uniquely treats Alexander's division of his empire and his last will and testament, the conqueror's attempt, as he tells his men, to "quethe myne quede" (7892). Aware of the calamities that await his subjects and having built such an impressively multicultural empire, he reduces it to its previous elements by bestowing it to his countrymen and barbarous conquered foes alike, as his beneficiaries include two "Greeks" (Perdiccas and Ptolemy), two Romans (named Mark and Tiberius), a former hostage named Antioch, an Arcadian (Aymes), a Syrian (Sampson), and, most notably, an Indian (Philoth) and a Persian (Salome, Darius's brother-in-law), who receive their respective native lands and newfound sovereignty over them.[32] In the passages from the Continental French *Roman d'Alexandre* interpolated into the Cambridge, Paris, and Durham manuscripts of the *Roman de toute chevalerie*, Alexander distributes portions of his empire to the *douzeperes*. His barons are thus granted their final reward for many years of service in the king's invasion of Asia, and the poor are left to suffer an extended and bloody civil war. *Kyng Alisaunder*, however, "appears to take an interest in wider sections of the population than the narrow aristocratic circle to which [Alexander's] contacts are all but confined" in its Anglo-Norman source. Whereas in Thomas of Kent's telling, Olympias warns her son about Antipater's treachery (compelling Alexander to summon him to Babylon), in the Middle English version the Macedonians complain to their king about Antipater's bad governance of the home front ("many man he had done shame. / þe londe-folk baden þe kyng / Of hym make remiweyng" [7813–15]), and whereas in the one Alexander allots his lands only to barons, in the other he divides his treasure among his knights, "sweyn" and "knave" (7962), men of lower rank as well.[33]

Yet when Alexander proves his generosity, he ensures that factions, not a unified empire, will follow upon his death, and no sooner does he grant nine successors control over portions of his lands than each of them fights for the right to bury the royal corpse in his newly inherited realm. Perdiccas, for example, wishes to inter his king's body in Macedon; Salome, the new (Persian) head of Persia, wants to take the corpse to Babylon; while the Indian barons wish to bury it in that easternmost land of the empire, until an anthropomorphized bird appears and instructs the men to convey the body to Alexandria, Egypt, and bury it in extravagant fashion in the temple of Apollo.[34] It is, the bird insists, God's will that Alexander be buried in Alexandria, and the poet comments on the subsequent interment that "neuere heþen kyng / Haue so riche a berȝing" (8006–7). The identification of Alexander as a pagan following a divine commandment dictating the location of his burial accords with the Christian distinction of Alexander, particularly in the thirteenth and fourteenth centuries, as a pre-eminent ruler of Antiquity and God's warrior against eastern forces of evil.[35]

The scribe of the Lincoln's Inn copy of *Kyng Alisaunder* expresses more emotive sympathy for the protagonist, as he concludes the poem with the couplet, "Alisaunder me reowiþ þyn ending / þat þou nadest dyȝed in cristenyng" (6745–6). However, Alexander is not a Christian warrior to be granted the spiritual redemption for which the poem's audience might hope. He is a pagan, and as *Kyng Alisaunder* draws to a close, the poet reminds that audience of the fate suffered by all pre-Christian rulers of Antiquity. Alexander lay in a lavish tomb in a city named for him, but such material monuments mean little, for his empire, dismembered by his successors, has passed into the annals of history:

Tholomeu haþ þe seisine.
God us lene wel to fyne!
Þoo þe kyng was ydelue,
Vche duk went to hym-selue,
And maden woo and cuntek ynouy.
Vche of hem neiy oþer slouy,
For to haue þe kynges quyde.
Michel bataille was hem myde.
Þus it fareþ in þe myddelerde,
Amonge þe lew[ed] and þe lerde!
Whan þe heued is yfalle,

Acumbred ben þe membres alle.
Þus ended Alisaunder þe king. (8008–20)

The allusion to the civil war among Alexander's survivors acknowledges the scene of discord in the final lines of the *Roman de toute chevalerie,* as does the proverbial reminder that with the passing of an authoritative leader, a succession crisis can dismember any empire. Yet the *Kyng Alisaunder*-poet does not concern himself with the ramifications of this civil war for the commoners of Alexander's empire, the poor and feeble who cannot shield themselves from the violence of the *douze peres* that will soon destroy their peace and sense of security once afforded by the conqueror. The Middle English poet rather emphasizes the ephemeral nature of Alexander's empire, reflective of earthly life as he reminds his audience throughout his lyrical interludes to the main action of his narrative. Alexander, like other rulers:

lyueden here a litel raas,
Ac sone forȝeten vchon was.
Þe leuedyes shene als þe glas,
And þise maidens, wiþ rody faas,
Passen sone als floure in gras;
So strong, so fair, neuere non nas
Þat he ne shal passe wiþ "allas!" (7824–30)

This passage does not condemn Alexander for his ambition or belligerence, nor does it blame him for his short-lived empire. While his successors are responsible for civil war once their leader dies, Alexander merely suffers the fate of all mortal creatures without either blame for how he has conducted his reign or opportunity for spiritual salvation. *Kyng Alisaunder* addresses, after all, battles and expeditions of the pagan past, and its poet does not attempt to contextualize his subject within the Christian concept of morality and redemption. Alexander's career is ultimately futile, as his empire is brought to ruin, but it is not reproachable.

Among the generation of writers after *Kyng Alisaunder* and the production of the Durham manuscript, which similarly draws attention to the transience of Alexander's accomplishments without spiritually condemning him, the brevity of the conqueror's reign, as suggested in the above passage, became an overarching theme of his reception. The three other Middle English Alexander romances, the so-called *Alexander A,*

Alexander B (both West Midlands, mid-fourteenth century),[36] and *The Wars of Alexander* (Northwest Midlands, ca. 1350–1450),[37] emphasize in their respective ways the themes of ambition, the brevity of Alexander's reign, and the role of divine authority over earthly kings, a reading of the conqueror's legend to be expected of clerical and monastic authors, but one, too, that pervades the secular Alexander legend in the fourteenth century.[38] *Alexander A* is a partial translation of the *Historia de preliis* I^2 recension that interpolates Orosius for the history of Macedon before the protagonist (resulting in a narrative that recalls Ralph Gubiun's interest in Macedonian history in the *St Albans Compilation*), while *Alexander B* features the epistolary debate between the conqueror and Indian philosopher-king Dindimus, based on the *Collatio cum Dindimo* but expanding this Latin source-text to underscore Alexander's acquiescence to divine providence. The *Wars* is a rendering of the I^3 recension of the *Historia de preliis*, which, as I argued in chapter 1, portrays Alexander in more cautionary, moralizing terms than its I^2 predecessor.

Christine Chism considers the audience of these Middle English Alexander romances by the late fourteenth century as the gentry that appreciated both the extent to which Alexander had been celebrated as the paradigm of chivalry, as romances of him had been enveloped with "the historical and ideological appurtenances of the English nobility," and just how unattainable that paradigm had become in their own time.[39] This audience, she argues, could admire but not emulate Alexander, because they "had been gradually but forcibly taught the futility of ambitions to conquer, regain, or convert the immense diversity of non-Christian lands to the east."[40] There is no question that Alexander remained an exemplary figure of the classical tradition, but neither do we lack for evidence that fourteenth-century writers frequently attributed this same "futility of ambitions" to the conqueror himself. The hero of *Kyng Alisaunder* is not an arrogant, egotistical conqueror who refuses to heed prophecies and warnings about the distinction between immortal and mortal authority, but a king who must develop self-confidence by putting the rumours of his father behind him, and when he builds a global empire he still cares about his common subjects, as well as his knights and barons. Still, for all of Alexander's admirable qualities, this empire is dismembered after his death.

Contemporaneous with *Kyng Alisaunder* and a generation before the Durham manuscript of the *Roman de toute chevalerie*, the emphasis on the transience of Alexander's career and empire is also apparent in the association of classical heroes with those from later historical periods, a motif established in Jacques de Longuyon's *Les Voeux du Paon* (ca. 1312), which introduced the motif of the Nine Worthies and anticipated the deliberate grouping of heroes in the Auchinleck manuscript. Contemporaneous with the Paris copy of the *Roman de toute chevalerie*, Jacques presents three pagan heroes (Hector, Alexander, and Julius Caesar), three Jewish ones (Joshua, David, and Judas Maccabeus), and three Christian ones (Arthur, Charlemagne, and Godfrey of Boullion).[41] The heroic ethos of this grouping held an influence on chivalric culture well beyond the fourteenth century, and after the *Voeux* was translated into Middle English,[42] its effect on Alexander's reception in fourteenth-century England is apparent in two surviving poems. In the first, "Parlement of the Thre Ages," Elde (Old Age) expounds on the Nine Worthies and laments Alexander as such:

> And there that pereles prynce was puysonede to dede,
> Thare he was dede of a drynke, as dole es to here,
> That the curssede Cassander in a cowpe hym broghte.
> He conquered with conqueste kyngdomes twelve,
> And dalte thaym to his dussypers when he the dethe tholede;
> And thus the worthieste of this werlde went to his ende. (399–404)[43]

The portrayal of Alexander's death as a tragedy is akin to the closing remarks of *Kyng Alisaunder*, but the notion that the *douze peres* received his apportioned empire peacefully is antithetical to both the *Roman de toute chevalerie* and its Middle English adaptation, both of which condemn the barons for destroying all that they had built with Alexander.

In a second example of the motif in Middle English, one that tellingly revises Jacque's intentions to celebrate the heroes by appropriating the Nine Worthies for a lesson in mortality, Arthur has a dream vision of Fortune's Wheel in the *Alliterative Morte Arthure*, a romance included alongside the *Prose Life of Alexander* in the Lincoln Thornton manuscript. Seeing, but not comprehending, the worthies whose ranks he will eventually join, Arthur is distraught at being cast from the wheel, and an interpreter explains the significance of the vision:

> "Freke," sais the philosophre, "thy fortune es passed;
> For thow sall fynd hir thi foom – frayste when the lykes!
> Thow arte at þe hegheste, I hette thee forsothe;
> Chalange nowe when thow will, thow cheuys no more.
> Thow has schedde myche bloed and schalkes distroyede,
> Sakeles, in cirquytrie, in sere kynges landis;
> Shryfe the of thy schame and schape for thyn ende;

Thow has a schewynge, Sir Kynge – take kepe ȝif the lyke;
For thow sall fersely fall within fyve wynters." (3394–402)[44]

The interpreter further explains the first person whom Arthur saw was Alexander, who appears as a decrepit, withered old man lamenting that:

"I was lorde," quod the lede, "of londes inewe,
And all ledis me lowttede that lengede in erthe;
And nowe es lefte me no lappe my lygham to hele,
But lightly now am I loste, leue iche mane the sothe." (3284–7)

Alexander's speech clearly evolves from the judgment of the philosophers at his tomb, an episode interpolated into the Durham manuscript of the *Roman de toute chevalerie*, but in the larger context of the dream, Arthur, like Alexander, receives a dire prophecy of his own death. Through warfare and the killing of the innocent, he has brought upon himself the wrath of Fortune and must spiritually prepare himself for the afterlife, having become an exemplum of the criminality and futility of warfare on the one hand and earthly life on the other. No longer simply a symbol of the futility of conquests and empires, Alexander is here appropriated for a lesson against wasting one's reign on war and material gain, a reception of his career that was significantly developed by the last identifiable reader of the *Roman de toute chevalerie*.

John Gower's *Roman de toute chevalerie*

Some two hundred years after Thomas of Kent wrote his romance, and just a generation after the Durham manuscript was produced, John Gower evidently considered the *Roman de toute chevalerie* still to be an authoritative source-text on Alexander, one that might be read as a narrative reflective of the dangers that threaten to undermine any king's reign, and an attractive Anglo-Norman Alexander romance in the face of three centuries of French competition.[45] Gower, like the Durham manuscript scribe and annotator, seems, too, to have considered Thomas's work as a vehicle for moral warnings, including both sorcery and irresponsible kingship in the Alexander legend (the one that he articulates in the story of Nectanabus in the *Confessio amantis* and the other throughout his treatment of Alexander), and the fleeting nature of mortal life and earthly authority. We cannot know if Gower's text of the *Roman de toute chevalerie* corresponded with the Durham manuscript or indeed any of the surviving copies of the poem, but he clearly did not hesitate to edit Thomas's work to suit his needs in the *Confessio amantis* or to consult the *Historia de preliis*, which had begun to circulate more widely in fourteenth-century England. Gower borrows from Thomas's poem the basic narrative of Nectanabus's abdication of his throne in Egypt, seduction of Olympias in Macedon, fathering of Alexander, and murder by the child. To conclude Book Six and its theme of gluttony, he presents two examples of sorcery, one involving Ulysses and the other Nectanabus, both undone by their lust and ignorance of their impending deaths; to accentuate the latter's villainy, he removes from his Thomas's poem Olympias's duplicity and eagerness to use the affair (and the son she will conceive) to gain power over Philip.[46] As Russell A. Peck argues, through his lust for Olympias and neglect of his own realm, Nectanabus represents bad kingship that Genius counters with the ethical teaching that Aristotle provided for Alexander, based on the *Secretum secretorum*, in Book Seven.[47] A man of earthly appetites, the Egyptian sorcerer is thus more than a sexualized con artist; he is also the antithesis of the proper kingship on which Gower expounds in his poem.

Yet Gower's précis of Nectanabus also invites the reader to consider larger issues of Alexander's reception in the fourteenth century. While the moral of the story is clear (Nectanabus's sorcery and prognostications cannot help him prevent his murder at the hands of Alexander, who justly kills him for his dishonesty) the theme of ignorance connects each of Gower's characters in the story. Nectanabus is unaware of the moment of his death, Olympias does not know until it is too late that the sorcerer has deceived her, Philip never knows the true paternity of the boy who will be his successor, and Alexander does not realize that his life and reign are determined by a destiny that surpasses the actions and intentions of everyone around him. As Peter Nicholson argues, Nectanabus's attempts to control the narrative through sorcery and prophecy "point beyond the limited world of the characters to the existence of a greater power,"[48] one that Gower identifies for his readership but that remains unknown to the players in his story.

In creating his backstory to deceive Olympias, for example, Nectanabus begins with the notion that Ammon, the god of Egypt, has preordained the conception of Alexander. He explains that during his scientific studies:

"It fell into mi consience
That I unto the temple wente,
And ther will al myn hole entente

As I mi sacrifice dede,
On of the goddes hath me bede
That I you warne prively,
So that ye make you redy,
And that ye be nothing agast;
For he such love hath to you cast,
That ye schul ben his oghne diere,
And schal be your beddefiere,
Til ye conceive and be with childe." (6.1914–17)[49]

Through his insistence on the god's genuine affection for Olympias, Nectanabus introduces romantic deception into the episode. While he seduces Olympias because of his baser lust, she in turn falls in love with the supposed god in May, the traditional month of such amatory feelings, and longs for his presence after their first night together (details that Gower finds in the *Roman de toute chevalerie*). Within the more intimate confines of the sorcerer and queen's relationship, this disparity between sexual desire and emotional attachment allows Gower to emphasize the victimization of Olympias, and yet Nectanabus's speech resonates within Gower's larger historical scheme as well.[50] The sorcerer certainly believes in his own abilities, and in fabricating the story of Ammon he insinuates that Alexander's very existence is predicated on the god's love for Olympias. It is this love, Nectanabus claims, that has set in motion a chain of events, including his flight from Egypt and arrival in Macedon, Olympias's seeming blessing in being elected to bear the conqueror of the world, and Philip's replacement by an illegitimate son who will quickly overshadow his reign. Through love:

"[Ammon] schal a Sone of you begete,
Which with his swerd schal winne and gete
The wyde world in lengthe and brede;
Alle erthli kinges schull him drede,
And in such wise, I you behote,
The god of erthe he schal be hote." (6.1935–40)

What Nectanabus does not reveal to Olympias, and presumably what he does not know, is that the glory of Alexander's career will be marred by the circumstances of his death in Babylon. Alexander will fulfil Nectanabus's promises of conquest, but he will die young and never return home. In fact, the prophecy of Alexander's murder never comes from the mouth of Gower's Nectanabus. Such insight is only provided by Philip's clerk, who explains to the king a strange occurrence, in which a bird drops an egg from the sky, and a serpent that wanders out of it quickly dies. For the clerk, the dying serpent and its broken egg signify that:

"He schal desire in his corage,
Whan al the world is in his hond,
To torn ayein into the lond
Wher he was bore, and in his weie
Homward he schal with puison deie." (6.2242–6)

It is surely important that a clerk, a man of philosophy and scholarship, rather than a sorcerer, understands the future that awaits Alexander. Excluding such knowledge from Nectanabus's stories and prophecies does not merely underscore the limitations of his sorcery as used to deceive the royal family of Macedon. Nectanabus's belief that he is solely responsible for bringing Alexander into the world and his claim to Olympias that Ammon has determined the child's destiny represent a collective perversion of Gower's vision of divine authority. The Egyptian is, for the purposes of Book Six, "a false creator who, in his usual prognostications, cut himself off from his true creator."[51]

In the introduction to the Nectanabus episode, for example, Gower explains that:

The hihe creatour of thinges,
Which is the king of alle kinges,
Ful many a wonder worldes chance
Let sylden under his suffraunce;
Ther wot noman the cause why,
Bot he the which is almyhty. (6.1789–94)

Although Gower immediately applies this principle to the case of Nectanabus (reiterated in modern scholarship), this fundamental mystery of providence is equally applicable to Alexander. Writing in the voice of a third-person commentator on his story, Gower excuses both Olympias for being seduced by the promises of a supposed god and Alexander for his disreputable origins. "Bot nathles it hapneth so," he insists:

Althogh sche were in part deceived,
Yit for al that sche hath conceived

The worthieste of alle kiththe,
Which evere was tofore or siththe
Of conqueste and chivalerie;
So that thurgh guile and Sorcerie
Ther was that noble knyht begunne,
Which al the world hath after wunne. (6.2085–92)

Everyone involved has a role to play: Olympias as the vessel of Alexander and his period of dominance, Alexander as the mighty warrior-king, and Nectanabus the deceptive and ultimately deceived sorcerer. Through these roles, a major era in history begins, and Gower continues in relating Nectanabus's guile and sexual congress with Olympias by stressing that "thus fell the thing which falle scholde" (6.2093). A higher power does, in fact, determine the outcome of the story of Nectanabus, well beyond his murder by the hands of his son, Olympias's shame over being tricked, Philip's awe at the seemingly divine paternity of the child, and even of Alexander's reign.

Each of these four characters remains ignorant of this power, but Gower expounds on the plan of divinely ordained history in the prologue to the *Confessio amantis*. Here, in what amounts to a grander vision of the work of the "hihe creatour" that begins the Nectanabus episode, Gower recounts the dream of Nebuchadnezzar, who sees a four-tiered statue with a golden head, silver chest and arms, brass torso, and steel legs leading to feet of earth (representing the Babylonians, the Medo-Persians, the Macedonians/Greeks, and the Romans). As the world passes from the age of silver to bronze:

thanne it fell to Perse thus,
That Alisaundre put hem under,
Which wroghte of armes many a wonder,
So that the Monarchie lefte
With Grecs, and here astat uplefte,
And Persiens gon under fote,
So soffre thei that nedes mote. (692–8)

Yet despite the extraordinary achievements of Alexander, Gower's survey of this new age emphasizes its temporality:

it befell that ate laste
This king, whan that his day was come,
With strengthe of deth was overcome.

And natheles yet er he dyde,
He schop his Regnes to divide
To knyhtes whiche him hadde served,
And after that thei have deserved
Yaf the conquestes that he wan;
Wherof gret werre tho began
Among hem that the Regnes hadde,
Thurgh proud Envie which hem ladde,
Til it befell ayein hem thus:
The noble Cesar Julius,
Which tho was king of Rome lond,
With gret bataille and with strong hond
Al Grece, Perse and ek Caldee
Wan and put under, so that he
Noght al only of thorient
Bot al the Marche of thoccident
Governeth under his empire. (702–21)

Alexander is relegated to being another name in the annals of history, and while he ascends to the head of Darius's empire and expands it, his realm in the East pales in comparison to that of Julius Caesar, who conquers the West as well.

This was not the first time that Gower had surveyed the progress of history, but Nebuchadnezzar's dream in the *Confessio amantis* offers a different theory of causation than that in the *Mirour de l'omme*. In this earlier work, Gower explains the transition from the Macedonians to the Romans in terms of both Fortune and human agency. Conqueror of Persia then ruler of the world, Alexander dies at the height of his power, and as Fortune turns her wheel:

Les gentz du Roy par covoitise
Començont guerre et grant debat,
Chascuns volt estre potestat,
Ce que l'un halce l'autre abat,
Siq'au darrein par halte enprise
La grande Rome ove ceaux combat
Et les venquist, dont leur estat
Fortune hosta de sa reprise.

Led by covetousness, the people of the king began to wage war and great strife against each other. Each one wanted power, and when one raised his station, another brought it down. At last, beginning their own impressive conquests, the Romans made war on them and defeated them, and so Fortune vanquished [the Macedonian] state as punishment.[52]

In a world dictated by Fortune, envy and murder propel one age into the next, an idea from which Gower does not necessarily depart in the *Confessio amantis*. Nebuchadnezzar's dream provides the general framework of history, but human characters still play their own roles. For the *Mirour de l'omme*, Alexander's successors must exhibit such destructive animosity in order for the Romans to begin their period of dominance, and for the *Confessio amantis* both Nectanabus's deception of Olympias and the animosity that divides the eastern world after Alexander's death eases the Roman appropriation of formerly Macedonian lands. As if in concentric circles, Nectanabus's arrival in Macedon lay at the centre of definitive moments in history, surrounded by Alexander's conquest of the East, Roman imperium, the age of Brass, and the other ages in succession over the course of human history. Nectanabus, in other words, is not merely ignorant of the fact that he has fathered his own killer (the immediate moral of his episode in Book Six) but of his small yet significant role in world history as well (Nebuchadnezzar's vision in the prologue).

Throughout the *Confessio amantis*, Gower considers Alexander in the moralizing terms popular in the fourteenth century. In cataloguing fashion, he includes the philosophers Diogenes and Dindimus, both ideologically opposed to Alexander (3.1201–1330 and 5.1453–96), the pirate who convinces the conqueror that they are both bandits at heart (3.2363–437), and a number of references to well-known characters and episodes in the conqueror's story. As I have argued elsewhere, however, Gower was no mere cataloguer of Alexander-themed exempla.[53] Over the course of his three major works, his conception of Alexander matured into an acutely critical judgment against the ruler whom he saw as a representative of misguided kingship built on continuous military campaigns. Devoting his life to warfare earns Alexander the dubious distinction of the anti-exemplary king, as Gower reflects in his last comment on the conqueror in the 1399 poem, "In Praise of Peace." He begins with Solomon, who prays for wisdom to govern his subjects, while Alexander, the poem relates:

Unto the god besoghte in other weie,
Of all the world to winne the victorie,

So that undir his swerd it myht obeie.
In werre he hadde al that he wolde preie,
The myghti god behight him that beheste,
The world he wan, and had it of conqweste.
Bot thogh it fel at thilke time so,
That Alisandre his axinge hath achieved,
This sinful world was al paiene tho,
Was non which hath the hihe god believed:
No wondir was thogh thilke world was grieved,
Thogh a tiraunt his pourpos myhte winne;
Al was vengance and infortune of sinne. (37–49)

Frank Grady argues of this passage that while it recalls "a familiar position for Alexander [in which] his conquests are often represented as allowed and approved by God," it also demonstrates Gower's inability or unwillingness to condemn Alexander by dismissing him as merely representative of a belligerent, pre-Christian era.[54] In the *Confessio amantis* Gower is not hesitant, however, to chastise Alexander for yielding to his individual will rather than heeding the voice of reason or that of Aristotle. Even with this education, Alexander "still became a tyrant and died wretchedly in exile," which offers Henry an exemplum of misguided and belligerent kingship.[55] Instead of excusing Alexander as simply living on the wrong side of "the Augustinian distinction between ancient pagan times and the modern, enlightened Christian period,"[56] Gower takes the Orosian stance that pagans were a contemptible lot in a time of self-induced miseries, seen above in the *Mirour de l'omme*.

Despite the identity of Alexander as "the worthieste of alle kiththe" in the Nectanabus episode, Gower's reception of the conqueror, indeed reminiscent of Orosius, is more accurately reflected in Book Three. Ruling by his individual will and desire for conquest, Alexander meets a fittingly violent end in Babylon. As Genius explains:

And as [Alexander] hath the world mistimed
Noght as he scholde with his wit,
Noght as he wolde it was aquit.
Thus was he slain that whilom slowh,
And he which riche was ynowh
This dai, tomorwe he hadde noght:
And in such wise as he hath wroght
In destorbance of worldes pes,

His werre he fond thanne endeles,
In which for evere desconfit
He was. (3.2458–68)[57]

As the final lines above insinuate, Alexander faces due punishment for his policy of war, for like his father Nectanabus, he is a criminal who is justly killed for his misdeeds. As Gower would later write of the sorcerer's deceit of Olympias in the Anglo-Norman *Traitié*, "le fin demoustre toute l'aventure" (the outcome reflects the whole story), a fitting epitaph for both father and son.[58] Moreover, the middle portion of the passage above suggests the same judgment on Alexander's death as expressed in the anecdote of the philosophers at his tomb in the Durham manuscript or Gower's own adaptation of the anecdote in the *Vox clamantis*:

Magnus erat Cesar totoque potencior orbe,
Nunc quem nec mundus ceperat, vrna capit.
Sic et Alexander fortissimus ille Macedo
Clauditur angusto, puluis et ossa, loco:
Maior erat magno mundo, modo nobile corpus
Exulis et victi vilis arena tegit.[59]

Mighty Caesar was greater than this entire globe, and now an urn contains this man, whom the world could not. So, too, is that mightiest Alexander of Macedon closed up – dust and bones – in a narrow space; he was greater than this vast world, and now a bit of sand covers the noble body of this exiled and conquered man.

Considered together, these facets of Gower's assessment of Alexander – his relegation to an era of influence merely between the Persians and the Romans (rather than being exalted above all rulers of Antiquity), his shameful belligerence, and his wretched ending because of it – both recall and exaggerate the attitude expressed towards Alexander in the Durham manuscript.

As a student of history and a reader of canonical historians in his own right, Thomas of Kent surely understood the transience of his protagonist and the Macedonian Empire, a quality seized upon by the *Kyng Alisaunder*-poet and the scribe of the Durham manuscript in the fourteenth century, as well as Gower. I do not believe that the fleeting nature of this empire necessarily dictated his poem, for Thomas seems more interested in the internal corruption of Macedon by animosity and deception, from the domestic tension between Philip and Olympias (which Gower removes so as to focus on Alexander as a child of sorcery and an innocent mother) to the treachery committed against the conqueror in Babylon and the ensuing baronial war. By the late fourteenth century the reception of Alexander, dictated by the brevity and futility of his reign, owed more to the Durham manuscript of the *Roman de toute chevalerie*, with its interpolations that underscored these themes, than to Thomas himself. In the age of Middle English Alexander romances, his influence on Alexander romances in England was both direct, because it inspired *Kyng Alisaunder*, and indirect, in that manuscripts of the *Roman de toute chevalerie* accumulated further perspectives on the conqueror well after its composition. Thomas's poem and the copies made of it thus anticipated many of the themes of Alexander's reception among the fourteenth-century Middle English romances of his career, even though it served as a source text for only one of them. The *Alexander A*-poet incorporated passages from Orosius in order to flesh out a narrative of the animosity between the protagonist's mother and father; *Alexander B*, based on the correspondence between Alexander and Dindimus, suggests the misguided ambition and regret for a life spent on conquests found in the Durham manuscript; and *The Wars of Alexander* is the most moralizing of all of the Middle English romances of his career, as it presents him as a man raised up and cast down by Fortune.[60] So it was that even as these romances continued certain aspects of Alexander's portrayal found already in Thomas's work and the manuscripts of it, they also explored their own, and the conqueror's reception among writers in England evolved for two centuries after the *Roman de toute chevalerie*.

Afterword: The Advent of the Continental Alexander

One could certainly argue that the interpolation of the *Fuerre de Gadres* and Alexander's division of his empire from the Continental *Roman d'Alexandre* into the three most complete manuscripts of the *Roman de toute chevalerie* represents the earliest attempt to assert the Continental Alexander over the Anglo-Norman one, but neither of these episodes transforms Thomas's narrative. His poem presents, as I read it, Alexander as the son of an aging, unaware king, a conniving sorcerer, and a queen who was the victim of both (albeit scheming in her own right), and while Thomas praises the conqueror as a feudal leader of his barons and as a king capable of humility and Christian virtue, Alexander is ultimately shortsighted in his understanding of human nature and politics. In the concluding lines, Thomas thereby reminds his readers that this misguided baronage was incapable of managing the empire that Alexander bequeathed to them and so all that the protagonist accomplished was for naught. The Continental interpolations in the manuscripts of the *Roman de toute chevalerie* do not detract from this reading, but the importation of lengthier, rather than episodic, French romances would, and this process of disseminating their view of Alexander as the predominant one in Atlantic Europe began between the production of the Paris and Durham manuscripts of Thomas's narrative.

In the late 1330s or 1340s, an unknown author produced for William I of Hainaut the voluminous romance known as *Perceforest*.[1] In the grand scheme of Continental French Alexander romances, this work long invited little commentary within what by the mid-fourteenth century was a well established, Insular network of Alexander texts, except for interest in its patron. William came from a region in the Low Countries where the conqueror's chivalric legacy was well established (the

Voeux du paon, Restor du paon, and the *Parfait du paon* were all written there), and he evidently inspired local writers to praise him as a noble who recalled Alexander's courtly qualities that earned him a spot in the Nine Worthies.[2] William was also well connected to the English royal family: his daughter Philippa married Edward III, and he played such a role in his future son-in-law's ascension to the Plantagenet throne that *Perceforest,* with its unification of Brutus, Alexander, and Arthur narratives to rewrite British history, may have celebrated his political machinations abroad. In Sylvia Huot's words, "the story of Alexander as saviour of England suffering from incompetent royal rule might well have been understood by its original audience as a flattering commentary on William's role in the removal of Edward II."[3] The identification of this "original audience" is key to understanding the changing trajectory of Alexander's reception in England, owing particularly to works commissioned by William and like-minded Continental aristocracy.

Perceforest offers in its first book a bewildering and bizarre Alexander romance, woven from the threads of various Continental texts (the *Fuerre de Gadres,* the *Voeux du Paon,* and the "vengeance" texts of Jehan le Nevelon and Gui de Cambrai) and the author's fanciful imagination. Taking its cue from the death of the hero Gadifer in the *Fuerre de Gadres,* the text recounts how Alexander agrees to care for his orphaned sons, Betis and Gadifer. After a storm carries the conqueror and his new wards to Britain, which he foresaw in a dream vision inspired by Venus, they wash ashore on the foreign land to find the locals gathered at a temple devoted to the goddess and expressing their fear "that the great king who'd conquered all the East might be coming to 'spread his wings' over them."[4] Seeing that Britain has fallen into political and social disarray, Alexander instead installs Betis (soon to become Perceforest) as king of England and Gadifer as king of Scotland, while he remains long enough to preach the virtues of justice and wise rule. Yet Britain is also a land of fairies, spirits, and strange occurrences, and before he returns to Asia to lead an assault on Babylon, Alexander falls in love with the sorceress Sebile, the Lady of the Lake. Unlike the two marginal female characters in the *Pseudo-Callisthenes* and medieval Alexander romances – Darius's daughter (and Alexander's Persian bride) Roxane and the queen Candace[5] – Sebile plays a crucial role in the history presented by *Perceforest.* Recalling the plot of Jehan le Nevelon's *La Venjance Alixandre,* in which Candace's son learns that Alexander is his father and leads the barons against Antipater, the second book reveals that the sorceress and the conqueror also had a son, who learns of his father's identity only after Alexander's murder in Babylon. He grows up to marry Perceforest's daughter, with whom he fathers a daughter in turn, before he is killed in battle, and the girl, Alexander's granddaughter, marries one of Gadifer's grandsons. It is from this royal union that the bloodline of Arthur is established and *Perceforest* unifies two romance traditions.

Alexander thus serves two roles in this massive text. During his time in Britain, he must save the people there from corruption and the tyranny of the enchanter Darnant, establish Perceforest and Gadifer as kings, and instil in both the necessity of good rule. He explains to the brothers that if they rule justly and ensure a dynasty built on kingly virtues, then they can avoid internecine violence and the threat of civil war, "in which the first to suffer destruction are the common folk, to whom we are servants, for we have promised to protect them and keep the peace in return for the revenues we receive from them."[6] Although his advice is suspect, of course, for the reader, given that Alexander cannot do the same, through his coronation of the brothers in Britain and his moral teaching, he ensures that as he departs for Babylon, where his own empire will soon be dismembered, "he takes comfort in the thought that his Occidental Empire is flourishing under Perceforest's wise rule."[7] He also unknowingly establishes his "eastern" lineage in western Europe through his son with Sebile.[8] In creating a larger, classically themed construct for British history, *Perceforest* presents Alexander as the restorer of civilization and moral superiority to a land fallen into discord since the days of Brutus[9] and the leader of a group of "founding fathers not just of a civilization, but of a dynasty which culminates, across the cyclic vicissitudes of the kingdom of Britain, in Arthur."[10]

It has recently been argued that *Perceforest* represents the conquest of Arthurian romance by Alexander romance,[11] but the text can also be considered the first step in the sustained, late medieval invasion of Thomas's Anglo-Norman Alexander by its Continental counterpart. Although the *Fuerre de Gadres* and Alexander's deathbed partitioning of his empire made for lengthy, Continental interpolations in the manuscripts of the *Roman de toute chevalerie*, neither episode ultimately undermines Thomas's portrayal of the conqueror. Rather, both can be read in support of the moralizing theme of Alexander's fleeting reign and empire in the poem. The *Fuerre de Gadres* offers another scene of chivalrous exploits among many others in the manuscript, although it recounts a campaign of needless death, as the invading Macedonian forces that set out into the Levant without their leader are routed by the enemy and saved only by Alexander's arrival. At the same time, any celebration of valour to be found in this episode, as is the case with all of the campaigns and expeditions in the *Roman de toute chevalerie*, is negated by the collapse of Alexander's empire at the end of the poem, a collapse rooted in the political schism emphasized by the interpolation of the conqueror's careful division of his lands among his barons. For *Perceforest*, however, the *Fuerre de Gadres* represents the beginning of a new dynastic era for Europe, the bringing together of the conqueror of the Middle East and Asia and the future kings of Britain and the unification of two pillars of the romance tradition within one bloodline. *Perceforest* does not fail to apply the sort of moral warnings to Alexander that were already popular among fourteenth-century Insular writers and their readers – in a reminder that he is a pagan, for example, he is forbidden access to a sacred temple because he is "stained with misbelief and other sins" and told a prophecy of his imminent demise that recalls the "Wonderstone" episode[12] – but such warnings do not prevent Alexander from enjoying his reception as the paragon of kingly virtue and the worthy ancestor of Arthur. In *Perceforest*, his ambition and desire to conquer the whole of Asia "is balanced, or better, *atoned for* by the wisdom and the genuine generosity ... that he demonstrates in England."[13]

Perceforest is about both the end of Alexander's own empire and its dynastic importance for later eras of British history, notably that of Arthur, for whom the Macedonian lays the foundation for tournaments, courtly love, and even the sword in the stone.[14] Nor does the romance aim to criticize Alexander and his officers but to establish them as the collective paragon of courtly behaviour and appropriate them into the British ancestral and literary record. But as an alternative narrative of British history and its classical origins, *Perceforest* is neither written by an Insular author nor reflective of the Insular reception of Alexander since the twelfth century. It rather marks a turning point in that reception in a manner foreign (in more ways than one) to Anglo-Latin, Anglo-Norman, and Middle English texts of preceding generations. Not only does *Perceforest* overwrite the collapse of the Macedonian Empire with its vital legacy for British history, but it also found in the royal family a new Insular audience for tales of the conqueror. When she married Edward III, William's daughter Philippa brought to England from Hainaut an interest in the Nine Worthies and Continental Alexander romance,[15] and it is even possible that *Perceforest* inspired the design for Edward's House of the Round Table.[16] After this importation of the Continental Alexander into Edward and Philippa's England, the fashion for similar representations of the conqueror is evident for well over a century, into the Yorkist and even Tudor courts. Edward IV and his family owned multiple copies of Vasco da Lucena's French history of Alexander, written for Charles the Bold to establish the Macedonian as a paradigm for contemporary nobility,[17] Continental French romances of his career were favoured by Henry VIII,[18] and Alexander was known primarily to fifteenth- and sixteenth-century English royalty as a figure celebrated for his chivalry in the manner popularized under William's literary influence.[19]

Alongside this emerging fashion for Continental Alexander narratives, or perhaps because of it, the textual transmission of Alexander romances in England evolved as well. The Paris and Durham manuscripts and the Oxford and London fragments suggest that Thomas's poem was quite popular across the fourteenth century, yet this popularity would not last. The sheer number of manuscripts of French Alexander romances in this century and the next were widely exported and would soon considerably outnumber the copies of the *Roman de toute chevalerie*. A variety of texts and a stream of codices, including Alexandre de Paris's *Roman d'Alexandre*, the thirteenth-century Old French prose *Roman d'Alexandre*,[20] the *Histoire ancienne jusqu'à César*, and ultimately Vasco da Lucena's fifteenth-century translation of Curtius Rufus's biography of Alexander would be disseminated in large, increasingly elaborate illustrated copies and would ensure that telling Alexander's story in French was a Continental, not an Insular, enterprise.[21]

With the emerging fashion for Continental Alexander narratives, the creation and transmission of texts regarding the conqueror changed trajectory in England. The Latin recensions and descendants of the *Pseudo-Callisthenes*, notably the Valerius *Epitome* and the versions of the *Historia de preliis*, continued to circulate broadly, but popular vernacular texts were predominantly Continental French. After *Kyng Alisaunder*, Alexander romances written in England survive in few numbers. The three alliterative poems, the so-called *Alexander A* and *B* and *The Wars of Alexander*, are known to us in one, one, and two manuscripts respectively, and there remains a single copy of the Thornton *Prose Life of Alexander*. Expanding this survey to include the British Alexander yields three more manuscripts of Scottish texts, including one of the *Buik of Alexander* (a translation of French poems no less) and two of the *Buik of King Alexander the Conquerour* (also based in part on a French source, the *Roman d'Alexandre*),[22] both of which attest to the increasing dominance of Continental French Alexander romances and the diminishing popularity of the lone Anglo-Norman one. After Gower's reading of the *Roman de toute chevalerie* to inform the *Confessio amantis*, no English writer would take up a sustained examination of Alexander. Chaucer briefly sketched the conqueror's career as an exemplum of Fortune's whims in the *Monk's Tale*,[23] a model appropriated by John Lydgate for the *Fall of Princes*,[24] but Alexander did not receive the prolonged, impactful attention such as that enjoyed, for example, by the Arthurian legend in the English vernacular. Rather than finding a late medieval rival in English, the *Roman de toute chevalerie* could still be copied into the fourteenth century as a definitive account of the Macedonian conqueror. At the same time, although no surviving copy of Thomas's poem was produced on the European Continent, it is equally noteworthy that by the mid-fourteenth century (the date of the Durham manuscript) we have no evidence of a copy of the Continental *Roman d'Alexandre* having been produced in England, other than the episodic interpolations in the manuscripts of Thomas's poem. His narrative evidently served the audience for French Alexander romance in Angevin and Plantagenet England from the late twelfth to the mid- or late fourteenth century and both inspired a Middle English translation and provided John Gower with a source for his own account of the conqueror, some two centuries after Thomas wrote it. Given the wealth of Alexander romances in circulation in this period, that is no small accomplishment, no matter how neglected the poet and poem today.

Notes

Introduction

1 The vulgate histories include two written in Latin (Quintus Curtius Rufus's *Historia Alexander Magni* and Justin's epitome of the *Philippic Histories* by Pompeius Trogus) and three in Greek (Diodorus Siculus's *Bibliotheca historica*, Arrian's *Anabasis Alexandri*, and Plutarch's *Parallel Lives*). The *Pseudo-Callisthenes* likely dates to the third century AD.
2 See, e.g., Spencer, *The Roman Alexander*, xiv.
3 Cary, *The Medieval Alexander*, 24–58. Although scholars of the classical Alexander often identify these Greek, Latin, and Hebrew narratives as "romances," a book intended for medievalists has to take into account both the linguistic and generic connotations of the word, especially in discussing twelfth-century literature. Alexander narratives survive in several vernaculars of medieval Europe from this century onward, and while these works took their cue from texts composed in the classical languages, I do not wish to cause undue confusion for the reader.
4 Brucker, "Le personnage de Frédéric II dans la poésie lyrique d'oc du XIIIe siècle," 2: 40.
5 David Williams, "Alexandre le Grand dans la littérature anglaise médiévale," 356.
6 Georgianna, "Coming to Terms with the Norman Conquest," 50.
7 Burgess, "The Term 'Chevalerie' in Twelfth-Century French," 357, identifies "body of knights," "a military act or series of acts performed by a chevalier," and "the possession of the skills required to perform such acts" as the three primary meanings of "chevalerie."
8 See Weynand, *Der Roman de Toute chevalerie des Thomas von Kent in seinem verhaltnis zu seinen quellen*; Foster, "The *Roman de toute chevalerie* and Its

Date and Author," 156–7; and Legge, *Anglo-Norman in the Cloisters*, 35–6 for the confusion.

9 Legge, *Anglo-Norman Literature and its Background*, 106; and *Anglo-Norman in the Cloisters*, 37. Meuwese, "The Exploits of Alexander the Great in Trinity College," 129, argues that the identification of Thomas as a "maistre" implies that he is a cleric and that two portraits of the author in a Benedictine habit in Paris, Bibliothèque Nationale MS fr. 24364 do not correspond to the portrait in the Cambridge copy.

10 Busby, "Codices manuscriptos nudos tenemus," 267.

11 Short, "Patrons and Polyglots," 235–7.

12 Meyer, *Alexandre le Grand dans la littérature française du moyen âge*, 2: 281.

13 Foster, "The *Roman de toute chevalerie*," 2: 154–5.

14 Foulet, "La date du *Roman de toute chevalerie*," 2: 1,210.

15 Thomas of Kent, *The Anglo-Norman Alexander = Le roman de toute chevalerie*, ed. Foster, 2: 73–6 (hereafter cited as *Anglo-Norman Alex.*).

16 Gosman, "La genese du *Roman d'Alexandre*: quelque aspects," 25; and *La légende d'Alexandre le Grand dans la littérature française du 12e siècle*, 293.

17 *Anglo-Norman Alex.*, 2: 90, notes the scribal confusion of Pompeius Trogus (whose *Philippic Histories* Thomas used in the form of Justin's epitome) with Pompey, the rival of Julius Caesar – hence the reference to the latter's name above.

18 Meyer, *Alexandre le Grand dans la littérature française*, 2: 273: "c'est une œuvre également dépourvue d'originalité et de style." Agard, "Anglo-Norman Versification and the *Roman de toute chevalerie*," 235, extends linguistic criticism to the manuscripts of the work as well, codices whose prosody he cites as "not an evolution but a disintegration."

19 Gaullier-Bougassas, *Les romans d'Alexandre*, 184.

20 Legge, *Anglo-Norman Literature*, 105.

21 Salter, *English and International*, 29.

22 Blacker, *The Faces of Time*, 55, notes the comparison of classical and contemporary leaders in twelfth-century historiography.

23 Raynaud, "Les répresentations du pouvoir royal du XIIIe au XVe siècle: le cas d'Alexandre," 67.

24 Gosman, *La légende d'Alexandre le Grand*, 315; see also, Gosman, "La genèse du *Roman d'Alexandre*," 33.

25 Blacker, "'La geste est grande, longue et grieve a translater': History for Henry II," 394.

26 Ashe, *Fiction and History in England, 1066–1200*, 95.

27 Gaunt, "French Literature Abroad," 58.

28 Two fourteenth-century fragments survive, one folio in Oxford, Bodleian

Library, Lat. misc.b.17 and two in London, British Museum, Add. 46701. For descriptions of the individual manuscripts, see Schneegans, "Die handschriftliche Gestaltung des Alexanders-Romans von Eustache von Kent," 240–65; and *Anglo-Norman Alex.*, 2: 3–14.

29 Gosman, *La légende d'Alexandre le Grand*, 290 ("La consequence de l'opération [of the Foster and Short edition] est que le *RTCh* ne nous est que partiellement accessible") and 336 ("Le résultat … est une édition 'à la médiévale' qui nous cache ce qui est vraiment médiévale").

30 Busby, *Codex and Context*, 1: 284.

31 Thomas of Kent, *Le roman d'Alexandre,* trans. Gaullier-Bougassas and Harf-Lancner.

32 Trotter, review of *Le roman d'Alexandre, ou, Le roman de toute chevalerie,* trans. Gaullier-Bougassas and Harf-Lancner, 180.

33 Cruse, *Illuminating the Roman d'Alexandre*, 197.

34 See Stone, *From Tyrant to Philosopher King*.

1. Alexander Romance in Twelfth-Century Europe

1 White, Jr., *Latin Monasticism in Norman Sicily*, 47; and Matthew, *The Norman Kingdom of Sicily*, 106–7

2 Martin, *Italies normandes, XIe–XIIe siècles*, 287.

3 Douglas, *The Norman Fate, 1100–1154*, 145.

4 See especially Stoneman, *Alexander the Great*; and Goukowsky, *Essai sur les origines du mythe d'Alexandre 336-270 av. J.C.*

5 The *Pseudo-Callisthenes* likely dates to the third century AD. For a translation, see Stoneman, *The Greek Alexander Romance.*

6 Merkelbach, *Die Quellen des Griechischen Alexanderromans*, offers a helpful discussion of the recensions.

7 Three other Latin apocryphal texts were written around the same time: the *Itinerarium Alexandri Magni*, the *Metz Epitome* (an independent abridgement of the *Pseudo-Callisthenes*), and the *Liber de morte Alexandri testimentoque eius*. For Valerius's text and its reception, see Callu, "Lire Julius Valère."

8 Callu and Festy, "L''Alexandre latin': Léon de Naples et sa première interpolation (J^1)," 49.

9 See Zink, "The Prologue to the *Historia de Preliis*," for Leo's agenda in preparing his translation. In Pfister, ed., *Der Alexanderroman des Archipresbyters Leo*, 45, Leo explains in his preface for Duke John that although a pagan, Alexander maintained faith in his gods and was wise and pious, qualities for secular and sacred readers alike to admire.

10 *The Greek Alexander Romance*, trans. Stoneman, 28–9.

11 Leo's text also travelled to Hohenstaufen Germany and France. Ross, "A New Manuscript of Archpriest Leo of Naples," 1–3, identifies a copy written ca. 1300 in France, presumably the result of the text's migration from Naples to Germany, where two twelfth-century copies were produced.

12 For the manuscripts, see Hilka and Magoun, "A List of Manuscripts Containing Texts of the *Historia de Preliis Alexandri Magni, Recensions* I^1, I^2, I^3," 84–6; and Ross, "Some Unrecorded Manuscripts of the *Historia de Preliis*."

13 Bergmeister, ed., *Die Historia de preliis Alexandri Magni (Der lateinische Alexanderroman des Mittelalters)*, viia–ixa, surveys the sources of the *Historia* recensions.

14 Kratz, trans., *The Romances of Alexander*, xxi–xxiii.

15 Campopiano, "Parcours de la légende d'Alexandre en Italie," 69–72; and "*Gentes, monstra, fere*," 240–1.

16 Dionisotti, "The Letter of Mardochaeus the Jew to Alexander the Great," 3, argues that the Tartars, referenced as the "Tartari" in the Gog and Magog story of the I^3 text, only became "a recognizable entity" ca. 1218, after the Siege of Damietta. In 1236 Quilichino of Spoleto translated the I^3 into a verse epic.

17 Takayama, "Law and Monarchy in the South," 58. Roth, *The History of the Jews of Italy*, 92–3, adds that the region was equally important for transmitting classical texts. Chazan, *The Jews of Medieval Western Christendom, 1000–1500*, 119, assesses the later twelfth century in southern Italy as the age of Jewish scribal effort towards translating "a Latin corpus."

18 See Ausfeld, ed., *Der Griechische Alexanderroman*, 15–17.

19 Van Bekkum, ed., *A Hebrew Alexander Romance According to MS London, Jews' College no. 145*, 12. Van Bekkum, "Alexander the Great in Medieval Hebrew Literature," 220, assesses the Rabbinical reception of him as "an exemplary ruler over the world, a conqueror and overlord *par excellence*."

20 Rothschild, "L'*Iter ad Paradisum* entre homélie rabbinique, roman, traité d'apologétique et exemplum," 93–4.

21 Dönitz, "Alexander the Great in Medieval Hebrew Traditions," 23–4. For Jewish legends of Alexander, see also Simon, "Alexandre le Grand, juif et Chrétien"; and Kazis, ed., *The Book of the Gests of Alexander of Macedon*, 2.

22 Momigliano, "Flavius Josephus and Alexander's Visit to Jerusalem," 446.

23 See Josephus, *Jewish Antiquities*, 6: 11.6.

24 Hilka and Steffens, eds., *Historia Alexandri Magni (Historia de preliis), Rezension* J^1, 50.

25 Michael, "Typological Problems in Medieval Alexander Literature," 133.
26 Gero, "The Legend of Alexander the Great in the Christian Orient," 9.
27 See Anderson, *Alexander's Gate, Gog and Magog, and the Inclosed Nations*, for a comprehensive discussion of the episode, as well as McGinn, *Visions of the End*, 70–3.
28 Peter Comestor, *Historia scholastica*, col. 1498: "Cumque [Alexander] quaesisset causam captivitatis, accepit eos recessisse aperte a Deo Israel."
29 Ibid., col. 1498: "videns laborem humanum non sufficere, oravit Deum Israel, ut opus illud compleret."
30 Ibid., col. 1498: "Et, ut ait Josephus, Deus quid facturus est pro fidelibus suis, si tantum fecit pro infideli?"
31 Bildhauer, "Blood, Jews and Monsters in Medieval Culture," 85.
32 See ibid., 80, for their identification as Jews. See Dionisotti, "The Letter of Mardochaeus," 3; and Burnett and Dalché, "Attitudes towards the Mongols in Medieval Literature," for the association of Gog and Magog with the Mongols.
33 Unlike in Persian romances, in which Alexander is roundly celebrated as a philosopher-king and permitted to reach paradise. See Southgate, "Portrait of Alexander in Persian Alexander-Romances of the Islamic Era"; Polignac, "L'image d'Alexandre dans la littérature arabe"; Masroori, "Alexander in the City of the Excellent"; and Stoneman, Erickson, and Netton, *The Alexander Romance in Persia and the East*.
34 Gunderson, "Early Elements in the Alexander Romance," 358.
35 Zacher, ed., *Alexandri Magni Iter ad Paradisum*, 20.
36 Ibid., 32.
37 Boffito, "La leggenda aviatoria di Alessandro Magno," 327; and Schmidt, *A Legend and Its Image*, 16, cite mosaics of Alexander dressed in Byzantine royal fashion in Taranto and Venice, respectively. Dimitrokalis, "L'ascensione di Alessandro Magno nell'Italia del Medioevo," cites several other examples of Alexander mosaics in Italy. For a collated reading of the Greek versions of the scene, see Millet, "L'Ascension d'Alexandre."
38 Morosini, "The Alexander Romance in Italy," 333.
39 Castiñeiras, "L'Alessandro anglonormanno e il mosaico di Otranto," 44–5.
40 Abulafia, *Frederick II*, 34.
41 Tronzo, "The Mantle of Roger II of Sicily."
42 Britt, "Roger II of Sicily," 26.
43 Tabacco, *The Struggle for Power in Medieval Italy*, 243.
44 Steffens, ed., *Die Historia de preliis Alexandri Magni*, 2–4.
45 Quilichinus de Spoleto, *Historia Alexandri Magni*, ed. Wolfgang Kirsch, 193: "cur deus fecit omnia mutabilia et inconstancia, cum ipse sit constans

et inuariabilis ... inducit exemplum de Alexandro, qui, cum fuerit potentissimus, non potuit stare in firmo statu, nec potuit se defendere a modica gutta ueneni."

46 See Pfister, ed., *Kleine texte zum Alexanderroman*.

47 For a listing, see Ross, "A Check-List of Three Alexander Texts." As Gaullier-Bougassas, "Quêtes d'immortalité ou de salut," 18–19, notes, Brahman texts also continued to circulate in Italy and Byzantium.

48 Kuebler, ed., *Juli Valeri Alexandri Polemi, Res Gestae Alexandri Macedonis*, 183.

49 Friedman, *The Monstrous Races in Medieval Art and Thought*, 167–8.

50 Callu, trans., *Julius Valère, Roman d'Alexandre*, 21, argues that in these early romances Alexander grows more tolerant and peaceful as his expedition evolves from a military campaign to a search for knowledge.

51 Boer, ed., *Epistola Alexandri ad Aristotelem*, 59–60.

52 Baumgartner, "Figures du Destinateur," 2.

53 The text of the older version of Lamprecht's translation, the *Vorau Alexander*, ends after Darius's death.

54 Buschinger, "German Alexander Romances," 300.

55 Campopiano, "Parcours de la légende d'Alexandre," 75.

56 See Aerts, "Alexander the Great in 'Exempla' and 'Similitudines' in Byzantine Literature," for a survey of perspectives east of Italy. Orosius, *Historiarum adversum paganos libri VII*, ed. Zangemeister, 3.7: "ille gurges miseriarum atque atrocissimus turbo totius orientis" (that whirlpool of miseries and most atrocious whirlwind of the entire East), which also indicates a clear geographical perspective on the conqueror.

57 For Alexander's appropriation by moralists, see Cary, *The Medieval Alexander*, 80–117.

58 Gosman, "La genèse du *Roman d'Alexandre*," 25.

59 Meyer, *Alexandre le Grand dans la littérature française*, 2: 212–13.

60 Busby, "Codices manuscriptos nudos tenemus," 259.

61 Gaullier-Bougassas, *Les romans d'Alexandre*, 185–6.

62 These romances are edited in Armstrong, ed., *The Medieval French Roman d'Alexandre*: for Albéric, see Foulet, ed., 3: 37–60; for the *Alexandre décasyllabique*, see ibid., 61–100; for Lambert le Tort's *Alexandre en orient*, see Foulet, ed., 6: 88–93; for the *Fuerre de Gadres*, see Armstrong and Foulet, eds., 4: 89–103; and for the *Mort Alixandre*, see Armstrong, ed., 7: 27–35 (the series is hereafter cited as *MFRA*).

63 This "archetype" text does not survive, but the best witnesses to this original form are Paris, Bibliothèque de l'Arsenal MS 3472; Venice, Museo Civico MS VI, 665; and Paris, Bibliothèque Nationale MS 789. For the text of the first two, see La Du, ed., *MFRA*, 1.

64 See Petit, "Les romans antiques et Alexandre"; and Suard, "Alexandre est-il un personnage de roman?"
65 Verner, *The Epistemology of the Monstrous in the Middle Ages*, 78–89; and Le Goff, *The Medieval Imagination*, 37.
66 Baumgartner, "La formation du mythe d'Alexandre au XIIe siècle."
67 The French romances inform such a statement as that made by Bunt, "An Exemplary Hero: Alexander the Great," 50: "in all romances Alexander is a great and admirable hero and a magnanimous and generous leader of men."
68 For a survey of the Nectanabus tradition in the twelfth century, see Friede, "Alexanders Kindheit in der französischen Zehnsilberfassung und in *Roman d'Alexandre*."
69 Abril, "Les Enfances d'Alexandre," 3.
70 For the evolution of the Nectanabus legend, see Perry, "The Egyptian Legend of Nectanabus." As Jouanno, *Naissance et métamorphosis du Roman d'Alexandre, Domaine grec*, 62, argues, in the original version of the *Pseudo-Callisthenes*, Nectanabus predicts that Alexander will be as much Egyptian as Macedonian and will forge, by extension, an Egyptian empire.
71 Raynaud, "Les répresentations du pouvoir royal," 67.
72 *MFRA*, 3: lines 27–32: "Dicunt alquant estrobatour / quel reys fud filz d'encantatour. / Mentent, fellon losengetour. / Mal en credreyz nec un de lour, / Qu'anz fud de ling d'enperatour / Et filz al rey macedonor."
73 Albéric's text is not extant at this point but is translated by Kinzel, ed., *Lamprechts Alexander*, 42–3. *MFRA*, 3: 42–60, provides a modern French translation of Lamprecht's passage. Earlier in Kinzel, ed., *Lamprechts Alexander*, lines 10–12, the poet relies on biblical authority to reject the story of Nectanabus: "Philippus was sîn vater genant. / diz mugit ir wol hôren / in libro Machabeorum."
74 So reads the Venice MS in *MFRA*, 1: lines 74–83. Cf., 3: lines 61–7.
75 Zacher, ed., *Julii Valerii epitome*, 19–20 (hereafter cited as *Zacher Epitome*).
76 Armstrong, Buffun, Edwards, and Lowe, eds., *MFRA*, 2: lines 364–6.
77 Gaullier-Bougassas, *Les Romans d'Alexandre*, 346.
78 Ibid., 361.
79 Gosman, "The French Background," 12.
80 Ibid.
81 Gaullier-Bougassas, *Les Romans d'Alexandre*, 505.
82 *MFRA*, 7: lines 115–27: "Li uns voldra aveir tota la segnorie, / Si coma li lïuns a la chere hardie; / L'autra, qui est leuparz, lunc lui ne cosent mie; / Li terz si est li ors qui contra cels grongdie; / Li quarz est li dragons qui

contr'aus treis foudrie; / E li quinz, qui lops est, la rapine polplie.' / 'Deus! Ce dist Alixandres, com faite desverie ... / Trahisons est amee e lehautez hahie, / Avarice est montee e largece fallie, / Lausengë est en cort, vertez en est pertie. / Encors sera el mont si granz la felonie / Que ja hom n'avra cure ne d'ami ne d'amie." Cf. *Zacher Epitome*, 62: the upper, "iam putrida ac semiviva" (already rotted and half-alive) portion of the body represents Alexander, while the lower part, "quae ferinis capitibus cingitur" (covered in beastly hair) signifies that "ut hae ferae inter dissident, sic quoque post mortem tuam hi inter se discordes erunt" (just as wild beasts fight amongst themselves, so after your death [Alexander] will there be discord amongst [your officers].)

83 See, respectively, *MFRA*, 1: 334–42 and 7: 48–55. The Venice manuscript of the "archetype" *Roman d'Alexandre*, in ibid., 1: 471–95, adds a lengthy narrative of the vengeance exacted against Alexander's assassins.

84 See Gui de Cambrai, *Le Vengement Alixandre.*

85 Benton, "The Court of Charlemagne as a Literary Center," 22–3.

86 See Jehan le Nevelon, *La Venjance Alixandre.*

87 Walter of Châtillon, *The Alexandreis: A Twelfth-Century Epic*, trans. Townsend, 15, settles on 1171–81 as the probable date range.

88 Dennis M. Kratz, *Mocking Epic*, 78.

89 Townsend, trans., *The Alexandreis*, 21.

90 Ashurst, "Alexander the Great," 28.

91 Townsend, trans. of Walter of Châtillon, *The Alexandreis*, lines 5.580–99. The original, in Marvin L. Colker, ed., *Galteri de Castellione Alexandreis*, lines 5.500–16, reads: "Si fide recolas quam raro milite contra / Victores mundi tenero sub flore iuuentae / Quanta sit aggressus Macedo, quam tempore paruo / Totus Alexandri genibus se fuderit orbis ... Si gemitu commota pio uotisque suorum / Flebilibus diuina daret clementia talem / Francorum regem, toto radiaret in orbe / Haut mora uera fides, et nostris fracta sub armis / Parthia baptismo renouari posceret ultro, / Queque diu iacuit effusis minibus alta / Ad nomen Christi Kartago resurgeret."

92 See Colker, *Galteri de Castellione Alexandreis*, lines 6.24–35.

93 Kratz, *Mocking Epic*, 82, reads this *virtus* as both Aristotelian and Christian.

94 Gaullier-Bougassas, *Les Romans d'Alexandre*, 509.

95 Townsend, trans., *The Alexandreis*, lines 10.228–30.

96 Ibid., lines 10.537–9.

97 Ibid., 15.

98 Lafferty, *Walter of Châtillon's Alexandreis*, 174.

99 Godman, "The Archpoet and the Emperor," 41.

100 Baldwin, *The Government of Philip Augustus*, 362–6.
101 Kelly, *The Art of Medieval French Romance*, 215–16, notes that Bodel wrote *Saisnes* as "an adaptation of Charlemagne to the ideals and ambitions of the French crown of around 1200." Busby, "Narrative Genres," 140, adds that Bodel saw the Matters of Britain, Rome, and France as providing "Arthurian entertainment, classical edification, and French history."
102 Namely the *Histoire ancienne jusqu'à César* and the *Old French Prose Alexander*. See Lynde-Recchia, *Prose, Verse, and Truth-Telling in the Thirteenth Century*, 25–9; and Spiegel, *Romancing the Past*, 107–8.
103 Reis, "The 'Other' Medieval French Alexander," 356.
104 Godman, "Transmontani," 200–1.
105 Weiss, "Emperors and Antichrists," 95.
106 Heer, *The Holy Roman Empire*, 73.
107 Weiss, "Emperors and Antichrists," 95.
108 Abulafia, *Frederick II*, 78–9.
109 Lomax, "Frederick II, His Saracens, and the Papacy," 176; and Weiler, "Reasserting Power," 249–51.
110 Shaw, "Friedrich II as the 'Last Emperor'"; and McGinn, *Visions of the End*, 168–79.
111 Kinoshita, *Medieval Boundaries*, 3.
112 Noble, "Romance in England and Normandy in the Twelfth Century," 76.

2. Alexander in Anglo-Norman England: The Latin Texts

1 Stone, *From Tyrant to Philosopher-King*, 77–110. For the pairing of the two histories, see Seel, "Die justinischen Handschriftenklassen und ihr Verhältness zu Orosius"; and Mortensen, "Orosius and Justinus in One Volume."
2 See Orchard, *Pride and Prodigies*, 116–39; Orchard, *A Critical Companion to Beowulf*, 24–39; Tristram, "Der Insulare Alexander"; and Tristram, "More Talk of Alexander."
3 The *Parva recapitulatio* includes a third episode, Alexander's visit to Jerusalem, where he was read the prophecy of his conquest of Persia in the Book of Daniel. For a discussion of the manuscripts, see Stone, *From Tyrant to Philosopher-King*, 63–75. For an edition of the Latin and Middle English versions, see Ross, "'*Parva recapitulatio*,' An English Collection of Texts relating to Alexander the Great"; Hill, "The Middle English and Latin Versions of the *Parva recapitulatio*"; DiMarco and Perelman, eds, *The Middle English Letter of Alexander to Aristotle*; and Hahn, "The Middle English Letter of Alexander to Aristotle."

4 See Stone, *From Tyrant to Philosopher-King*, 77–110.
5 Shopkow, *History and Community*, 225.
6 All manuscripts are of English origin: London, British Library MSS Royal 13. A. i (late eleventh century), Royal 15. C. vi (twelfth century), Cotton, Cleopatra D. v (thirteenth century), and Harley 5054 (fifteenth century); Cambridge, University Library MSS Mm. V. 29 (twelfth century) and Dd. X. 24 (fifteenth century). Crick, *The Historia Regum Britannie of Geoffrey of Monmouth*, 4: 26–7, adds Lincoln, Cathedral Library MS 98 (late thirteenth or early fourteenth century).
7 London, British Library, MS Royal 13. A. i, fols 94v–95v.
8 See Carney, *Olympias, Mother of Alexander the Great*, 104–24.
9 London, British Library, MS Royal 13. A. i, fol. 98r.
10 Ibid., fol. 98v.
11 Cambridge, Corpus Christi College MS 219, fol. 1r: "Incipit hystoria regis Macedonum Philippi, filiique eius Alexandri magni, excerpta de libris Pompeii Trogi, Orosii, Josephi, Jeronimi, Solini, Augustini, Bede, et Ysidori" (this manuscript is hereafter cited as CCCC, MS 219).
12 Clark, *A Monastic Renaissance at St Albans*, 79. As Rodney Thomson argues in the essays of *England and the Twelfth-Century Renaissance*, an impressive collection of Roman literature was copied and transmitted in post-Conquest England, particularly at the libraries of Bury St Edmunds and St Albans.
13 For the manuscripts, see James, *A Catalogue of the Manuscripts in Gonville and Caius College, Cambridge*, 77; Ker, *Medieval Libraries of Great Britain*, 340; and Stone, "Investigating Macedon in Medieval England," 108–9. For the Anglo-Norman translation in the early-thirteenth-century Cambridge, Fitzwilliam Museum MS 20, see Magoun, "The *St Albans Compilation* and the *Old French Prose Alexander*"; and Arnold, "The Prophecy of Daniel in the *Old French Prose Alexander*."
14 Skeat, ed., *The Romance of William of Palerne*, xxxiii–xxxiv: "Radulphus de Sto Albano eiusdem fani Albani monachus et Abbas … hanc historiam de rebus gestis Alexandri Macedonis edidit; obit anno domini MCLI, in eodem coenobio sepultus, sub Stephano Anglorum rege" (Ralph of St Albans, monk and abbot of the same abbey of St Albans … produced this history of the deeds of Alexander of Macedon; he died in the year of the Lord 1151, in the reign of Stephen, King of the English, and is buried in the same cloister).
15 R.M. Thomson, *Manuscripts from St Albans Abbey 1066–1235*, 1: 28.
16 CCCC, MS 219, fols 37r–7v.
17 CCCC, MS 219, fol 38r.

18 Ibid., fol 38v.
19 Ibid., fol 39r.
20 Ibid., fol 55r.
21 Ibid., fol. 63v.
22 Bisson, *The Crisis of the Twelfth Century*, 281.
23 Binski, *Medieval Death*, 35–50.
24 Van Houts, ed. and trans., *The Gesta Normannorum Ducum of William of Jumièges, Orderic Vitalis, and Robert of Torigni*, 2: 185–7.
25 Chibnall, ed. and trans., *The Ecclesiastical History of Orderic Vitalis*, 4: 83.
26 Fahlin, ed., *Chronique des ducs de Normandie*, 2: lines V.41,763–5. Closer to Thomas of Kent's composition of the *Roman de toute chevalerie*, Jordan Fantosme (whose work Thomas knew) comments on another king's failure to ensure a peaceful allocation of power. In Johnston, ed. and trans., *Jordan Fantosme's Chronicle*, 3, he recalls that between Henry II and Henry the Young King "arose deadly ill will, which brought about the deaths of many a noble knight."
27 Burgess, trans., *The History of the Norman People*, 194.
28 See Judith A. Green, *Henry I, King of England and Duke of Normandy*, 316; and Newman, *The Anglo-Norman Nobility in the Reign of Henry I*, 16.
29 See, e.g., the classicizing tones of Henry of Huntingdon, *Historia Anglorum*, 493: "King Henry is dead, once the pride, now the sorrow of the world. The divine powers lament the passing of his divinity. They sigh – Mercury less eloquent than he, Apollo less strong in mind, Jupiter less commanding, and Mars less vigorous. Janus less cautious, Alcides less valiant, Pallas less in combat, Minerva less in art – they sigh."
30 Van Houts, ed. and trans., *The Gesta Normannorum ducum*, 2: 259.
31 Chibnall, ed. and trans., *The Ecclesiastical History of Orderic Vitalis*, 6: 453. Cf., Robert of Torigni's complaints over civilian casualties after Henry I's death in Van Houts, ed. and trans., *The Gesta Normannorum Ducum*, 2: 259: "After the father of his people, who brought peace and love, defence of the weak, / himself a devout man succumbed, impious men raged, oppressed and burned."
32 Potter, ed. and trans., *Gesta Stephani*, 3. The two priors of the Augustinian priory of Hexham, Ralph and John, also give voice to the figurative death of peace and justice and the rise of violence against the innocent population. See Stephenson, trans. *Contemporary Chronicles of the Middle Ages*, 53, for the former and Arnold, ed., *Symeonis Monachi Opera Omnia*, 2: 286, for the latter.
33 Chibnall, ed. and trans., *The Ecclesiastical History of Orderic Vitalis*, 6: 451.

34 Darlington and McGurk, eds. and Bray and McGurk, trans., *The Chronicle of John Worcester*, 3: 217.

35 See Garnett, *Conquered England*, 188–90. As Thomas, *The English and the Normans*, 257, suggests, monastic historians expressed a general outrage against the suffering of religious and civilian communities that had long lingered over their similar displeasure over the behaviour of the Norman invaders of England.

3. The *Roman de toute chevalerie*: Sources, Influences, and Innovations

1 Busby, "Neither Flesh nor Fish, Nor Good Red Herring," 403.

2 Calin, *The French Tradition*, 20, lists French biblical translation, hagiography, the miracle, the chronicle, theatre, science, biography, the lai, and possibly romance as originating in England.

3 As Ailes, "What's in a Name?" 74, claims, "there is no impermeable barrier between Anglo-Norman and continental texts."

4 See Dean, *Anglo-Norman Literature*, 51–7 (hereafter cited as *Anglo-Norman Lit.*).

5 Gransden, *Historical Writing in England c550 to c1307*, 219.

6 Gillingham, "Events and Opinions," 60.

7 See *Anglo-Norman Alex.*, line P46: "En romanz oi l'epistre d'Alisandre retraire / Qu'il tramist Aristotle son bon mestre gramaire" (the lines are missing from the Cambridge manuscript). I cite Foster's edition throughout this chapter, when the passages in question do not represent unique readings of a given manuscript of Thomas's work.

8 Damian-Grint, *The New Historians*, 31.

9 Ibid., 19.

10 Ibid., 152.

11 Gaullier-Bougassas, *Les romans d'Alexandre*, 182–6.

12 For a guide to Thomas's Latin sources, see Weynand, *Der Roman de Toute chevalerie*. Citing a small selection of Thomas's sources, Howlett, *The English Origins of Old French Literature*, 127, still contextualizes the *Roman de toute chevalerie* within the intellectual tradition established by Ralph Gubiun.

13 Damian-Grint, "*Estoire* as Word and Genre," 190–2.

14 Damian-Grint, *The New Historians*, 261–2, surveys the use of "livre" in the larger context of authorial *auctoritas*.

15 Gaullier-Bougassas, *Les romans d'Alexandre*, 187, notes that Thomas frequently uses the verb "trover" in referring to his source material research; this would semantically insinuate both composing and discovering.

16 Cf., *Anglo-Norman Alex.*, lines 6657–64: "Quant Solin e Trege averez tot reverse / E Ysidre, qe fu de langage estoré, / Jerome e Ethike, Orosye l'escrié, / E Dyonis de Inde, Magesten le barbé, / E l'epistre Alisandre qu'il tramist par chereté / A mestre Aristotle qui l'out endoctriné, / E les autres liveres a cestui assemble, / Donc saverez [vous] pur voir qe n'est pas contrive." The last four lines again grant the *Epistola Alexandri ad Aristotelem* the same stature as the classical sources listed and thereby suggest Thomas's additional authority in relying on a text removed from Roman and ecclesiastical traditions.

17 Gransden, *Legends, Traditions and History in Medieval England*, 142. In Anglo-Latin texts, see, e.g., William of Malmsbury, *Gesta regum Anglorum*, 1: 17, in which William of Malmesbury warns that "I guarantee the truth of nothing in past time except the sequence of events; the credit of my narrative must rest with my authorities"; and Wright, ed., *The Historia regum Britannie of Geoffrey of Monmouth*, 1: 1, in which Geoffrey claims that he translated "Britannici sermonis librum vetustissimum" (a very ancient book in the language of the Britons).

18 Short, ed. and trans., *Geffrei Gaimar, Estoire des Engleis*, xv.

19 Burgess, trans., *The History of the Norman People*, 91.

20 Bennett, "Poetry as History?" 23.

21 Le Saux, "The Languages of England," 188.

22 Johnston, ed., *Jordan Fantosme's Chronicle*, 1.

23 Rollo, *Historical Fabrication, Ethnic Fable and French Romance in Twelfth-Century England*, 15, comments on twelfth-century historiography that "the facts of the past, then as now, were the primary objects of retrieval and documentation, and any falsification of history, then as now, was viewed as fundamentally transgressive." For the question of authority and mendacity among twelfth-century historiographers, see also Partner, *Serious Entertainments*; and Beer, *Narrative Conventions of Truth in the Middle Ages*.

24 Galbraith, *Historical Research in Medieval England*, 27.

25 Clanchy, *From Memory to Written Record*, 200–1.

26 As Bunt. "Alexander's Last Days," 209, notes, there is a certain level of irony in the reception of the *Roman de toute chevalerie*, as the *Kyng Alisaunder*-poet, who translated Thomas's work in the thirteenth century, places his trust in his Latin sources when he identifies a discrepancy between them and the French "gest."

27 D.H. Green, *The Beginnings of Medieval Romance*, 165–6.

28 Ibid., 187, identifies such gaps as the textual or historical "lacunae" into which romance writers insert fictions.

29 Gaullier-Bougassas, *Les romans d'Alexandre*, 206–7: "[Alexandre de Paris] reste en effet fidèle à la conception de l'*estoire* comme beau récit édifiant, où l'historicité des faits se subordonne à leur valeur d'exemple."

30 Weiss, "Insular Beginnings," 32. Rector, "'Faites le mien desir,'" 316–17, notes that Thomas cites a maxim on learning from others' punishment that also appears in Fantosme's chronicle and that "is used to invite an audience to use historical reading as an exercise of correction and persuasion."

31 Bruckner, *Shaping Romance*, 208.

32 Spiegel, *Romancing the Past*, 102, argues of Continental romance: "by transforming ancient history into a metaphoric equivalent of French chivalric society, romance authors established an implicit, metaphorically effected connection to ancient civilization that enabled them to convert that past from a cultural legacy into a social patrimony."

33 Damian-Grint, *The New Historians*, 205.

34 Gosman, "La Matière 'classique' dans la littérature française," 273.

35 Furrow, "*Chanson de geste* as Romance in England," 63–6.

36 Noble, "Romance in England and Normandy in the Twelfth Century," 75. Kay, *The Chansons de geste in the Age of Romance*, 49–50, distinguishes continuous, unresolved conflicts as another characteristic of the genre. This aspect of the Alexander narrative, for example, likely inspired the French romances dealing with the wars among his successors and surviving family members.

37 Ibid., 605. See also Camargo, "The Metamorphosis of Candace"; and de Weever, "Candace in the Alexander Romances."

38 Short, "Language and Literature," 207.

39 Field, "The Anglo-Norman Background to Alliterative Romance," 60.

40 Weiss, "Emperors and Antichrists," 32–3.

41 Legge, *Anglo-Norman Literature*, 86.

42 Green, *The Aristocracy of Norman England*, 437.

43 Radulescu, "Genealogy in Insular Romance," 8.

44 Field, "'Pur les francs homes amender,'" 182. Dannenbaum, "Anglo-Norman Romances of English Heroes," 604, identifies this as the "departure and return" pattern popular in Anglo-Norman romances of Thomas's generation.

45 Sturges, *Medieval Interpretation*, 26, argues that in romances, unlike *chansons de geste*, "divine immanence is withdrawn from the world, or only from the literary work, [and] authoritative truth and certain knowledge must also withdraw from the realm of human action, to be replaced by multiple human interpretations of the ambiguities that result."

46 Zink, *Medieval French Literature*, 51, classifies Alexander romance within the twelfth-century interest in classical subjects but excludes it from the genealogical romances established by Wace and Benoit. As Blumenfeld-Kosinski, *Reading Myth*, 10, argues, the intent of *romans antiques* was to make classical epics "a part of history, sometimes even of medieval national history." As Green, *The Beginnings of Medieval Romance*, 166, notes, however, there were some historians in the ninth and tenth centuries who traced the lineage of the Franks and Saxons to the Macedonians.

47 Ramey, *Christian, Saracen and Genre in Medieval French Literature*, 36.

48 Weiss, "Insular Beginnings," 29.

49 Baswell, "Marvels of Translation and Crises of Transition in the Romances of Antiquity," 37–8.

50 Over, *Kingship, Conquest, and Patria*, 81. Compare, for example, Warren, *History on the Edge*, 163, who notes that earlier in the century Wace's *Roman de Brut* positively reflected Henry II's ambitions in the figure of Arthur.

51 Batt and Field, "The Romance Tradition," 68–81.

52 Maddox, *The Arthurian Romances of Chretien de Troyes*, 119.

53 Sargent-Baur, "Dux bellorum / rex militum / roi fainéant," 359.

54 Fries, "Boethian Themes and Tragic Structure in Geoffrey of Monmouth's *Historia Regum Britanniae*."

55 Guerin, *The Fall of Kings and Princes*, 19.

56 Patricia Clare Ingham, *Sovereign Fantasies*, 3.

57 Ibid., 526.

58 CCCC, MS 219, fol. 59v.

59 Ibid., fol. 59v.

60 Ibid., fol. 60r. Orosius, *Pauli Orosii Historiarum adversum paganos libri VII*, ed. Zangemeister, 94, adds, "et ipsa Olympias continuo meritas crudelitatis poenas luit: nam cum muliebri audacia multas principum caedes ageret."

61 Gaullier-Bougassas, *Les romans d'Alexandre*, 196. In prefacing the brief affair between Alexander and Candace, Thomas relates the dangers of love and feminine wiles. In *Anglo-Norman Alex.*, lines 7611–43 of the Foster edition, Thomas cites a range of biblical examples of men who suffered because of women.

62 See, e.g., *Anglo-Norman Alex.*, line 279, when Thomas explains that Olympias did not know that she was being deceived ("ele n'entendoit mie en li la traison") and line 282, when she admits to Nectanabus that the love of a god is preferable to that of a knight ("mielz vaut l'amur de dieu qe de nul chevaler").

63 See ibid., lines 23–5.

64 The original text of Rosellini, ed., *Iuli Valeri Res gestae Alexandri Macedonis translatae ex Aesopo Graeco*, 28–9, only offers further information on Cleopatra's lineage and a lengthier insult from Lysias. Thomas did not, then, consult this narrative beyond its far more popular *Epitome*.

65 See *Anglo-Norman Alex.*, lines 636–47.

66 Gosman, *La légende d'Alexandre le Grand*, 311.

67 *Zacher Epitome*, 26–7: "Enimvero interea Pausanias quidam nomine, opibus et diutiis affluens, in Olympiadis desiderium amoremque prolapsus est. Qui cum per internuntios adtemptaret et mulier consentiret, scilicet ut deserto Philippo ad illum transnuberet ... Quibus cognitis irruens regiam deprehendit Pausaniae violentiam. Cumque eum iaculo destinaret, tenereturque formidine matris vulnerandae, Olympias sic eum adhortatur: "Iaculare," inquit, "fili! iaculare ne dubites!"

68 Ibid., 10.

69 Ibid., 29: "His Alexander auditis statuam complexus patrem salutat, eiusque se filium profitetur."

70 This episode ultimately derives from Alexander's historical (and well known) visit in 331 BCE to the Oasis of Siwah, where he was proclaimed by the resident priests to be the son of Ammon (equivalent to the Greek Zeus) and thus a rightful pharaoh of Egypt.

71 See *Anglo-Norman Alex.*, lines 1,005–7: "Alisandre saisist [Pausanias], a Phelippon le rent, / Le brant li met al poing e il fiert durement. / Tuit le chef ly trenche e le corps ensement."

72 Ibid., lines 1009–11: "[Phelippe] dit a Alisandre: 'Bien ait ton talent / Qe ma mort vengeroies par ton hardement.'"

73 See ibid., lines 1401–25.

74 *Zacher Epitome*, 51.

4. The Two Deaths of Alexander in Cambridge, Trinity College MS O. 9. 34

1 James, *The Western Manuscripts in the Library of Trinity College, Cambridge*, 3: 482.

2 For this counter-argument, see Ross, "A Thirteenth Century Anglo-Norman Workshop," 1: 689–94; Morgan, *Early Gothic Manuscripts*, 1: 129; Avril and Stirnemann, *Manuscrits enluminés d'origine insulaire, vii*[e]*–xx*[e] *siècle*, 137; and Meuwese, "The Exploits of Alexander the Great in Trinity College," 130.

3 *Anglo-Norman Alex.*, 2: 12.

4 Schneegans, "Die handschriftliche Gestaltung des Alexander-Romans," 242.

5 *Anglo-Norman Alex.*, 2: 3.

6 Thomas's narrative ends on fol. 39v, at which point the French interpolation begins with branch IV, line 53 (laisse 5 in Armstrong, Buffum, Edwards, and Lowe, eds, *MFRA*, 2) continuing to line 719 (laisse 37) on fol. 43v. The text then skips ahead to lines 766–92 (laisse 39) before incorporating and rearranging segments of laisses 50–1. On fol. 44r the text returns to laisse 38, then picks up with line 1135–201 (laisse 53).

7 *Anglo-Norman Alex.*, 2: 23.

8 See Boer, ed., *Epistola Alexandri*, 48–9.

9 The passage, and quite a bit of the subsequent text, is missing, owing to a lacuna in the Trinity College manuscript, so I rely on the Foster edition.

10 Boer, ed., *Epistola Alexandri*, 51–2: "de tempore vitae meae reticui, ne a commilitionibus meis redditus desperationi in alienis dirumperer locis. Eas vero voces, quas ex responsis una mecum audierunt … silentio ex sua fide et meo tegebant consilio."

11 See *Anglo Norman Alex.*, lines 210–13 and 270–3, for Nectanabus's remarks, and line 420 for Philip's ominous assessment of Alexander's birth.

12 *Zacher Epitome*, 63.

13 See Stone, *From Tyrant to Philosopher-King*, 104–10.

14 Cf., Short, ed. and trans., *Geffrei Gaimar, Estoire des Engleis*, 345, when upon William II's death, his barons "tore their hair and were uncontrolled in their grief that was greater than any that has been witnessed since. Robert fitz Haimo, a powerful, noble, and aristocratic baron, arrived on the scene, and he also showed and gave vent to great grief. He kept repeating: 'I wish I were dead! I would rather die than carry on living!' Whereupon he fell to the ground in a swoon. And when he came to, he wrung his hands, and grew so weak and faint that he almost collapsed a second time. Great grieving was heard on every side, and the attendants and the huntsmen shed bitter tears."

15 The Valerius *Epitome* ends, for example, with Alexander's funeral and a list of the Alexandrias that he established.

16 *MFRA*, 2: lines 1675–8.

17 Influenced by Byzantine exemplars of the Virgin surrounded by attendants, Ottonian artists of illuminated manuscripts and then painters and mosaic artists in Norman Italy and Sicily adapted the scene of burial and public mourning into the mid-twelfth century. See Weitzmann, *Art in the Medieval West*, 16, plate 27; Pächt, *The Rise of Pictorial Narrative in Twelfth-Century England*, plate 5; and Saxl and Wittkower, *British Art and the Mediterranean*, 24. As Oakeshott, *Classical Inspiration in Medieval*

Art, 136–7, notes, the motif was imported into England in the same century, when it first appeared in English Romanesque manuscripts. As Ortenberg, *The English Church and the Continent*, 79, argues, this Byzantine motif arrived there via the Carolingian and Ottonian Empires and Norman Sicily. See also Robb, *The Art of the Illuminated Manuscript*, 197; and Oakeshott, *The Artists of the Winchester Bible and Sigena*.

18 Avril and Stirnemann, *Manuscrits enluminés*, 137.

19 The four parts of this account in Luard, ed., *Chronica majora*, 1: 61–3 are entitled "De Alexandro Magno, rege Macedonum" (On Alexander the Great, King of the Macedonians), "De gloriosa victoria Alexandri contra Darium regem Persarum, et de numero interfectorum" (On Alexander's glorious victory against Darius, King of the Persians, and on the number of casualties), "Ut regnum Persarum cessit Macedonibus" (How the Persian empire fell to the Macedonians), and "De divisione regni Alexandri post mortem ipsius" (On the division of Alexander's kingdom after his death).

20 See the marginal citations in Luard, ed., *Chronica Majora*, 1: 61–3. Lewis, *The Art of Matthew Paris in the Chronica Majora*, 138, wrongly suggests Peter Comestor's *Historia scholastica*. This possibly owes to Luard's decision to include a lengthy interpolation from Peter Comestor in London, Lambeth Palace MS 1106 in his critical edition of Roger's *Flores historiarum*.

21 Hewlett, ed., *Liber qui dicitur Flores Historiarum*, 1: 67.

22 CCCC, MS 219, fol. 16r.

23 Hewlett, ed., *Liber qui dicitur Flores Historiarum*, 1: 68.

24 Ibid., 1: 63: "illico translato vel disperso in multis imperio."

25 See Stone, "Investigating Macedon in Medieval England," 12–13. Walsingham's text, which interpolates the Valerius *Epitome* into the *St Albans Compilation*, survives in Oxford, Bodleian Library MS 299.

26 Amid the attitudes of Roger Wendover and especially Matthew Paris towards Alexander, cf. the contemporary dismissal (expected of a sacred text and audience) of the conqueror's inability to escape death in Baker and Bell, eds., *St. Modwenna*, lines 709–12: "Alisaundre le cunquerant / Ne li autre rei poant / Pur ren, qu'il usent en lur vivant, / De mort ne poent aver garant."

27 Gransden, *Historical Writing in England c 550 to c 1307*, 404.

28 For Matthew's criticism of Henry III, see Vaughan, *Matthew Paris*, 139–40, particularly for his feelings on taxation and extortion.

29 Lewis, *The Art of Matthew Paris*, 139.

30 Luard, ed., *Chronica majora*, 1: 50.

31 Ibid., 4: 77–8. This is Matthew's original history, beyond what Roger had penned in his lifetime.

32 This belief in Alexander as God's agent in the battle against infidels and agents of evil was not universally held. As Strickland, *Saracens, Demons, and Jews*, 186, suggests, "given the medieval theological view of Alexander as alternately a prideful figure of unbridled power, the Devil, and a precursor of Antichrist, the rather pessimistic belief conveyed by such imagery [as Alexander battling eastern monsters] is that such monstrous enemies may be defeated only by the Devil himself."

33 Lewis, *The Art of Matthew Paris*, 138. The Psalm is one of divine protection: "super aspidem et basilicum calcabis conculcabis leonem et draconem" (You will walk upon the asp and the basilisk, and you will trample underfoot the lion and the dragon).

34 Blurton, "From *Chanson de Geste* to Magna Carta," 119.

35 Galbraith, *Matthew Paris and Roger Wendover*, 20; and Holt, "The St Albans Chroniclers and Magna Carta," 77.

36 See, e.g., Hewlett, ed., *Flores historiarum*, 2: 166: "Haec fuit in Anglia persecutio generalis, dum patres a filiis, fratres a fratribus, cives a civibus, ad supplicia vendebantur. Nundinae cum mercatis cessabant, res venales in coemeteriis agebantur; agricultura quievit, nec quisquam ecclesiarum limites egredi ausus erat" (In England, there was widespread persecution, as fathers were sold over for punishment by their sons, brothers by brothers, and citizens by fellow citizens. Business at the market-place stopped, transactions were conducted in cemeteries, and farming ceased, because no one dared to walk beyond the thresholds of the churches).

37 E.g., at ibid., 2: 162, Roger recounts John's campaign of devastating the barons' estates around London and in the North, which involved burning, pillaging, and the torture of the elderly and infirm captives.

38 David Matthews, *Writing to the King*, 43.

39 Dean, ed. *Anglo-Norman Lit.*, 52.

40 Ibid., 53.

41 Ibid., 56.

42 Ibid., 54.

43 Ibid., 54–5.

44 Ibid., 55.

45 Rouse, *The Idea of Anglo-Saxon England*, 75.

46 Schmolke-Hasselmann, *The Evolution of Arthurian Romance*, 247.

47 Ibid., 229.

48 Jane H.M. Taylor, "The Thirteenth-Century Arthur," 67.

49 Gosman, "The French Background," 12, notes that in the *Fuerre de Gadres* interpolation in the *Roman de toute chevalerie*, Alexander is distant from the main action, and his barons take centre stage.
50 *Anglo-Norman Lit.*, 89–91.
51 Ibid., 99.
52 Holden, ed., Gregory and Crouch, trans., *History of William Marshal*, 1: 39.
53 Legge, *Anglo-Norman Literature*, 107, notes the reference to Gadifer, the protagonist of the *Fuerre de Gadres*. See Holden, ed., Gregory, and Crouch, trans., *History of William Marshal*, 3: lines 1004–6. At ibid., 3: lines 3576–8, the poet compares William thus: "never did Arthur or Alexander, / whose lives were noted for their noble deeds, / perform so many in such [a short] time."
54 Bedford, "*Fouke le Fitz Waryn*," 101.
55 Rock, "*Fouke le Fitz Waryn* and King John: Rebellion and Reconciliation," 75.
56 Harding, *England in the Thirteenth Century*, 267.
57 Marvin, *The Oldest Anglo-Norman Prose Brut Chronicle*, 41–3. For the baronial attitude towards Arthurian literature, see Field, "The Anglo-Norman Background to Alliterative Romance," 64.
58 Ibid., 295.
59 Marvin, "John and Henry III in the Anglo-Norman Prose *Brut*," 178.
60 Marvin, "The English *Brut* Tradition," 232.
61 Marvin, *The Oldest Anglo-Norman Prose Brut Chronicle*, 11.
62 Although Weiss, "Ineffectual Monarchs," 56, notes that "the inert or ineffectual monarch becomes a recurrent topos in narrative from the mid twelfth century," such criticism was not generally aimed at Alexander.
63 *Anglo-Norman Lit.*, 91.
64 Weiss, "Emperors and Antichrists," 98.
65 Ibid., 99.
66 Ibid., 90.
67 Holden, ed., *Le Roman de Waldef*, lines 15533–8: "Allas! quel duel e quel damage / Ke il ne vesquist par eage; / N'oïmes unc de roi parler / Qui tant se feïst renumer, / Fors sulement roi Alisandre, / Celi qui tant fist sanc espandre."
68 *Anglo-Norman Lit.*, 90–1.
69 Weiss, "Insular Beginnings," 38.
70 The *Prose Lancelot* survives in two fourteenth-century Anglo-Norman copies, *Percival* in one, *Octavian et Dagobert* in a late-thirteenth-century copy, and *Partonopeus* in two thirteenth- and one fourteenth-century manuscripts. See *Anglo-Norman Lit.*, 100–1.

71 Weiss, "Ineffectual Monarchs," 63.
72 Over, *Kingship, Conquest, and Patria*, 81.
73 Maddox, *The Arthurian Romances of Chretien de Troyes*, 119.
74 Carpenter, "A Noble in Politics," 203.

5. Paris, Bibliothèque Nationale MS 24364: Alexander, Chivalry, and the Wars of Edward I

1 For the murals, see Borenius, "The Cycle of Images in the Palaces and Castles of Henry III"; and Stone, *From Tyrant to Philosopher-King*, 126–8. Salter, *English and International*, 89; and Lethaby, "English Primitives IV," 138, suggest that the scenes were modelled on romances.
2 Barrett, "Roland and Crusade Imagery in an English Royal Chapel," 145.
3 See Whatley, "Romance, Crusade, and the Orient."
4 Binski, "The Painted Chamber at Westminster," 135. For his earlier work on the murals, see *The Painted Chamber at Westminster*; and *Westminster Abbey and the Plantagenets*.
5 For a general guide to the text, see Williams, *The Secret of Secrets*.
6 Williams, "Roger Bacon and His Edition of the Pseudo-Aristotelian *Secretum secretorum*," 66–7.
7 Steele, ed., *Opera hactenus inedita Rogeri Baconi*, 5: 37–8.
8 Ibid., 5: 65.
9 Binski, "The Painted Chamber at Westminster," 147.
10 Harding, *England in the Thirteenth Century*, 309. See also Matthews, *Writing to the King*, 53–63.
11 William Aldis Wright, ed., *The Metrical Chronicle of Robert of Gloucester*, 2: 735.
12 Saul, *Chivalry in Medieval England*, 77–84.
13 Thomas Wright, ed. and trans., *The Political Songs of England*, 128.
14 Prestwich, *Plantagenet England, 1225–1360*, 165.
15 Thomas Wright, ed. and trans., *The Chronicle of Pierre de Langtoft*, 2: 329. The French original, in ibid., 2: 328, reads "A ses barons Engleis, par droite quantitez, / La tere de pité scà fust en ses poestez, / E pardurablement les soens heritez." As John Taylor, *English Historical Literature in the Fourteenth Century*, 157, argues, Langtoft employs the Arthurian legend "to justify Edward's policy in Scotland."
16 Taylor, *English Historical Literature in the Fourteenth Century*, 242.
17 Zettl, ed., *An Anonymous Short English Metrical Chronicle*, 624.
18 Prestwich, *The Three Edwards*, 84.
19 Stubbs, ed., *Chronicles of the Reigns of Edward I and Edward II*, 2: 12–14. See, too, Smalley, *English Friars and Antiquity in the Early Fourteenth Century*, 9.

20 D'Avray, *Death and the Prince*, 71.
21 Matthews, *Writing to the King*, 92.
22 Childs, ed. and trans., *Vita Edwardi Secundi*, 69.
23 Fryde, *The Tyranny*, 15; and Prestwich, "The Ordinances of 1311," 9.
24 Fryde, *The Tyranny*, 14.
25 Ibid., 239, n. 10.
26 Ibid., 17.
27 Haines, *King Edward II*, 60.
28 Douglas, *English Historical Documents III*, 3: 526. Stubbs, ed., *Chronicles of the Reigns of Edward I and Edward II*, 154, prints the original: "est liez par seon serement de gouerner seon poeple et les ligez loiez de governer oueqe lui en aide de lui."
29 Phillips, *Aymer de Valence*, 316: "les oppressiouns que ount estre feit et uncore se fount de jour en jour a soen poeple de redrescer et mettre pur amendement al honour de Deu et de nostre seigneur le Roy et de tout son people."
30 Prestwich, *The Three Edwards*, 82–3.
31 Douglas, *English Historical Documents III*, 3: 527.
32 Prestwich, "The Ordinances of 1311," 5.
33 Avril and Stirnemann, *Manuscrits enluminés*, 136–7; and Harf-Lancner, "From Alexander to Marco Polo, from Text to Image," 238.
34 For a description of the manuscript, see *Anglo-Norman Alex.*, 2: 6–10; Avril and Stirnemann, *Manuscrits enluminés*, 126–38; and Schneegans, "Die handschriftliche Gestaltung des Alexander-Romans," 240–1. Dean, ed., *Anglo-Norman Literature*, 98, identifies a contemporary fragment of the *Roman de toute chevalerie* in Oxford, Bodleian Library MS Lat. Misc. b. 17 as "possibly Continental."
35 Avril and Stirnemann, *Manuscrits enluminés*, 137.
36 Sanders, *English Baronies*, 49.
37 Gibbs, ed., *Complete Peerage*, 2: 10.
38 Richardson, *Magna Carta Ancestry*, 45, 449.
39 Avril and Stirnemann, *Manuscrits enluminés*, 137.
40 Richardson, *Magna Carta Ancestry*, 45.
41 Gough, ed., *Scotland in 1298*, 145.
42 Wright, ed., *The Roll of Arms*, 13.
43 Nicolas, ed., *The Siege of Carlaverock*, 199.
44 Rothwell, ed., *The Chronicle of Walter of Guisborough*, 345: "quod a prima institucione regni Anglie reges eiusdem regni tam temporibus Britonum quam Anglorum superius et directum dominium regni Scocie habuerunt."
45 Haines, *King Edward II*, 64.
46 Fryde, *The Tyranny*, 22.

47 As Richard Ingham, "The Persistence of Anglo-Norman 1230–1362, 44, notes, Continental scribes are known to have emended Anglo-Norman manuscripts.
48 Galbraith, "Nationality and Language in Medieval England," 124; and Calin, *The French Tradition*, 123.
49 Heng, "The Romance of England," 155.
50 Ibid., 157.
51 Calin, *The French Tradition*, 20. One notable example just before the Paris manuscript is the French prose redaction of the Anglo-Norman *Gui de Warewic* (ca. 1300); see Franks, "Taste and Patronage."
52 Lucas, "The Growth and Development of English Literary Patronage," 222.
53 Binski, *The Painted Chamber at Westminster*, 93–103; Tudor-Craig, "The Painted Chamber at Westminster"; and Prestwich, *Edward I*, 119.
54 Salter, *English and International*, 30.
55 Crick, *The Historia Regum Britannie of Geoffrey of Monmouth*, 4: 22–9, catalogues manuscripts featuring texts of both Alexander and Arthur.
56 Salter, *English and International*, 29–30.
57 *Zacher Epitome*, 38–41.
58 Heng, *Empire of Magic*, 66.
59 Akbari, *Idols in the East*, 95.
60 Prestwich, *War, Politics and Finance under Edward I*, 78, 91.
61 Jahner, "The Poetry of the Second Barons' War," 200–3.
62 Matthews, *Writing to the King*, 37.
63 Ibid., 38–9.
64 Kendrick, "On Reading Medieval Political Verse," 188.
65 Smallwood, "The Prophecy of the Six Kings," 575.
66 Simpkin, "The English Army and the Scottish Campaign of 1310–1311," 28; and Richardson, *Magna Carta Ancestry*, 45.
67 Furrow, "*Chanson de geste* as Romance in England," 72.
68 Prestwich, *Plantagenet England*, 165.
69 Turville-Petre, *England the Nation*, 13. Bothwell, *Edward III and the English Peerage*, 3, defines the period between 1308–12 (the years of the Piers Gaveston crisis and the date range assigned to the Paris manuscript) and this failed baronial uprising of 1322 as the summation of Edward II's "unmitigated disaster as king" that would complicate his son's own sovereignty.

6. Moralizing Alexander in Durham Cathedral Library MS C.IV.27B

1 See, however, chapter 3, p. 57 and note 46.
2 Busby, *Codex and Context*, 1: 322–3. As *Anglo-Norman Alex.*, 2: 4, notes, although the manuscript lacks the illustrations of the Cambridge and

Paris copies, it retains their captions as chapter-headings, listed also in a table of contents in the first six folios of the manuscript.

3 The passages from Josephus, *Antiquitates Judaicae* are found on fols 77v and 116v; those from Orosius, *Historiae adversum paganos* on fols 85r, 88r, 105v, 107v, and 113r.

4 A fifth annotation on fol. 184v, likely drawn from the Valerius *Epitome*, refers to Candace's entrapment of the disguised Alexander in her palace: "Michi Alexander eris ceteris Antigonus uocaberis" (You will remain "Alexander" to me, but I will call you "Antigonus" in front of others).

5 Rud, *Codicum manuscriptorum Ecclesiae Cathedralis Dunelmensis catalogus classicus*, 312–13.

6 Busby, "Codices manuscriptos nudos tenemus," 266.

7 *Anglo-Norman Alex.*, 2: 70–2. In Ernest Thomas, trans., *The Love of Books*, 9, Richard muses that "Alexander, the conqueror of the earth ... would now have been unknown to fame, if the aid of books had been wanting."

8 "Richard de Bury's Books," 177. Cheney, "Richard de Bury, Borrower of Books," 325 notes that "after his death his executors allowed St Albans to buy back some [books] cheaply."

9 *Catalogi veteres librorum Ecclesiae cathedralis dunelm*, 1–10. The Cathedral Library also holds twelfth- and thirteenth-century copies of the *Antiquitates Judaicae* and Peter Comestor's *Historia scholastica*; see Ker, ed., *Medieval Libraries of Great Britain*, 66–7.

10 Lawrence-Mathers, *Manuscripts in Northumbria*, 19.

11 Piper, "The Libraries of the Monks of Durham," 220. For the inventories of 1391 and 1395 of the Spendiment and cloister books, respectively, see *Catalogi veteres*, 31–2, 56.

12 Kekewich, "Edward IV, William Caxton, and Literary Patronage in Yorkist England," 481.

13 In the assessment of Matthew, *Britain and the Continent 1000–1300*, 21, "language was not a shibboleth before 1300."

14 The introduction to Wogan-Browne, Watson, Taylor, and Evans, *The Idea of the Vernacular*, 4, notes that until 1370, "French was still a serious alternative vernacular for writers and audiences," and the question of writing in French or English remained "a social issue rather than a stylistic one." Miller, "The Death of French in Medieval England," 146, bluntly declares Anglo-Norman literature "dead" in England by ca. 1400.

15 Lodge, "The Sources of Standardisation in French – Written or Spoken?" 26.

16 See Marvin, "The Vitality of Anglo-Norman in Late Medieval England," 311.

17 *Anglo-Norman Alex.*, 2: 5–6.

18 Akbari, "Alexander in the Orient," 109.
19 Burton, *Monastic and Religious Orders in Britain 1000–1300*, 196–7.
20 See Schubert, *Jewish Historiography and Iconography*, 76–7; Gameson, *The Manuscripts of Early Norman England*, 24–5, 56; and Webber, "The Patristic Content," 197–9.
21 Baumgartner, "The Raid on Gaza in Alexandre de Paris's Romance," 37.
22 The interpolated passage transitions from this heartfelt exchange to the visit to Jerusalem rather awkwardly by identifying Darius as "proud" (l'orgoillus) and "arrogant" (buffois [fol. 116v]).
23 Legros, "Alexandre dans le *Roman de Toute Chevalerie*," 515.
24 See Dean, "Nicholas Trevet, Historian," for a survey of Trevet's sources. The *Historia ab origine mundi* (which Dean also refers to as the *Annales*) is unedited.
25 London, British Library, MS Royal 13. B. xvi, fols 150rv.
26 Cary, *The Medieval Alexander*, 19–21.
27 Here I take issues with Legros, "Alexandre dans le *Roman de Toute Chevalerie*," 523, who claims that Alexander does renounce his previous behaviour.
28 de Weever, "Candace in the Alexander Romances," 539, reads, for example, Candace's opulence and manner of dress as evocative of the whore of Babylon and argues that after encountering didactic opportunities to embrace humility and his own mortality, Alexander enjoys his lone sexual affair just before his murder in Babylon. The *Kyng Alisaunder*-poet, on the other hand, transforms Candace from a temptress into a lover; see Camargo, "The Metamorphosis of Candace."
29 Peckham and La Du, eds, *La Prise de Defur*, lii.
30 Ibid., lines 1581–4: "Quant un roialme as pris et mis en ton demaine, / S'un autre ne conquiers, ne vaus une castaingne; / Puis le tierc, puis le quart; oels est de tel diaigne / Quant qu'il voit tout couvoite, fais fu de male ouvraingne."
31 Ibid., lines 313–48.
32 Ibid., lines 341–4: "mais ses sens le detient, nel laisse desreer / Ne la dolour qu'il a dedens son cuer moustrer. / Trop est fiers Alixandres, qui trop ne se demente / De la mort."
33 Gosman, "Le *Roman d'Alexandre*," 69.
34 Zacher, ed., *Alexandri Magni Iter ad Paradisum*, 31–2. See above, chapter 1, 7.
35 Migne, ed., *Historia scholastica*, col. 1454.
36 See Bunt, "Alexander and the Universal Chronicle."
37 Lumby, ed., *Polychronicon Ranulphi Higden*, 3: 476.
38 Ibid., 4: 6.
39 Ibid., 4: 8.

40 Given-Wilson, *Chronicles*, 118.

41 See Hedicke, ed., *Q. Curti Rufi Historiarum Alexandri Magni libri qui supersunt*, 333 (9.6.25).

42 See Hilka and Söderhjelm, eds., *Petri Alfonsi Disciplina Clericalis*, 44–5.

43 Tubach, *Index Exemplorum: A Handbook of Medieval Religious Tales*, 15–19, lists an impressive fifty-nine types of anecdotes directly related to Alexander. To cite the most voluminous example, the *Gesta Romanorum*, perhaps compiled in England not long before the Paris manuscript of the *Roman de toute chevalerie*, refigures the well-known episode of Alexander dining incognito at his rival's banquet table (here Porus rather than Darius) and stealing his golden goblets as an allegory for Christ (Alexander) recovering lost souls (the drinking vessels) from Satan (Porus), one of several spiritually themed applications of the conqueror's career (Oesterley, ed., *Gesta Romanorum*, 610–11). See also ibid., 329–30, 334–6, 422, 504–5, 610–11, and 615 for anecdotes of Alexander.

44 Banks, ed., *An Alphabet of Tales*, 1: 33–4. For the transmission of the *Alphabet of Tales*, see Welter, *L'Exemplum dans la littérature religieuse*, 313–14, and Bunt, *Alexander the Great in the Literature of Medieval Britain*, 81–5.

45 *An Alphabet of Tales*, 2: 349–50.

46 See Loomis, "Alexander the Great's Celestial Journey," 136–40 ("Western" examples) and 177–85 ("Eastern" examples); and Schmidt, *A Legend and Its Image*. Wood, *Wooden Images*, 63–5, discusses its appearance on misericords in English cathedrals.

47 Ormrod, *Edward III*, 45–7.

48 See Stone, *From Tyrant to Philosopher-King*, 136–9.

49 See Hanna, *London Literature*, 116–17; and Michael, "A Manuscript Wedding Gift."

50 Vale, *Edward III and Chivalry*, 57–75.

51 Staniland, "Court Style, Painters, and the Great Wardrobe," 243, identifies a pillow of the king's decorated with scenes of Alexander's career.

52 Matthews, *Writing to the King*, 108.

53 Hanna, *London Literature*, 268.

54 Nederman, ed., *Political Thought in Early Fourteenth-Century England*, 122.

55 Ormrod, *Political Life in Medieval England*, 62.

56 Ibid., 63.

57 See especially McKendrick, *The History of Alexander the Great*; and Blondeau, *Un conquérant pour quatre ducs*.

58 Gellrich, *Discourse and Dominion*, 123–4.

59 The last folios of the Durham manuscript are mutilated or lost; for this passage, see *Anglo-Norman Alex.*, lines 7975–83.

60 McKisack, *The Fourteenth Century*, 96.
61 Goldberg, *Medieval England*, 163. See, e.g., Tait, ed., *Chronica Johannis de Reading*, 110–11 for the belief in the plague as divine punishment. Horrox, ed. and trans., *The Black Death*, 62–84, offers a range of contemporary responses to the outbreak of 1348.
62 Preest, trans., *The Chronicle of Geoffrey le Baker of Swinbrook*, 29–32.
63 Bryant, trans., *The True Chronicles of Jean le Bel*, 22. Cf., Johnes, trans., *Sir John Froissart's Chronicles*, 1: 4.
64 So reads "The Pipewell Chronicle on the deposition of Edward II, 1327," in *English Historical Documents III*, 3: 288. Cf., Thompson, ed., *Adae Murimuth Continuatio Chronicarum*, 1: 51.
65 Pope and Lodge, ed. and trans., *Life of the Black Prince*, 170.
66 Tyson, "The Epitaph of Edward the Black Prince," 99.
67 Brie, ed., *The Brut*, 1: 242–7.
68 To this list could be added *Piers Plowman*, which, as Jewell, "*Piers Plowman* – A Poem of Crisis," 59–80, argues, similarly reflects the social and political unrest caused by the Black Death and the reigns of Edward III and Richard II.
69 Lerner, *The Age of Adversity*, 31.

7. From Anglo-Norman to Middle English Alexander Romance

1 See Smithers, ed., *Kyng Alisaunder*, 2: 4–8 for a description of the Auchinleck and printed copies of the poem. All citations to *Kyng Alisaunder* refer to this edition (hereafter cited as *KA*).
2 *KA*, 2: 16–28, and Bunt, *Alexander the Great in the Literature of Medieval Britain*, 21.
3 Heng, "The Romance of England," 155.
4 Machan, *English in the Middle Ages*, 24–5.
5 Miller, "The Death of French in Medieval England," 147, notes that in a letter of 1295 Edward I declared that the French were "bent on wiping the English language off the earth."
6 Heng, "The Romance of England," 157.
7 Bunt, *Alexander the Great*, 20–1, discusses these unique omissions of the Indian wonders. This copy also features a B-text of *Piers Plowman*, a text that suggests a similar rationale for organizing this codex as that behind Bodley MS Laud Misc. 622.
8 Whitelock, ed., *The Seven Sages of Rome*, xii–xviii. For an alternative version of the text, see Brunner, ed., *The Seven Sages of Rome (Southern Version)*.

9 *KA*, 2: 40–1, argues that one author accounted for *Kyng Alisaunder*, *Richard Coer de Lion*, and *Of Arthour and Merlin*, but Macrae-Gibson ed., *Of Arthour and Merlin*, 2: 65–75, presents a thorough counter-argument.

10 Brunner, ed., *Der mittelenglische Versroman über Richard Löwenherz*, lines 7–20.

11 Ibid., lines 21–2.

12 Macrae-Gibson, ed., *Of Arthour and Merlin*, lines 18–30. Butler, "A Failure to Communicate," reads this, however, as a criticism, rather than praise for the dominance of English at the expense of the other two languages.

13 Finlayson, "'*Richard, Coer de Lyon*,'" 157. For the development of the romance Richard in the mid-thirteenth century, see Gillingham, "Some Legends of Richard the Lionheart"; and "The Unromantic Death of Richard I"; and Broughton, *The Legends of King Richard I, Coeur de Lion*.

14 Finlayson, "Legendary Ancestors," 306.

15 See Nicholson, *Chronicle of the Third Crusade*, 148. Ambroise, roughly contemporaneous with Thomas, cites Alexander in Ailes and Barber, eds, *The History of the Holy War*, 89, only in terms of his death ("Alexander, whose death aroused such strong feelings").

16 Calkin, "Violence, Saracens, and English Identity." Ramey, *Christian, Saracen and Genre in Medieval French Literature*, 44, notes that Saracens in romances can refer to various types of enemies.

17 Finlayson, "'Richard, Coer de Lyon,'" 179.

18 McDonald, "Eating People," 129–30.

19 Turville-Petre, *England the Nation*, 115.

20 Ambrisco, "Cannibalism and Cultural Encounters in *Richard Coeur de Lion*," 508, argues that Richard's cannibalism and curious mother in the A-version transform him into a ghoulish figure in his own right. Akbari, "The Hunger for National Identity," 201, offers another reading of Richard's eastern ancestry that further associates him with Alexander: "Richard's ability to be a western conqueror comes from his eastern origin. The territory he seeks to conquer, in a sense, already belongs to him."

21 Brunner, ed., *Der mittelenglische Versroman über Richard Löwenherz*, lines 6335–44.

22 Ibid., lines 7207–8.

23 Ibid., lines 7251–2.

24 Turville-Petre, *England the Nation*, 115.

25 These vivid lyrical portraits of the seasons and courtly life appear throughout *Kyng Alisaunder*. See Pearsall and Salter, *Landscapes and Seasons*, 136–9; and Scattergood, "Validating the High Life."

26 *Zacher Epitome*, 29: "His Alexander auditis statuam complexus patrem salutat, eiusque se filium profitetur."

27 Cf., Justin, *Epitome of the Philippic History of Pompeius Trogus*, 51–2, in which Alexander bribes the priests at the temple of Jupiter Ammon to proclaim that he is the god's son.

28 *KA*, lines 91–100. The success of Nectanabus, who has used sorcery to ward off previous invaders, inspires "grete onde" in other kings, including Philip, plagued by "grete thede." In the *Valerius Epitome* and the *Roman de toute chevalerie*, the coalition comes – without provocation – from as far away as India.

29 Chism, "Winning Women in Two Middle English Alexander Poems," 24.

30 See Stone, "'Many man he shal do woo.'"

31 Cf., Justin, *Epitome of the Philippic History of Pompeius Trogus*, 60–2, wherein Alexander kills his veteran general Clitus, and in his grief, secludes himself and refuses to eat, until his men implore him to put aside his guilt and lead them out of hostile lands.

32 Bunt, "Alexander's Last Days in the Middle English *Kyng Alisaunder*," offers the most detailed discussion of Alexander's unique will and death in this romance.

33 Ibid., 219.

34 In *Zacher Epitome*, 63, this compromise is commanded by the oracle of Apollo; and in *Anglo-Norman Alex.*, lines 7975–6, a divine voice tells Alexander's successors to end their quarrels and quickly fulfil the will of God by burying the corpse in Alexandria.

35 *KA*, lines 8006–7.

36 The first two alliterative romances are edited, respectively, in Skeat, ed., *The Romance of William of Palerne*, 177–218; and Skeat, ed., *Alexander and Dindimus*.

37 Duggan and Turville-Petre, eds., *The Wars of Alexander*, xlii, date the poem from the mid-fourteenth century to ca. 1450, when its earlier manuscript, Oxford, Bodley MS Ashmole 44, was compiled.

38 Chism, *Alliterative Revivals*, 37, and Duggan and Turville-Petre, eds., *The Wars of Alexander*, xlii.

39 Chism, *Alliterative Revivals*, 129.

40 Chism, "Too Close for Chivalry," 118.

41 For a survey of the Nine Worthies, see Schroeder, *Der Topos der Nine Worthies*.

42 Turville-Petre, "A Lost Alliterative Alexander Romance," identifies the fragments of the now missing Middle English translation of the *Voeux du paon*.

43 Lampe, "The Poetic Strategy of *The Parlement of the Thre Ages,*" 182. See also Peck, "The Careful Hunter in *The Parlement of the Thre Ages,*" 338.
44 Krishna, ed., *The Alliterative Morte Arthure.*
45 Porter, "Gower's Ethical Microcosm and Political Macrocosm," 152, argues, for example, that in the accounts of Alexander as the son of Nectanabus in Book Six and the student of Aristotle in Book Seven, "there is clear evidence that Gower planned his poem to culminate in an explicit 'mirror for princes.'"
46 For a detailed study of Gower's alteration to the *Roman de toute chevalerie,* see Beidler, "Diabolical Treachery in the Tale of Nectanabus."
47 Peck, *Kingship and Common Profit,* 137.
48 Nicholson, *Love and Ethics in Gower's Confessio Amantis,* 328.
49 All citations refer to Macaulay, ed., *The English Works of John Gower.*
50 Although as Olsson, *John Gower and the Structures of Conversion,* 188, argues, in her excitement over the possibility of bearing a mighty king and in her promise to bestow riches upon Nectanabus, "[Olympias's] is hardly a humble, restrained, or modest submission to a god's will."
51 Peck, *Kingship and Common Profit,* 136.
52 Macaulay, ed., *The Complete Works of John Gower,* 1: lines 22073–80.
53 See Stone, *From Tyrant to Philosopher-King,* 141–63.
54 Grady, "The Lancastrian Gower," 563–4.
55 Peck, "The Politics and Psychology of Governance in Gower," 237.
56 Grady, "The Lancastrian Gower," 564.
57 Cf. Orosius, *Pauli Orosii Historiarum adversum paganos,* ed. Zangemeister, 88: "Alexander uero apud Babylonam, cum adhuc sanguinem sitiens male castigata auiditate ministri insidiis uenenum potasset, interiit" (Alexander died in Babylon, when he was still thirsting for blood and in drinking poison his greed was foully punished by the treachery of an attendant).
58 Macaulay, ed., *The Complete Works of John Gower,* 1: 6.7, 14, 21.
59 Ibid., 4: lines 6.1107–12.
60 One other Middle English Alexander text survives from the fifteenth century: see Westlake, ed., *The Prose Life of Alexander from the Thornton MS,* which is a translation of the same source-text (the *I*[3] recension of the *Historia de preliis*) used for *The Wars of Alexander.*

Afterword

1 *Perceforest* survives in four manuscripts of the second half of the fifteenth century: Paris, Bibliothèque Nationale MSS fr. 109, 345, 346, and 347.

2 Huot, *Postcolonial Fictions*, 2.
3 Ibid., 7–8.
4 Bryant, *Perceforest*, 36.
5 Jane H.M. Taylor, "Alexander Amoroso," 226.
6 Bryant, *Perceforest*, 145.
7 Szkilnik, "Conquering Alexander," 213.
8 Gaullier-Bougassas, "Alexandre le Grand," 411.
9 Lods, *Le Roman Perceforest*," 259.
10 Jane H.M. Taylor, "The Sense of a Beginning," 108–9.
11 Szkilnik, "Conquering Alexander," 203.
12 Bryant, *Perceforest*, 55. An old man at the temple explains to Alexander that "eleven years ago there appeared a bird in Greece that has since grown to an unimaginable size, and by the last day of this year it will have grown so great that it will have outgrown the world, spreading its wings over all the earth, but the next day I could cover that bird with my mantle." Gaullier-Bougassas, "Alexandre le Grand," 415–16, argues that Alexander both accepts his mortal limitations in the romance and acknowledges that the gods control his fate.
13 Szkilnik, "Conquering Alexander," 214.
14 Huot, *Postcolonial Fictions*, 9.
15 Vale, *Edward III and Chivalry*, 45.
16 Barber, "Imaginary Buildings."
17 "The Library of Margaret of York," 262.
18 Carley, *The Libraries of King Henry VIII*, 3.
19 Ibid., 112, n. 37.
20 See Arnold, "The Prophecy of Daniel"; Magoun, "The *St Albans Compilation*"; and Ross, "Some Notes on the Old French Alexander Romance in Prose."
21 See Ross, *Alexander Historiatus*, 11–12, 18–20, 54–7, and 69–71, for a catalogue of the illustrated manuscripts of these works, many of which date to the fourteenth and fifteenth century.
22 Ritchie, ed., *The Buik of Alexander*; and Cartwright, ed., *The Buik of King Alexander the Conquerour*.
23 See Stone, "Chaucer's Alexander the Great and the Monk's Tale."
24 See Stone, *From Tyrant to Philosopher-King*, 168–80; and Bunt, *Alexander the Great in the Literature of Medieval Britain*, 43–52.

Works Cited

Manuscripts

Parva recapitulatio de eodem Alexandro et de suis. Cambridge, University Library MSS Mm. V. 29, fols 155r–6v.

Parva recapitulatio de eodem Alexandro et de suis. London, British Library, MS Royal 15. C. vi, fols 129v–30v.

Parva recapitulatio de eodem Alexandro et de suis. Cambridge, University Library, MS Dd. X. 24, fols 169v–70v.

Parva recapitulatio de eodem Alexandro et de suis. London, British Library, MS Cotton, Cleopatra D. v, fols 181v–3r.

Parva recapitulatio de eodem Alexandro et de suis. London, British Library, MS Harley 5054, fols 178r–81r.

Parva recapitulatio de eodem Alexandro et de suis. London, British Library, MS Royal 13. A. i, fols 94v–8v.

St Albans Compilation. Cambridge, Corpus Christi College, MS 219, fols 1r–64r.

Thomas of Kent. *Roman de toute chevalerie.* Cambridge, Trinity College, MS O.9.34.

Thomas of Kent. *Roman de toute chevalerie.* Durham, Cathedral Library, MS C.IV.27B.

Thomas of Kent. *Roman de toute chevalerie.* Oxford, Bodleian Library, MS Lat. Misc. b. 17.

Thomas of Kent. *Roman de toute chevalerie.* Paris, Bibliothèque nationale de France, MS fr. 24364.

Trevet, Nicolas. *Historia ab origine mundi.* London, British Library, MS Royal 13. B. xvi.

Primary Sources

Ailes, Marianne, and Malcolm Barber, eds. *The History of the Holy War: Ambroise's Estoire de la guerre sainte*. Woodbridge: Boydell, 2003.

Armstrong, E.C., ed. *The Medieval French Roman d'Alexandre*. 7 vols. Princeton: Princeton University Press, 1937–76.

Armstrong, E.C., ed. *Version of Alexandre de Paris: Variants and Notes to Branch IV*. Vol. 7 of *The Medieval French Roman d'Alexander*, edited by E.C. Armstrong. Princeton: Princeton University Press, 1955.

Armstrong, E.C., and Alfred Foulet, eds. *Le roman du fuerre de gadres d'Eustache essai d'établissement de ce poème du XIIe siècle tel qu'il existé avant d'être incorporé dans le Roman d'Alexandre, avec les deux récits latins qui lui sont apparentés*. Vol. 4 of *The Medieval French Roman d'Alexander*, edited by E.C. Armstrong. Princeton: Princeton University Press, 1942.

Armstrong, E.C., D.L. Buffum, Bateman Edwards, and L.F.H. Lowe, eds. *Version of Alexandre de Paris: Text*. Vol. 2 of *The Medieval French Roman d'Alexander*, edited by E.C. Armstrong. Princeton: Princeton University Press, 1937.

Arnold, T., ed. *Symeonis Monachi Opera Omnia*. 2 vols. Rolls Series 75. London: Longman, 1882–5.

Ausfeld, Adolf, ed. *Der Griechische Alexanderroman*. Leipzig: Teubner, 1907.

Baker, A.T., and Alexander Bell, eds. *St. Modwenna*. Anglo-Norman Text Society 7. London: Anglo-Norman Text Society, 1947.

Banks, Mary MacLeod, ed. *An Alphabet of Tales: An English 15th Century Translation of the Alphabetum narrationum of Etienne de Besançon, from additional ms. 25, 719 of the British Museum*. 2 vols. EETS 126–7. London: Kegan Paul, Trench, Trüber & Co., 1904–5.

Bergmeister, Hermann-Josef, ed. *Die Historia de preliis Alexandri Magni (Der lateinische Alexanderroman des Mittelalters): Synoptische Edition der Rezensionen des Leo Archipresbyter und der interpolierten Fassungen I1, I2, I3 (Buch I und II)*. Beiträge zur Klassischen Philologie 65. Meisenheim am Glan: Hain, 1975.

Boer, W. Walther, ed. *Epistola Alexandri ad Aristotelem*. Beiträge zur klassischen Philologie 50. Meisenheim am Glan: Hain, 1973.

Brewer, J.S., ed. *Giraldi Cambrensis opera*. 8 vols. Rolls Series 21. London, 1861–91.

Brie, Friedrich W.D., ed. *The Brut or the Chronicles of England*. 2 vols. EETS 131, 136. London: Kegan Paul, Trubner, 1906–8.

Brunner, Karl, ed. *Der mittelenglische Versroman über Richard Löwenherz*. Wiener Beiträge zur englischen Philologie 42. Vienna: Wilhelm Braumuller, 1913.

Brunner, Karl, ed. *The Seven Sages of Rome (Southern Version)*. EETS 191. London: H. Milford, 1933.

Bryant, Nigel. *Perceforest: The Prehistory of King Arthur's Britain.* Cambridge: D.S. Brewer, 2011.

Burgess, Glyn S., trans. *The History of the Norman People: Wace's Roman de Rou.* Woodbridge: Boydell Press, 2004.

Callu, Jean-Pierre, trans. *Julius Valère, Roman d'Alexandre.* Turnhout: Brepols, 2010.

Cartwright, John, ed. *The Buik of King Alexander the Conquerour.* 2 vols. STS, 4th series 16, 18. Edinburgh: Scottish Text Society, 1986–90.

Chibnall, Marjorie, ed. and trans. *The Ecclesiastical History of Orderic Vitalis.* 6 vols. Oxford: Clarendon Press, 1969–80.

Childs, Wendy R., ed. and trans. *Vita Edwardi Secundi: The Life of Edward the Second.* Oxford: Clarendon Press, 2005.

Darlington, R.R., and P. McGurk, eds. and Jennifer Bray and P. McGurk, trans. *The Chronicle of John of Worcester.* 3 vols. Oxford: Clarendon Press, 1995–8.

DiMarco, Vincent, and Leslie Perelman, eds. *The Middle English Letter of Alexander to Aristotle.* Amsterdam: Rodopi, 1978.

Duggan, Hoyt N., and Thorlac Turville-Petre, eds. *The Wars of Alexander.* EETS SS 10. Oxford: Oxford University Press, 1989.

Fahlin, Carin, ed. *Chronique des ducs de Normandie.* Uppsala: Almquist & Wiksells, 1951–67.

Foulet, Alfred, ed. *Version of Alexandre de Paris: Introduction and Notes to Branch III.* Vol. 6 of *The Medieval French Roman d'Alexander,* edited by E.C. Armstrong. Princeton: Princeton University Press, 1976.

Foulet, Alfred, ed. *Version of Alexandre de Paris: Variants and Notes to Branch I.* Vol. 3 of *The Medieval French Roman d'Alexander,* edited by E.C. Armstrong. Princeton: Princeton University Press, 1949.

Gibbs, Vicary, ed. *Complete Peerage of England, Scotland, Ireland, Great Britain and the United Kingdom, extant, extinct or dormant.* 2nd ed. 13 vols. London: St Catherine Press, 1910–98.

Gough, Henry, ed. *Scotland in 1298: Documents Relating to the Campaign of King Edward the First.* London: A. Gardner, 1888.

Gui de Cambrai. *Le Vengement Alixandre.* Edited by Bateman Edwards. Elliott Monographs 23. New York: Kraus Reprint, 1965.

Hedicke, Edmund, ed. *Q. Curti Rufi Historiarum Alexandri Magni libri qui supersunt.* Leipzig: Teubner, 1908.

Henry of Huntingdon. *Historia Anglorum: The History of the English People.* Edited and translated by Diana Greenway. Oxford: Clarendon Press, 1993.

Hewlett, H.G., ed. *Liber qui dicitur Flores Historiarum ab anno Domini MCLIV annoque Henrici Anglorum regis Secundi primo.* 3 vols. Rolls Series 84. London: Longman, 1886–9.

Hilka, Alfons, ed. *Historia Alexandri Magni (Historia de preliis): Rezension J*[2] *(Orosius-Rezension)*. 2 vols. Beiträge zur klassischen Philologie 79, 89. Meisenheim am Glan, 1976–7.

Hilka, Alfons, and Karl Steffens, eds. *Historia Alexandri Magni (Historia de preliis), Rezension J*[1]. Beiträge zur Klassischen Philologie 107. Meisenheim am Glan: Hain, 1979.

Hilka, Alfons, and Werner Söderhjelm, eds. *Petri Alfonsi Disciplina Clericalis*. Acta societatis scientiarum fennicae 38, no. 4. Helsingfors: Druckerci der Finnischen-Litteratur-Geselschaft, 1911.

Holden, A.J., ed. *Le Roman de Waldef (Cod. Bodmer 168)*. Texte (Bibliotheca Bodmeriana) 5. Cologne: Fondation Martin Bodmer, 1984.

Holden, A.J., ed., S. Gregory, and D. Crouch, trans. *History of William Marshal*. 3 vols. Anglo-Norman Text Society Occasional Publications 4–6. London: Anglo-Norman Text Society, 2002–6.

Horrox, Rosemary, ed. and trans. *The Black Death*. Manchester: Manchester University Press, 1994.

James, M.R., ed. *A Catalogue of the Manuscripts in Gonville and Caius College, Cambridge*. Cambridge: Cambridge University Press, 1914.

James, M.R., ed. *The Western Manuscripts in the Library of Trinity College, Cambridge*. 4 vols. Cambridge: Cambridge University Press, 1904.

Jehan le Nevelon. *La Venjance Alixandre*. Edited by Edward Billings Ham. Princeton: Princeton University Press, 1931.

Johnes, Thomas, trans. *Sir John Froissart's Chronicles of England, France and the Adjoining Countries*. 2 vols. London: Longman & Co., 1812.

Johnston, R.C., ed. *Jordan Fantosme's Chronicle*. Oxford: Clarendon Press, 1981.

Josephus. *Jewish Antiquities*. Translated by Ralph Marcus. 10 vols. London: W. Heinemann, 1926–81.

Justin. *Epitome of the Philippic History of Pompeius Trogus, Books 11–12: Alexander the Great*. Translated by J.C. Yardley. Oxford: Oxford University Press, 1997.

Kazis, Israel J., ed. *The Book of the Gests of Alexander of Macedon: Sefer Toledot Alexandros ha-Makdoni*. Cambridge, MA: The Mediaeval Academy of America, 1962.

Ker, N.R., ed. *Medieval Libraries of Great Britain: A List of Surviving Books*. London: Royal Historical Society, 1987.

Kinzel, Karl, ed. *Lamprechts Alexander*. Halle: Waisenhaus, 1884.

Kratz, Dennis M., trans. *The Romances of Alexander*. New York: Garland, 1991.

Krishna, Valerie, ed. *The Alliterative Morte Arthure: A Critical Edition*. New York: Burt Franklin, 1976.

Kuebler, Bernard, ed. *Juli Valeri Alexandri Polemi, Res Gestae Alexandri Macedonis*. Leipzig: Teubner, 1888.

La Du, Milan Sylvanus, ed. *Text of the Arsenal and Venice Versions*. Vol. 1 of *The Medieval French Roman d'Alexander*, edited by E.C. Armstrong. Princeton: Princeton University Press, 1937.

Luard, H.R., ed. *Matthaei Parisiensis, Monachi Sancti Albani. Chronica Majora*. 7 vols. Rolls Series 57. London: Longman, 1872–84.

Lumby, J.R., ed. *Polychronicon Ranulphi Higden, Monachi Cestrensis; together with the English Translation of John of Trevisa and of an unknown writer in the 15th century*. 9 vols. Rolls Series 41. London: Longman, 1865–6.

Macaulay, G.C., ed. *The Complete Works of John Gower*. 4 vols. Oxford: Clarendon Press, 1899–1902.

Macaulay, G.C., ed. *The English works of John Gower*. 2 vols. EETS 81–2. London: K. Paul, Trench, Trübner & Co., 1900–1.

Macrae-Gibson, O.D., ed. *Of Arthour and Merlin*. 2 vols. EETS 268, 279. Oxford: Oxford University Press, 1973–9.

Marvin, Julia. *The Oldest Anglo-Norman Prose Brut Chronicle: An Edition and Translation*. Woodbridge: Boydell Press, 2006.

Nederman, Cary J., ed and trans. *Political Thought in Early Fourteenth-Century England: Treatises by Walter of Milemete, William of Pagula, and William of Ockham*. Tempe: Arizona Center for Medieval and Renaissance Studies, 2002.

Nicholson, Helen J. *Chronicle of the Third Crusade: A Translation of the Itinerarium peregrinorum et Gesta Regis Ricardi*. Aldershot: Ashgate, 1997.

Nicolas, Nicholas Harris, ed. *The Siege of Carlaverock*. London: J.B. Nichols, 1828.

Oesterley, Hermann, ed. *Gesta Romanorum*. Berlin: Weidmann, 1872.

Orosius. *Historiarum adversum paganos libri VII*. Edited by Karl Zangemeister. Corpus scriptorum ecclesiasticorum Latinorum 5. Leipzig: Teubner, 1882.

Peckham, Lawton P.G., and Milan S. La Du, eds. *La Prise de Defur and Le Voyage d'Alexandre au paradis terrestre*. Elliott Monographs 35. New York: Kraus Reprint, 1965.

Peter Comestor. *Historia scholastica*. Patrologia Latina 198, ed. J.P. Migne. Turnhout: Brepols, 1855.

Pfister, Friedrich, ed. *Der Alexanderroman des Archipresbyters Leo*. Heidelberg: C. Winter, 1913.

Pfister, Friedrich, ed. *Kleine texte zum Alexanderroman: Commonitorium Palladii, Briefwechsel zwischen Alexander und Dindimus, Brief Alexanders über die Wunder Indiens*. Heidelberg: C. Winter, 1910.

Pope, Mildred K., and Eleanor C. Lodge, eds. and trans. *Life of the Black Prince by the Herald of Sir John Chandos*. Oxford: Clarendon Press, 1910.

Preest, David, trans. *The Chronicle of Geoffrey le Baker of Swinbrook*. Woodbridge: Boydell & Brewer, 2012.

Quilichinus de Spoleto. *Historia Alexandri Magni*. Edited by Wolfgang Kirsch. Skopje: Univerzitetska pečatnica, 1971.

Ritchie, R.L. Graeme, ed. *The Buik of Alexander*. 4 vols. STS, NS 12, 17, 21, 25. Edinburgh: Blackwood, 1921–9.

Rosellini, Michaela, ed. *Iuli Valeri Res gestae Alexandri Macedonis translatae ex Aesopo Graeco*. Stuttgart: Teubner, 1993.

Rothwell, Harry, ed. *The Chronicle of Walter of Guisborough*. Camden Series 89. London: Royal Historical Society, 1957.

Short, Ian, ed. and trans. *Geffrei Gaimar, Estoire des Engleis: History of the English*. Oxford: Oxford University Press, 2009.

Skeat, Walter W., ed. *Alexander and Dindimus: or, The letters of Alexander to Dindimus, King of the Brahmans, with the replies of Dindimus; being a second fragment of the alliterative romance of Alisaunder*. EETS ES 31. London: N. Trübner & Co., 1878.

Skeat, Walter W., ed. *The Romance of William of Palerne*. EETS ES 1. London: Kegan Paul, Trench, Trübner, 1890.

Smithers, G.V., ed. *Kyng Alisaunder*. 2 vols. EETS 227, 237. London, 1952–7.

Steele, Robert, ed. *Opera hactenus inedita Rogeri Baconi*. 16 vols. Oxford: Clarendon Press, 1909–41.

Steffens, Karl, ed. *Die Historia de preliis Alexandri Magni: Rezension J3*. Beiträge zur klassischen Philologie 73. Meisenheim am Glan: Hain, 1975.

Stephenson, Joseph, trans. *Contemporary Chronicles of the Middle Ages: Sources of Twelfth-Century History*. Dyfed: Llanerch Enterprises, 1988.

Stoneman, Richard, trans. *The Greek Alexander Romance*. New York: Penguin, 1991.

Stubbs, William, ed. *Chronicles of the Reigns of Edward I and Edward II*. 2 vols. Rolls Series 76. London: Longman & Co., 1883.

Tait, James, ed. *Chronica Johannis de Reading et anonymi Cantuariensis, 1346–1367*. Manchester: Manchester University Press, 1914.

Thomas of Kent. *The Anglo-Norman Alexander = Le roman de toute chevalerie*. Edited by Brian Foster, with the assistance of Ian Short. 2 vols. London: Anglo-Norman Text Society, 1976–7.

Thomas of Kent. *Le roman d'Alexandre, ou, Le roman de toute chevalerie*. Translated by Catherine Gaullier-Bougassas and Laurence Harf-Lancner. Paris: H. Champion, 2003.

Thomas, Ernest, trans. *The Love of Books: The Philobiblion of Richard de Bury*. London: Moring, 1907.

Thompson, E.M., ed. *Adae Murimuth Continuatio Chronicarum. Robertus de Avesbury De gestis mirabililbus regis Edwardi Tertii*. Rolls Series 93. London: Eyre and Spottiswoode, 1889.

Van Bekkum, W. Jac., ed. *A Hebrew Alexander Romance according to MS London, Jews' College no. 145*. Orientalia Lovaniensia Analecta 47. Leuven: Peeters, 1992.

Van Houts, Elisabeth M.C., ed. and trans. *The Gesta Normannorum Ducum of William of Jumièges, Orderic Vitalis, and Robert of Torigni*. 2 vols. Oxford: Clarendon Press, 1992.

Walter of Châtillon. *The Alexandreis*. Edited by Marvin L. Colker. Padua: Antenore, 1978.

Walter of Châtillon. *The Alexandreis: A Twelfth-Century Epic*. Translated by David Townsend. Philadelphia: University of Pennsylvania Press, 2007.

Westlake, J.S., ed. *The Prose Life of Alexander from the Thornton MS*. EETS 143. London: Kegan Paul, Trench, Trübner, 1913.

Whitelock, Jill, ed. *The Seven Sages of Rome (Midland Version)*. EETS 324. Oxford: Oxford University Press, 2005.

William of Malmesbury, *Gesta regum Anglorum, The History of the English Kings*. Edited and translated by R.A.B. Mynors. 2 vols. Oxford: Clarendon Press, 1998–9.

Wright, Neil, ed. *The Historia regum Britannie of Geoffrey of Monmouth*. 5 vols. Cambridge: D.S. Brewer, 1984–91.

Wright, Thomas, ed. and trans. *The Chronicle of Pierre de Langtoft*. 2 vols. Rolls Series 47. London: Longmans, Green, Reader, and Dyer, 1868.

Wright, Thomas, ed. and trans. *The Political Songs of England, from the Reign of John to that of Edward II*. Camden Society 6. London: J.B. Nichols and Son, 1839.

Wright, Thomas, ed. *The Roll of Arms of the Princes, Barons, and Knights who attended King Edward I to the Siege of Caerlaverock in 1300*. London: J.C. Hotten, 1864.

Wright, William Aldis, ed. *The Metrical Chronicle of Robert of Gloucester*. 2 vols. Rolls Series 86. London: Eyre and Spottiswoode, 1887.

Zacher, Julius, ed. *Alexandri Magni Iter ad Paradisum*. Königsberg: T. Theile, 1859.

Zacher, Julius, ed. *Julii Valerii epitome*. Halle: Waisenhaus, 1867.

Zettl, Ewald, ed. *An Anonymous Short English Metrical Chronicle*. EETS OS 196. London: Oxford University Press, 1935.

Secondary Sources

Abril, Christine. "Les Enfances d'Alexandre: Essai de comparaison entre le *Roman d'Alexandre* et le *Libro de Alexandre*." *Pris-ma* 13 (1997): 1–12.

Abulafia, David. *Frederick II: A Medieval Emperor*. New York: Oxford University Press, 1988.

Aerts, W.J. "Alexander the Great in 'Exempla' and 'Similitudines' in Byzantine Literature." In *Exemplum et Similitudo: Alexander the Great and Other Heroes as Points of Reference in Medieval Literature*, edited by W.J. Aerts and M. Gosman, 1–18. Groningen: Forsten, 1988.

Agard, Frederick B. "Anglo-Norman Versification and the *Roman de toute chevalerie.*" *Romanic Review* 33 (1942): 216–35.

Ailes, Marianne. "What's in a Name? Anglo-Norman Romances or *Chansons de geste?*" In *Medieval Romance, Medieval Contexts*, edited by Rhiannon Purdie and Michael Cichon, 61–75. Cambridge: Cambridge University Press, 2011.

Akbari, Suzanne Conklin. "Alexander in the Orient: Bodies and Boundaries." In *Postcolonial Approaches to the European Middle Ages: Translating Cultures*, edited by Ananya Jahanara Kabir and Deanne Williams, 105–26. Cambridge: Cambridge University Press, 2005.

Akbari, Suzanne Conklin. "The Hunger for National Identity in *Richard Coer de Lion.*" In *Reading Medieval Culture: Essays in Honor of Robert W. Hanning*, edited by Robert M. Stein and Sandra Pierson Prior, 198–227. Notre Dame: University of Notre Dame Press, 2005.

Akbari, Suzanne Conklin. *Idols in the East: European Presentations of Islam and the Orient, 1100–1450.* Ithaca: Cornell University Press, 2009.

Ambrisco, Alan S. "Cannibalism and Cultural Encounters in *Richard Coeur de Lion.*" *Journal of Medieval and Early Modern Studies* 29, no. 3 (1999): 499–528.

Anderson, A.R. *Alexander's Gate, Gog and Magog, and the Inclosed Nations.* Cambridge, MA: The Mediaeval Academy of America, 1932.

Arnold, F. "The Prophecy of Daniel in the *Old French Prose Alexander.*" *French Studies* 17 (1963): 324–30.

Ashe, Laura. *Fiction and History in England, 1066–1200.* Cambridge: Cambridge University Press, 2007.

Ashurst, David. "Alexander the Great." In *Heroes and Anti-Heroes in Medieval Romance*, edited by Neil Cartlidge, 27–41. Cambridge: D.S. Brewer, 2012.

Avril, François, and Patricia Danz Stirnemann, eds. *Manuscrits enluminés d'origine insulaire, viie–xxe siècle.* Paris: Bibliothéque nationale, 1987.

Baldwin, John W. *The Government of Philip Augustus: Foundations of French Royal Power in the Middle Ages.* Berkeley: University of California Press, 1986.

Barber, Richard. "Imaginary Buildings." In *Edward III's Round Table at Windsor: The House of the Round Table and the Windsor Festival of 1344*, edited by Julian Munby, Richard Barber, and Richard Brown, 100–16. Woodbridge: Boydell & Brewer, 2007.

Barrett, Christopher. "Roland and Crusade Imagery in an English Royal Chapel: Early Thirteenth-Century Wall Paintings in Claverley Church, Shropshire." *The Antiquaries Journal* 92 (2012): 129–68.

Baswell, Christopher. "Marvels of Translation and Crises of Transition in the Romances of Antiquity." In *The Cambridge Companion to Medieval Romance*, edited by Roberta L. Krueger, 29–44. Cambridge: Cambridge University Press, 2000.

Batt, Catherine, and Rosalind Field. "The Romance Tradition." In *The Arthur of the English: The Arthurian Legend in Medieval English Life and Literature*, edited by W.R.J. Barron, 59–70. Cardiff: University of Wales Press, 2001.

Baumgartner, Emmanuèle. "Figures du Destinateur: Salomon, Arthur, le roi Henri d'Angleterre." In *Anglo-Norman Anniversary Essays*, edited by Ian Short, 1–10. Anglo-Norman Text Society Occasional Publications Series 2. London: Anglo-Norman Text Society, 1993.

Baumgartner, Emmanuèle. "La formation du mythe d'Alexandre au XIIe siècle: Le *Roman d'Alexandre* et l'exotisme." In *Conter de Troie et d'Alexandre: pour Emmanuèle Baumgartner*, edited by Laurence Harf-Lancner, and Michelle Szkilnik, 146–53. Paris: Presses Sorbonne nouvelle, 2006.

Baumgartner, Emmanuèle. "The Raid on Gaza in Alexandre de Paris's Romance." In *The Medieval French Alexander*, edited by Donald Maddox and Sara Sturm-Maddox, 29–38. Albany: State University of New York Press, 2002.

Bedford, Kathryn. "Fouke le Fitz Waryn: Outlaw or Chivalric Hero?" In *British Outlaws of Literature and History: Essays on Medieval and Early Modern Figures from Robin Hood to Twm Shon Catty*, edited by Alexander L. Kaufman, 97–113. Jefferson: McFarland & Co., 2011.

Beer, Jeanette M.A. *Narrative Conventions of Truth in the Middle Ages*. Geneva: Librairie Droz, 1981.

Beidler, Peter G. "Diabolical Treachery in the Tale of Nectanabus." In *John Gower's Literary Transformations in the Confessio Amantis: Original Articles and Translations*, edited by Peter G. Beidler, 83–90. Washington, DC: University Press of America, 1982.

Bennett, Matthew. "Poetry as History? The 'Roman de Rou' of Wace as a Source for the Norman Conquest." In *Anglo-Norman Studies V: Proceedings of the Battle Conference*, edited by R. Allen Brown, 21–39. Woodbridge: Boydell Press, 1982.

Benton, John F. "The Court of Charlemagne as a Literary Center." In *Culture, Power and Personality in Medieval France*, edited by Thomas N. Bisson, 3–43. London: Hambledon Continuum, 1991.

Bildhauer, Bettina. "Blood, Jews and Monsters in Medieval Culture." In *The Monstrous Middle Ages*, edited by Bettina Bildhauer and Robert Mills, 75–96. Toronto: University of Toronto Press, 2003.

Binski, Paul. *Medieval Death: Ritual and Representation*. Ithaca: Cornell University Press, 1996.

Binski, Paul. *The Painted Chamber at Westminster*. London: The Society of Antiquaries of London, 1986.

Binski, Paul. "The Painted Chamber at Westminster, the Fall of Tyrants and the English Literary Model of Governance." *Journal of the Warburg and Courtauld Institutes* 74 (2011): 121–54.

Binski, Paul. *Westminster Abbey and the Plantagenets: Kingship and the Representation of Power, 1200–1400*. New Haven: Yale University Press, 1995.

Bisson, Thomas N. *The Crisis of the Twelfth Century: Power, Lordship, and the Origins of European Government*. Princeton: Princeton University Press, 2009.

Blacker, Jean. *The Faces of Time: Portrayal of the Past in Old French and Latin Historical Narrative of the Anglo-Norman Regnum*. Austin: University of Texas Press, 1994.

Blacker, Jean. "'La geste est grande, longue et grieve a translater': History for Henry II." *Romance Quarterly* 37, no. 4 (1990): 387–96.

Blondeau, Chrystèle. *Un conquérant pour quatre ducs: Alexandre le Grand à la cour de Bourgogne*. Paris: CTHS-Institut national d'Histoire de l'Art, 2009.

Blumenfeld-Kosinski, Renate. *Reading Myth: Classical Mythology and Its Interpretations in Medieval French Literature*. Palo Alto: Stanford University Press, 1997.

Blurton, Heather. "From *Chanson de Geste* to Magna Carta: Genre and the Barons in Matthew Paris's *Chronica Majora*." *New Medieval Literatures* 9 (2007): 117–38.

Boffito, G. "La leggenda aviatoria di Alessandro Magno." *La Bibliofilia* 23 (1921–2): 316–30.

Borenius, Tancred. "The Cycle of Images in the Palaces and Castles of Henry III." *Journal of the Warburg and Courtauld Institutes* 6 (1943): 40–50.

Bothwell, J.S. *Edward III and the English Peerage: Royal Patronage, Social Mobility and Political Control in Fourteenth-Century England*. Woodbridge: Boydell & Brewer, 2004.

Britt, Karen C. "Roger II of Sicily: Rex, Basileus, and Khalif? Identity, Politics, and Propaganda in the Cappella Palatina." *Mediterranean Studies* 16 (2007): 21–45.

Broughton, Bradford B. *The Legends of King Richard I, Coeur de Lion: A Study of Sources and Variations to the Year 1600*. The Hague: Mouton, 1966.

Brucker, Charles. "Le personnage de Frédéric II dans la poésie lyrique d'oc du XIIIe siècle." In *Studia Occitanica in memoriam Paul Remy*, edited by Hans-Erich Keller, 1: 31–44. Kalamazoo: Medieval Institute Publications, 1986.

Bruckner, Matilda Tomaryn. *Shaping Romance: Interpretation, Truth, and Closure in Twelfth-Century French Fictions*. Philadelphia: University of Pennsylvania Press, 1993.

Bryant, Nigel, trans., *The True Chronicles of Jean le Bel, 1290–1360*. Woodbridge: Boydell & Brewer, 2011.

Bunt, G.H.V. "Alexander and the Universal Chronicle: Scholars and Translators." In *The Medieval Alexander Legend and Romance Epic*, edited by Peter Noble, Lucie Polak, and Claire Isoz, 1–10. Millwood: Kraus International, 1982.

Bunt, G.H.V. "Alexander's Last Days in the Middle English *Kyng Alisaunder*." In *Alexander the Great in the Middle Ages: Ten Studies on the Last Days of Alexander in Literary and Historical Writing*, edited by W.J. Aerts, Jos. M.M. Hermans, and Elizabeth Visser, 202–29. Nijmegen: Alfa Nijmegan, 1978.

Bunt, G.H.V. *Alexander the Great in the Literature of Medieval Britain*. Groningen: E. Forsten, 1994.

Bunt, G.H.V. "An Exemplary Hero: Alexander the Great." In *Companion to Middle English Romance*, edited by Henk Aertsen and Alasdair A. MacDonald, 30–55. Amsterdam: VU University Press, 1990.

Burgess, Glyn S. "The Term 'Chevalerie' in Twelfth-Century French." In *Medieval Codicology, Iconography, Literature, and Translation: Studies for Keith Val Sinclair*, edited by Peter Rolfe Monks and D.D.R. Owen, 343–58. Leiden: Brill, 1994.

Burnett, Charles, and Patrick Gautier Dalché. "Attitudes Towards the Mongols in Medieval Literature: The XXII Kings of Gog and Magog from the Court of Frederick II to Jean de Mandeville." *Viator* 22 (1991): 153–67.

Burton, Janet. *Monastic and Religious Orders in Britain 1000–1300*. Cambridge: Cambridge University Press, 1994.

Busby, Keith. *Codex and Context Reading Old French Verse Narrative in Manuscript*. 2 vols. Amsterdam: Rodopi, 2002.

Busby, Keith. "Codices manuscriptos nudos tenemus: Alexander and the New Codicology." In *The Medieval French Alexander*, Edited by Donald Maddox and Sara Sturm-Maddox, 259–73. Albany: State University of New York Press, 2002.

Busby, Keith. "Narrative Genres." In *The Cambridge Companion to Medieval French Literature*, edited by Simon Gaunt and Sarah Kay, 139–52. Cambridge: Cambridge University Press, 2008.

Busby, Keith. "'Neither Flesh nor Fish, Nor Good Red Herring': The Case of Anglo-Norman Literature." In *Studies in Honor of Hans-Erich Keller: Medieval*

French and Occitan Literature and Romance Linguistics, edited by Rupert T. Pickens, 399–417. Kalamazoo: Western Michigan University, 1993.

Buschinger, Danielle. "German Alexander Romances." In *A Companion to Alexander Literature in the Middle Ages*, edited by Z. David Zuwiyya, 291–314. Leiden: Brill, 2011.

Butler, Patrick. "A Failure to Communicate: Multilingualism in the Prologue to *Of Arthour and of Merlin*." In *The Auchinleck Manuscript: New Perspectives*, edited by Susanna Fein, 52–66. York: York Medieval Press, 2016.

Calin, William. *The French Tradition and the Literature of Medieval England*. Toronto: University of Toronto Press, 1994.

Calkin, Siobhain Bly. "Violence, Saracens, and English Identity in *Of Arthour and of Merlin*." *Arthuriana* 14, no. 2 (2004): 17–36.

Callu, Jean-Pierre. "Lire Julius Valère." In *L'historiographie médiévale d'Alexandre le Grand*, edited by Catherine Gaullier-Bougassas, 37–47. Turnhout: Brepols, 2011.

Callu, Jean-Pierre, and Michel Festy. "L''Alexandre latin': Léon de Naples et sa première interpolation (J[1])." In *L'historiographie médiévale d'Alexandre le Grand*, edited by Catherine Gaullier-Bougassas, 49–64. Turnhout: Brepols, 2011.

Camargo, Martin. "The Metamorphosis of Candace and the Earliest English Love Epistle." In *Court and Poet: Selected Proceedings of the Third Congress of the International Courtly Literature Society (Liverpool 1980)*, edited by Glyn S. Burgess, 101–11. Liverpool: Francis Cairns, 1981.

Campopiano, Michele. "*Gentes, monstra, fere*: l'*Histoire d'Alexandre* dans une encyclopédie du XIIe siècle." In *Conter de Troie et d'Alexandre: pour Emmanuèle Baumgartner*, edited by Laurence Harf-Lancner, Laurence Mathey-Maille, and Michelle Szkilnik, 233–52. Paris: Presses Sorbonne nouvelle, 2006.

Campopiano, Michele. "Parcours de la légende d'Alexandre en Italie. Réflexions sur la réception italienne de l'*Historia de preliis* J2 (XIIe–XVe siècle)." In *L'historiographie médiévale d'Alexandre le Grand*, edited by Catherine Gaullier-Bougassas, 65–83. Turnhout: Brepols, 2011.

Carley, James P. *The Libraries of King Henry VIII*. Corpus of British Medieval Library Catalogues 7. London: British Library, 2000.

Carney, Elizabeth. *Olympias, Mother of Alexander the Great*. New York: Routledge, 2006.

Carpenter, D.A. "A Noble in Politics: Roger Mortimer in the Period of Baronial Reform and Rebellion, 1258–1265." In *Nobles and Nobility in Medieval Europe: Concepts, Origins, Transformations*, edited by Anne J. Duggan, 183–204. Woodbridge: Boydell Press, 2000.

Cary, George. *The Medieval Alexander*. Edited by D.J.A. Ross. Cambridge: Cambridge University Press, 1956.

Castiñeiras, Manuel. "L'Alessandro anglonormanno e il mosaico di Otranto: Una ekphrasis monumentale?" *Troianalexandrina* 4 (2004): 41–86.

Catalogi veteres librorum Ecclesiae cathedralis dunelm. London: J.B Nichols and Son, 1838.

Chazan, Robert. *The Jews of Medieval Western Christendom, 1000–1500*. Cambridge: Cambridge University Press, 2006.

Cheney, Christopher R. "Richard de Bury, Borrower of Books." *Speculum* 48, no. 2 (1973): 325–8.

Chism, Christine. *Alliterative Revivals*. Philadelphia: University of Pennsylvania Press, 2002.

Chism, Christine. "Too Close for Chivalry: Dis-Orienting Chivalry in the *Wars of Alexander*." In *Text and Territory: Geographical Imagination in the European Middle Ages*, edited by Sylvia Tomasch and Sealy Gilles, 116–39. Philadelphia: University of Pennsylvania Press, 1998.

Chism, Christine. "Winning Women in Two Middle English Alexander Poems." In *Women and Medieval Epic: Gender, Genre, and the Limits of Epic Masculinity*, edited by Sara S. Poor and Jana K. Schulman, 15–39. New York: Palgrave Macmillan, 2007.

Clanchy, M.T. *From Memory to Written Record*. 2nd ed. Oxford: Blackwell, 1993.

Clark, James. *A Monastic Renaissance at St Albans: Thomas Walsingham and His Circle, c. 1350–1440*. Oxford: Oxford University Press, 2004.

Crawford, Donna. "Prophecy and Paternity in *The Wars of Alexander*." *English Studies* 73, no. 5 (1992): 406–16.

Crick, Julia C. *The Historia Regum Britannie of Geoffrey of Monmouth IV: Dissemination and Reception in the Later Middle Ages*. Cambridge: D.S. Brewer, 1991.

Cruse, Mark. *Illuminating the Roman d'Alexandre: Oxford, Bodleian Library, MS Bodley 264: The Manuscript as Monument*. Gallica 22. Cambridge: Cambridge University Press, 2011.

D'Avray, D.L. *Death and the Prince: Memorial Preaching before 1350*. Oxford: Clarendon Press, 1994.

Damian-Grint, Peter. "*Estoire* as Word and Genre: Meaning and Literary Usage in the Twelfth Century." *Medium Aevum* 66, no. 2 (1997): 189–206.

Damian-Grint, Peter. *The New Historians of the Twelfth-Century Renaissance: Inventing Vernacular Authority*. Woodbridge: Boydell Press, 1999.

Dannenbaum, Susan. "Anglo-Norman Romances of English Heroes: 'Ancestral Romance'?" *Romance Philology* 35, no. 4 (1982): 601–8.

de Weever, Jaqueline. "Candace in the Alexander Romances: Variations on the Portrait Theme." *Romance Philology* 43 (1990): 529–46.

Dean, Ruth J., ed. *Anglo-Norman Literature: A Guide to Texts and Manuscripts.* Anglo-Norman Text Society, Occasional Publications Series 3. London: Anglo-Norman Text Society, 1999.

Dean, Ruth. "Nicholas Trevet, Historian." In *Medieval Learning and Literature: Essays Presented to R.W. Hunt*, edited by J.J.G. Alexander and M.T. Gibson, 328–52. Oxford: Clarendon Press, 1976.

Dimitrokalis, Giorgio. "L'ascensione di Alessandro Magno nell'Italia del Medioevo." *Thesaurismata* 4 (1967): 214–22.

Dionisotti, A.C. "The Letter of Mardochaeus the Jew to Alexander the Great." *Journal of the Warburg and Courtauld Institutes* 51 (1988): 1–13.

Dönitz, Saskia. "Alexander the Great in Medieval Hebrew Traditions." In *A Companion to Alexander Literature in the Middle Ages*, edited by Z. David Zuwiyya, 21–39. Leiden: Brill, 2011.

Douglas, Davis, C., ed. *English Historical Documents, III: 1189–1327.* Edited by Harry Rothwell. London: Routledge, 1975.

Douglas, David C. *The Norman Fate, 1100–1154.* Berkeley: University of California Press, 1976.

Field, Rosalind. "The Anglo-Norman Background to Alliterative Romance." In *Middle English Alliterative Poetry and Its Literary Background: Seven Essays*, edited by David Lawton, 54–69. Woodbridge: D.S. Brewer, 1982.

Field, Rosalind. "'Pur les francs homes amender': Clerical Authors and the Thirteenth-Century Context of Historical Romance." In *Medieval Romance, Medieval Contexts*, edited by Rhiannon Purdie and Michael Cichon, 175–88. Cambridge: Cambridge University Press, 2011.

Finlayson, John. "Legendary Ancestors and the Expansion of Romance in Richard, Coer de Lyon." *English Studies* 79, no. 4 (1998): 299–308.

Finlayson, John. "Richard, Coer de Lyon: Romance, History or Something in Between?" *Studies in Philology* 87, no. 2 (1990): 156–80.

Foster, Brian. "The *Roman de toute chevalerie* and Its Date and Author." *French Studies* 9 (1955): 154–8.

Foulet, Alfred. "La date du *Roman de toute chevalerie.*" In *Mélanges offerts à Rita Lejeune, professeur à l'Université de Liège*, 2: 1205–10. Gembloux: Duculot, 1969.

Franks, John. "Taste and Patronage in Late Medieval England as Reflected in Versions in *Guy of Warwick.*" *Medium Aevum* 66 (1997): 80–93.

Friede, Susanne. "Alexanders Kindheit in der französischen Zehnsilberfassung und in *Roman d'Alexandre*: Fälle 'literarischer Nationalisierung' des Alexanderstoffs." In *Alexanderdichtungen im Mittelalter: kulturelle*

Selbstbestimmung im Kontext literarischer Beziehungen, edited by Jan Cölln, Susanne Friede, and Hartmut Wulfram, 82–136. Göttingen: Wallstein, 2000.

Friedman, John Block. *The Monstrous Races in Medieval Art and Thought*. Cambridge, MA: Harvard University Press, 1981.

Fries, Maureen. "Boethian Themes and Tragic Structure in Geoffrey of Monmouth's *Historia Regum Britanniae*." In *The Arthurian Tradition: Essays in Convergence*, edited by Mary Flowers Braswell and John Bugge, 29–42. Tuscaloosa: University of Alabama Press, 1988.

Fryde, Natalie. *The Tyranny and Fall of Edward II, 1321–1326*. Cambridge: Cambridge University Press, 1979.

Furrow, Melissa. "Chanson de geste as Romance in England." In *The Exploitations of Medieval Romance*, edited by Laura Ashe, Ivana Djordjević, and Judith Weiss, 57–72. Cambridge: Cambridge University Press, 2010.

Galbraith, V.H. *Historical Research in Medieval England*. London: Athlone Press, 1951.

Galbraith, V.H. *Matthew Paris and Roger Wendover*. Glasgow: University of Glasgow, 1944.

Galbraith, V.H. "Nationality and Language in Medieval England." *Transactions of the Royal Historical Society*, 4th series, 23 (1941): 113–28.

Gameson, Richard. *The Manuscripts of Early Norman England (c. 1066–1130)*. Oxford: Oxford University Press, 1999.

Garnett, George. *Conquered England: Kingship, Succession, and Tenure, 1066–1166*. Oxford: Oxford University Press, 2007.

Gaunt, Simon. "French Literature Abroad: Towards an Alternative History of French Literature." *Interfaces* 1 (2015): 25–61.

Gaullier-Bougassas, Catherine. "Alexandre le Grand et la conquête de l'Ouest dans les *Romans d'Alexandre* du XIIe siècle, leurs mises en prose au XVe siècle et le *Perceforest*." *Romania* 118 (2000): 83–104, 394–430.

Gaullier-Bougassas, Catherine. "Quêtes d'immortalité ou de salut: des origines grecque et hébraïque aux réinterprétations orientales." In *Les voyages d'Alexandre au paradis Orient et Occident*, edited by Catherine Gaullier-Bougassas and Margaret Bridges, 15–45. Turnhout: Brepols, 2013.

Gaullier-Bougassas, Catherine. *Les romans d'Alexandre: aux frontières de l'épique et du Romanesque*. Paris: H. Champion, 1998.

Gellrich, Jesse M. *Discourse and Dominion in the Fourteenth Century: Oral Contexts of Writing in Philosophy, Politics, and Poetry*. Princeton: Princeton University Press, 1995.

Georgianna, Linda. "Coming to Terms with the Norman Conquest: Nationalism and English Literary History." In *REAL: Yearbook of Research in English and*

American Literature 14: Literature and the Nation, edited by Brook Thomas, 33–53. Tübingen: Narr Francke Attempto, 1998.

Gero, Stephen. "The Legend of Alexander the Great in the Christian Orient." *Bulletin of the John Rylands University Library of Manchester* 75 (1993): 3–9.

Gillingham, John. "Events and Opinions: Norman and English Views of Aquitaine, c.1152–c.1204." In *The World of Eleanor of Aquitaine: Literature and Society in Southern France between the Eleventh and Thirteenth Centuries*, edited by Marcus Bull and Catherine Léglu, 75–101. Woodbridge: Boydell & Brewer, 2005.

Gillingham, John. "Some Legends of Richard the Lionheart: Their Development and Their Influence." In *Richard Coeur de Lion in History and Myth*, edited by Janet L. Nelson, 51–69. London: Centre for Late Antique and Medieval Studies, King's College, 1992.

Gillingham, John. "The Unromantic Death of Richard I." *Speculum* 54, no. 1 (1979): 18–41.

Given-Wilson, Chris. *Chronicles: The Writing of History in Medieval England*. London: Hambledon, 2004.

Godman, Peter. "The Archpoet and the Emperor." *Journal of the Warburg and Courtauld Institutes* 74 (2011): 31–58.

Godman, Peter. "Transmontani: Frederick Barbarossa, Rainald of Dassel, and Cultural Identity in the German Empire." *Beiträge zur Geschichte der Deutschen Sprache und Literatur* 132, no. 2 (2010): 200–29.

Goldberg, P.J.P. *Medieval England, A Social History, 1250–1550*. London: Arnold, 2004.

Gosman, Martin. "The French Background." In *Companion to Middle English Romance*, edited by Henk Aertsen and Alasdair A. MacDonald, 1–27. Amsterdam: VU University Press, 1990.

Gosman, Martin. "La genèse du *Roman d'Alexandre*: quelque aspects." *Bien dire et bien aprandre* 6 (1988): 25–44.

Gosman, Martin. *La légende d'Alexandre le Grand dans la littérature française du 12e siècle: une réécriture permanente*. Amsterdam: Rodopi, 1997.

Gosman, Martin. "La Matière 'classique' dans la littérature française: Les métacommentaires auctoriels (12e–16e siècles)." In *Mediaeval Antiquity*, edited by Andries Welkenhuysen, Herman Braet, and Werner Verbeke, 255–76. Mediaevalia Lovaniensia series 1, 24. Leuven: Leuven University Press, 1995.

Gosman, Martin. "Le *Roman d'Alexandre*. Les interpolations du XIIIe siècle." In *Le Roman antique au Moyen Age: actes du Colloque du Centre d'études médiévales de l'Université de Picardie, Amiens, 14–15 janvier 1989*, edited by Danielle Buschinger, 61–72. Göppinger Arbeiten zur Germanistik 549. Göppinger: Kümmerle, 1992.

Goukowsky, Paul. *Essai sur les origines du mythe d'Alexandre 336–270 av. J.C.* 2 vols. Nancy: Université de Nancy, 1978–81.

Grady, Frank. "The Lancastrian Gower and the Limits of Exemplarity." *Speculum* 70, no. 3 (1995): 552–75.

Gransden, Antonia. *Historical Writing in England*. 2 vols. Ithaca: Cornell University Press, 1974.

Gransden, Antonia. *Legends, Traditions and History in Medieval England*. London: Hambledon Press, 1992.

Green, D.H. *The Beginnings of Medieval Romance: Fact and Fiction 1150–1220*. Cambridge: Cambridge University Press, 2007.

Green, Judith A. *The Aristocracy of Norman England*. Cambridge: Cambridge University Press, 1997.

Green, Judith A. *Henry I, King of England and Duke of Normandy*. Cambridge: Cambridge University Press, 2006.

Guerin, M. Victoria. *The Fall of Kings and Princes: Structure and Destruction in Arthurian Tragedy*. Palo Alto: Stanford University Press, 1995.

Gunderson, Lloyd L. "Early Elements in the Alexander Romance." In *Ancient Macedonia: Papers Read at the First International Symposium Held in Thessaloniki, 26–29 August 1968*, edited by Basil Laourdas and Ch. Makaronas, 353–75. Thessaloniki: Institute for Balkan Studies, 1970.

Hahn, Thomas. "The Middle English Letter of Alexander to Aristotle." *Mediaeval Studies* 41 (1979): 117–45.

Haines, Roy Martin. *King Edward II: Edward of Caernarfon: His Life, His Reign, and Its Aftermath, 1284–1330*. Montreal: McGill-Queen's University Press, 2003.

Hanna, Ralph. *London Literature, 1300–1380*. Cambridge: Cambridge University Press, 2005.

Harding, Alan. *England in the Thirteenth Century*. Cambridge: Cambridge University Press, 1993.

Harf-Lancner, Laurence. "From Alexander to Marco Polo, from Text to Image: The Marvels of India." In *The Medieval French Alexander*, edited by Donald Maddox and Sara Sturm-Maddox, 235–57. Albany: State University of New York Press, 2002.

Heer, Friedrich. *The Holy Roman Empire*. Translated by Janet Sondheimer. New York: Praeger, 1968.

Heng, Geraldine. *Empire of Magic: Medieval Romance and the Politics of Cultural Fantasy*. New York: Columbia University Press, 2003.

Heng, Geraldine. "The Romance of England: Richard Coer de Lyon, Saracens, Jews, and the Politics of Race and Nation." In *The Postcolonial Middle Ages*, edited by Jeffrey Jerome Cohen, 135–71. New York: St Martin's Press, 2000.

Hilka, A., and F.P. Magoun. "A List of Manuscripts Containing Texts of the *Historia de Preliis Alexandri Magni, Recensions* I^1, I^2, I^3." *Speculum* 9 (1934): 84–6.

Hill, Betty. "The Middle English and Latin Versions of the *Parva recapitulation.*" *Notes and Queries* NS 27 (1980): 4–20.

Holt, J.C. "The St Albans Chroniclers and Magna Carta." *Transactions of the Royal Historical Society*, 5th Series, 14 (1964): 67–88.

Howlett, D.R. *The English Origins of Old French Literature*. Dublin: Four Courts, 1996.

Huot, Sylvia. *Postcolonial Fictions in the Roman de Perceforest: Cultural Identities and Hybridities*. Gallica 1. Woodbridge: D.S. Brewer, 2007.

Ingham, Patricia Clare. *Sovereign Fantasies: Arthurian Romance and the Making of Britain*. Philadelphia: University of Pennsylvania Press, 2001.

Ingham, Richard. "The Persistence of Anglo-Norman 1230–1362: A Linguistic Perspective." In *Language and Culture in Medieval Britain: The French of England c.1100–c.1500*, edited by Jocelyn Wogan-Browne, 44–54. Woodbridge: York Medieval Press, 2009.

Jahner, Jennifer. "The Poetry of the Second Barons' War: Some Manuscript Contexts." In *English Manuscripts before 1400*, edited by A.S.G. Edwards and Orietta Da Rold, 200–22. English Manuscript Studies, 1100–1700 17. London: British Library, 2012.

Jewell, Helen. "*Piers Plowman* – A Poem of Crisis: An Analysis of Political Instability in Langland's England." In *Politics and Crisis in Fourteenth-Century England*, edited by John Taylor and Wendy Childs, 59–80. Wolfeboro Falls: A. Sutton, 1990.

Jouanno, Corinne. *Naissance et metamorphosis du Roman d'Alexandre, Domaine grec*. Paris: CNRS Editions, 2002.

Kay, Sarah. *The Chansons de geste in the Age of Romance: Political Fictions*. Oxford: Oxford University Press, 1995.

Kekewich, Margaret. "Edward IV, William Caxton, and Literary Patronage in Yorkist England." *Modern Language Review* 66 (1971): 481–7.

Kelly, Douglas. *The Art of Medieval French Romance*. Madison: University of Wisconsin Press, 1992.

Kendrick, Laura. "On Reading Medieval Political Verse: Two Poems from the Reign of Edward II." *Mediaevalia* 5 (1979): 183–204.

Kinoshita, Sharon. *Medieval Boundaries: Rethinking Difference in Old French Literature*. Philadelphia: University of Pennsylvania Press, 2006.

Kratz, Dennis M. *Mocking Epic: Waltharius, Alexandreis and the Problem of Christian Heroism*. Madrid: Porrúa Turanzas, 1980.

Lafferty, Maura K. *Walter of Châtillon's Alexandreis: Epic and the Problem of Historical Understanding*. Turnhout: Brepols, 1998.

Lampe, David. "The Poetic Strategy of *The Parlement of the Thre Ages.*" *Chaucer Review* 7, no. 3 (1973): 173–83.

Lawrence-Mathers, Anne. *Manuscripts in Northumbria in the Eleventh and Twelfth Centuries.* Woodbridge: Brewer, 2003.

Le Goff, Jacques. *The Medieval Imagination*. Translated by Arthur Goldhammer. Chicago: University of Chicago Press, 1988.

Le Saux, Françoise H.M. "The Languages of England: The Multilingualism in the Work of Wace." In *Language and Culture in Medieval Britain: The French of England, c.1100–c.1500*, edited by Jocelyn Wogan-Browne, 188–97. Woodbridge: York Medieval Press, 2009.

Legge, M. Dominica. *Anglo-Norman in the Cloisters: The Influence of the Orders upon Anglo-Norman Literature*. Edinburgh: Edinburgh University Press, 1950.

Legge, M. Dominica. *Anglo-Norman Literature and Its Background*. Oxford: Clarendon Press, 1963.

Legros, Huguette. "Alexandre dans le *Roman de Toute Chevalerie* de Thomas de Kent, un itinéraire spirituel des dieux à Dieu." In *Romans d'antiquité et littérature du Nord: Mélanges offerts à Aimé Petit*, edited by Sarah Baudelle-Michels, Marie-Madeleine Castellani, Philippe Logié, and Emmanuelle Poulain-Gautret, 515–29. Paris: Champion, 2007.

Lerner, Robert E. *The Age of Adversity: The Fourteenth Century*. Ithaca: Cornell University Press, 1968.

Lethaby, W.R. "English Primitives IV: The Westminster and Chertsey Tiles." *Burlington Magazine for Connoisseurs* 30 (1917): 133–40.

Lewis, Suzanne. *The Art of Matthew Paris in the Chronica Majora*. Berkeley: University of California Press, 1987.

"The Library of Margaret of York and Some Related Books." In *Margaret of York, Simon Marmion, and the Visions of Tondal: Papers delivered at a symposium organized by the Department of Manuscripts of the J. Paul Getty Museum in collaboration with the Huntington Library and Art Collections, June 21–24, 1990*, edited by Thomas Kren, 257–62. Malibu: J. Paul Getty Museum, 1992.

Lodge, R. Anthony. "The Sources of Standardisation in French – Written or Spoken?" In *The Anglo-Norman Language and Its Contexts*, edited by Richard Ingham, 26–43. Woodbridge: York Medieval Press, 2010.

Lods, Jeanne. *Le Roman Perceforest: Origines, Composition, Caractères, Valeur et Influence*. Geneva: Droz, 1951.

Lomax, John Phillip. "Frederick II, His Saracens, and the Papacy." In *Medieval Christian Perceptions of Islam: A Book of Essays*, edited by John Victor Tolan, 175–97. New York: Taylor & Francis, 1996.

Loomis, R.S. "Alexander the Great's Celestial Journey ('Eastern' examples)." *Burlington Magazine for Connoisseurs* 32 (1918): 177–85.

Loomis, R.S. "Alexander the Great's Celestial Journey ('Western' examples)." *Burlington Magazine for Connoisseurs* 32 (1918): 136–40.

Lucas, Peter. "The Growth and Development of English Literary Patronage in the Later Middle Ages and Early Renaissance." *The Library*, 6th series, 4, no. 3 (1982): 219–48.

Lynde-Recchia, Molly. *Prose, Verse, and Truth-Telling in the Thirteenth Century: An Essay on Form and Function in Selected Texts, Accompanied by an Edition of the Prose Thebes as Found in the Histoire ancienne jusqu'à César*. Lexington, KY: French Forum, 2000.

Machan, Tim William. *English in the Middle Ages*. Oxford: Oxford University Press, 2003.

Maddox, Donald. *The Arthurian Romances of Chretien de Troyes: Once and Future Fictions*. Cambridge: Cambridge University Press, 1991.

Magoun, Francis. "The St Albans Compilation and the *Old French Prose Alexander*." *Speculum* 1 (1926): 225–32.

Martin, Jean-Marie. *Italies normandes, XIe–XIIe siècles*. Paris: Hachette, 1994.

Marvin, Julia. "The English *Brut* Tradition." In *A Companion to Arthurian Literature*, edited by Helen Fulton, 221–34. Malden: Wiley-Blackwell, 2009.

Marvin, Julia. "John and Henry III in the Anglo-Norman Prose *Brut*." In *Thirteenth Century England XIV: Proceedings of the Aberystwyth and Lampeter Conference, 2011*, edited by Janet Burton, Phillipp Schofield, and Björn Weiler, 169–82. Woodbridge: Boydell Press, 2013.

Marvin, Julia. "The Vitality of Anglo-Norman in Late Medieval England: The Case of the Prose *Brut* Chronicle." In *Language and Culture in Medieval Britain: The French of England c. 1100–c. 1500*, edited by Jocelyn Wogan-Browne, 303–19. Woodbridge: York Medieval Press, 2009.

Masroori, Cyrus. "Alexander in the City of the Excellent: A Persian Tradition of Utopia." *Utopian Studies* 24.1 (2013): 52–65.

Matthew, Donald. *Britain and the Continent 1000–1300*. London: Hodder Arnold, 2005.

Matthew, Donald. *The Norman Kingdom of Sicily*. Cambridge: Cambridge University Press, 1992.

Matthews, David. *Writing to the King: Nation, Kingship, and Literature in England, 1250–1350*. Cambridge Studies in Medieval Literature 77. Cambridge: Cambridge University Press, 2010.

McDonald, Nicola. "Eating People and the Alimentary Logic of *Richard Cœur de Lion*." In *Pulp Fictions of Medieval England: Essays in Popular Romance*, edited by Nicola McDonald, 124–50. Manchester: Manchester University Press, 2004.

McGinn, Bernard. *Visions of the End: Apocalyptic Traditions in the Middle Ages*. New York: Columbia University Press, 1979.

McKendrick, Scot. *The History of Alexander the Great: An Illuminated Manuscript of Vasco da Lucena's French Translation of the Ancient Text by Quintus Curtius Rufus*. Los Angeles: J. Paul Getty Museum, 1996.

McKisack, May. *The Fourteenth Century, 1307–1399*. Oxford: Clarendon Press, 1959.

Merkelbach, Reinhold. *Die Quellen des Griechischen Alexanderromans*. Munich: Beck, 1977.

Meuwese, Martine. "The Exploits of Alexander the Great in Trinity College." In *The Cambridge Illuminations: The Conference Papers*, edited by Stella Panayotova, 129–37. London: Harvey Miller, 2007.

Meyer, Paul. *Alexandre le Grand dans la littérature française du moyen âge*. 2 vols. Paris: Vieweg, 1886.

Michael, Ian. "Typological Problems in Medieval Alexander Literature: The Enclosure of Gog and Magog." In *The Medieval Alexander Legend and Romance Epic: Essays in Honour of David J.A. Ross*, edited by Peter Noble, Lucie Polak, and Claire Isoz, 131–47. Millwood: Kraus International, 1982.

Michael, Michael A. "A Manuscript Wedding Gift from Philippa of Hainault to Edward III." *Burlington Magazine* (1985): 582–99.

Miller, D. Gary. "The Death of French in Medieval England." In *Romance Phonology and Variation: Selected Papers from the 30th Linguistic Symposium on Romance Languages, Gainesville, Florida, February 2000*, edited by Caroline R. Wiltshire and Joaquim Camps, 145–59. Philadelphia: John Benjamins, 2002.

Millet, Gabriel. "L'Ascension d'Alexandre." *Syria* 4 (1923): 91–5.

Momigliano, Arnaldo. "Flavius Josephus and Alexander's Visit to Jerusalem." *Athenaeum* NS 57 (1979): 442–8.

Morgan, Nigel. *Early Gothic Manuscripts*. Survey of Manuscripts Illuminated in the British Isles 4. London: Harvey Miller, 1982.

Morosini, Roberta. "The Alexander Romance in Italy." In *A Companion to Alexander Literature in the Middle Ages*, edited by Z. David Zuwiyya, 329–64. Leiden: Brill, 2011.

Mortensen, Lars Boje. "Orosius and Justinus in One Volume: Post-Conquest Books across the Channel." *Cahiers de l'institut du Moyen-Âge grec et latin* 60 (1990): 388–99.

Newman, Charlotte A. *The Anglo-Norman Nobility in the Reign of Henry I: The Second Generation*. Philadelphia: University of Pennsylvania Press, 1988.

Nicholson, Peter. *Love and Ethics in Gower's Confessio Amantis*. Ann Arbor: University of Michigan Press, 2005.

Noble, Peter. "Romance in England and Normandy in the Twelfth Century." In *England and Normandy in the Middle Ages*, edited by David Bates and Anne Curry, 69–78. London: Hambledon Press, 1994.

Oakeshott, Walter. *The Artists of the Winchester Bible and Sigena: Romanesque Paintings in Spain and the Winchester Bible Artists*. London: Faber and Faber, 1945.

Oakeshott, Walter. *Classical Inspiration in Medieval Art*. New York: Praeger, 1960.

Olsson, Kurt. *John Gower and the Structures of Conversion: A Reading of the Confessio Amantis*. Cambridge: D.S. Brewer, 1992.

Orchard, Andy. *A Critical Companion to Beowulf*. Cambridge: D.S. Brewer, 2003.

Orchard, Andy. *Pride and Prodigies: Studies in the Monsters of the "Beowulf" Manuscript*. Cambridge: D.S. Brewer, 1995.

Ormrod, W.M. *Edward III*. New Haven: Yale University Press, 2011.

Ormrod, W.M. *Political Life in Medieval England, 1300–1450*. New York: St Martin's Press, 1995.

Ortenberg, Veronica. *The English Church and the Continent in Tenth and Eleventh Centuries*. Oxford: Clarendon Press, 1992.

Over, Kristen Lee. *Kingship, Conquest, and Patria: Literary and Cultural Identities in Medieval French and Welsh Arthurian Romance*. New York: Routledge, 2005.

Pächt, Otto. *The Rise of Pictorial Narrative in Twelfth-Century England*. Oxford: Clarendon Press, 1962.

Partner, Nancy F. *Serious Entertainments: The Writing of History in Twelfth-Century England*. Chicago: University of Chicago Press, 1977.

Pearsall, Derek, and Elizabeth Salter. *Landscapes and Seasons of the Medieval World*. Toronto: University of Toronto Press, 1973.

Peck, Russell A. "The Careful Hunter in *The Parlement of the Thre Ages*." *English Literary History* 39, no. 3 (1972): 332–41.

Peck, Russell A. *Kingship and Common Profit in Gower's Confessio Amantis*. Carbondale: Southern Illinois University Press, 1978.

Peck, Russell A. "The Politics and Psychology of Governance in Gower: Ideas of Kingship and Real Kings." In *A Companion to Gower*, edited by Sian Echard, 215–38. Cambridge: D.S. Brewer, 2004.

Perry, B.E. "The Egyptian Legend of Nectanabus." *Transactions and Proceedings of the American Philological Association* 97 (1966): 327–33.

Petit, Aimé. "Les romans antiques et Alexandre." In *Alexandre le Grand dans les littératures occidentales et proche-orientales: actes du colloque de Paris, 27–29 novembre 1999*, edited by Laurence Harf-Lancner, Claire Kappler, and Françoise Suard, 289–302. Nanterre: Centre des Sciences de la Littérature Université Paris X-Nanterre, 1999.

Phillips, J.R.S. *Aymer de Valence, Earl of Pembroke, 1307–1324: Baronial Politics in the Reign of Edward II*. Oxford: Clarendon Press, 1972.

Piper, A.J. "The Libraries of the Monks of Durham." In *Medieval Scribes, Manuscripts & Libraries: Essays Presented to N.R. Ker*, edited by M.B. Parkes and Andrew G. Watson, 213–50. London: Scolar Press, 1978.

Polignac, Fr. De. "L'image d'Alexandre dans la littérature arabe: l'Orient face à l'hellénisme?" *Arabica* 29, no. 3 (1982): 296–306.

Porter, Elizabeth. "Gower's Ethical Microcosm and Political Macrocosm." In *Gower's Confessio Amantis: Responses and Reassessments*, edited by A.J. Minnis, 135–62. Woodbridge: Brewer, 1983.

Potter, K.R, ed. and trans. *Gesta Stephani*. Oxford: Clarendon Press, 2004.

Prestwich, Michael. *Edward I*. New Haven: Yale University Press, 1997.

Prestwich, Michael. "The Ordinances of 1311 and the Politics of the Early Fourteenth Century." In *Politics and Crisis in Fourteenth-Century England*, edited by John Taylor and Wendy Childs, 1–18. Wolfeboro Falls: Sutton, 1990.

Prestwich, Michael. *Plantagenet England, 1225–1360*. Oxford: Oxford University Press, 2005.

Prestwich, Michael. *The Three Edwards: War and State in England, 1272–1377*. London: Methuen, 1980.

Prestwich, Michael. *War, Politics and Finance under Edward I*. Totowa: Rowman and Littlefield, 1972.

Radulescu, Raluca L. "Genealogy in Insular Romance." In *Broken Lines: Genealogical Literature in Late-Medieval Britain and France*, edited by Raluca L. Radulescu and Edward Donald Kennedy, 7–25. Turnhout: Brepols, 2008.

Ramey, Lynn Tarte. *Christian, Saracen and Genre in Medieval French Literature*. New York: Routledge, 2001.

Raynaud, Christiane. "Les répresentations du pouvoir royal du XIIIe au XVe siècle: le cas d'Alexandre." In *Images de l'Antiquité dans la littérature française: le texte et son illustration*, edited by Emmanuele Baumgartner and Laurence Harf-Lancner, 59–67. Paris: Presses de l'Ecole normale supérieure, 1993.

Rector, Geoff. "'Faites le mien desir': Studious Persuasion and Baronial Desire in Jordan Fantosme's *Chronicle*." *Journal of Medieval History* 34 (2008): 311–46.

Reis, Levilson C. "The 'Other' Medieval French Alexander: Arthurian Orientalism, Cross-Cultural Contact, and Transcultural Assimilation in Chrétien de Troyes's Cligés." *Romanische Forschungen* 125, no. 3 (2013): 353–66.

"Richard de Bury's Books from the Library of St. Albans." *The Bodleian Library Record* 3 (1950–1): 177–9.

Richardson, Douglas. *Magna Carta Ancestry: A Study in Colonial and Medieval Families*. Baltimore: Genealogical Pub Co., 2005.

Robb, David M. *The Art of the Illuminated Manuscript*. Philadelphia: Philadelphia Art Alliance, 1973.

Rock, Catherine A. "Fouke le Fitz Waryn and King John: Rebellion and Reconciliation." In *British Outlaws of Literature and History: Essays on Medieval and Early Modern Figures from Robin Hood to Twm Shon Catty*, edited by Alexander L. Kaufman, 67–96. Jefferson: McFarland, 2011.

Rollo, David. *Historical Fabrication, Ethnic Fable and French Romance in Twelfth-Century England*. Lexington, KY: French Forum, 1998.

Ross, D.J.A. *Alexander Historiatus: A Guide to Medieval Illustrated Alexander Literature*. London: The Warburg Institute, 1963.

Ross, D.J.A. "A Check-List of Three Alexander Texts: The Julius Valerius *Epitome*, the *Epistola ad Aristotelem* and the *Collatio cum Dindimo*." In his *Studies in the Alexander Romance*, 83–8. London: Pindar Press, 1985.

Ross, D.J.A. "A New Manuscript of Archpriest Leo of Naples: *Nativitas et victoria Alexandri Magni*." In his *Studies in the Alexander Romance*, 1–61. London: Pindar Press, 1985.

Ross, D.J.A. "'*Parva recapitulatio*,' An English Collection of Texts Relating to Alexander the Great." In his *Studies in the Alexander Romance*, 156–68. London: Pindar Press, 1985.

Ross, D.J.A. "Some Notes on the *Old French Alexander Romance* in Prose." *French Studies* 6 (1952): 135–47.

Ross, D.J.A. "Some Unrecorded Manuscripts of the *Historia de Preliis*." *Scriptorium* 9 (1955): 149–50.

Ross, D.J.A. "A Thirteenth Century Anglo-Norman Workshop Illustrating Secular Romances?" In *Mélanges offerts à Rita Lejeune, professeur à l'Université de Liège*, 1: 689–94. Gembloux: Duculot, 1969.

Roth, Cecil. *The History of the Jews of Italy*. Philadelphia: Jewish Publication Society of America, 1969.

Rothschild, John-Pierre. "L'*Iter ad Paradisum* entre homélie rabbinique, roman, traité d'apologétique et exemplum." In *Les voyages d'Alexandre au paradis Orient et Occident, regards croisés*, edited by Catherine Gaullier-Bougassas and Margaret Bridges, 93–125. Turnhout: Brepols, 2013.

Rouse, Robert Allen. *The Idea of Anglo-Saxon England in Middle English Romance*. Cambridge: Cambridge University Press, 2005.

Rud, Thomas. *Codicum manuscriptorum Ecclesiae Cathedralis Dunelmensis catalogus classicus*. Durham: Andrews, 1825.

Salter, Elizabeth. *English and International: Studies in the Literature, Art, and Patronage of Medieval England*. Edited by Derek Pearsall and Nicolette Zeeman. Cambridge: Cambridge University Press, 1988.

Sanders, I.J. *English Baronies: A Study of Their Origin and Descent, 1086–1327*. Oxford: Clarendon Press, 1960.

Sargent-Baur, Barbara Nelson. "Dux bellorum / rex militum / roi fainéant: la transformation d'Arthur au XIIe siècle." *Le Moyen âge* 90, no. 3–4 (1984): 357–73.

Saul, Nigel. *Chivalry in Medieval England*. Cambridge, MA: Harvard University Press, 2011.

Saxl, F., and R. Wittkower. *British Art and the Mediterranean*. London: Oxford University Press, 1948.

Scattergood, John. "Validating the High Life in *Of Arthour and of Merlin* and *Kyng Alisaunder*." *Essays in Criticism* 54, no. 4 (2004): 323–50.

Schmidt, Victor. *A Legend and Its Image: The Aerial Flight of Alexander the Great in Medieval Art*. Groningen: Forsten, 1995.

Schmolke-Hasselmann, Beate. *The Evolution of Arthurian Romance: The Verse Tradition from Chretien to Froissart*. Translated by Margaret and Roger Middleton. Cambridge: Cambridge University Press, 1998.

Schneegans, Heinrich. "Die handschriftliche Gestaltung des Alexanders-Romans von Eustache von Kent." *Zeitschrift für französische Sprache und Literatur* 30 (1906): 240–65.

Schroeder, Horst. *Der Topos der Nine Worthies in Literatur und bildender Kunst*. Göttingen: Vandenhoeck & Ruprecht, 1971.

Schubert, Kurt. *Jewish Historiography and Iconography in Early and Medieval Christianity*. Assen: Van Gorcum, 1992.

Seel, Otto. "Die justinischen Handschriftenklassen und ihr Verhältness zu Orosius." *Studii italiani di filologia classica* 11 (1934): 255–88 and 12 (1935): 5–40.

Shaw, Frank. "Friedrich II as the 'Last Emperor.'" *German History* 19, no. 3 (2001): 321–39.

Shopkow, Leah. *History and Community: Norman Historical Writing in the Eleventh and Twelfth Centuries*. Washington, DC: Catholic University of America Press, 1997.

Short, Ian. "Language and Literature." In *A Companion to the Anglo-Norman World*, edited by Christopher Harper-Bill and Elisabeth van Houts, 191–213. Woodbridge: Boydell Press, 2003.

Short, Ian. "Patrons and Polyglots: French Literature in Twelfth-Century England." In *Anglo-Norman Studies XIV: Proceedings of the Battle Conference, 1991*, edited by Marjorie Chibnall, 229–49. Woodbridge: Boydell, 1992.

Simon, M. "Alexandre le Grand, juif et Chrétien." *Revue d'histoire et de philosophie religieuses* 21 (1941): 177–91.

Simpkin, David. "The English Army and the Scottish Campaign of 1310–1311." In *England and Scotland in the Fourteenth Century: New Perspectives*, edited by Andy King and Michael A. Penman, 14–39. Woodbridge: Boydell Press, 2007.

Smalley, Beryl. *English Friars and Antiquity in the Early Fourteenth Century.* Oxford: Basil Blackwell, 1960.

Smallwood, T.M. "The Prophecy of the Six Kings." *Speculum* 60, no. 3 (1985): 571–92.

Southgate, Minoo S. "Portrait of Alexander in Persian Alexander-Romances of the Islamic Era." *Journal of the American Oriental Society* 97, no. 3 (1977): 278–84.

Spencer, Diana. *The Roman Alexander: Reading a Cultural Myth.* Exeter: University of Exeter Press, 2002.

Spiegel, Gabrielle. *Romancing the Past*: *The Rise of Vernacular Prose Historiography in Twentieth-Century France.* Berkeley: University of California Press, 1992.

Staniland, Kay. "Court Style, Painters, and the Great Wardrobe." In *England in the Fourteenth Century: Proceedings of the 1985 Harlaxton Symposium*, edited by W.M. Ormrod, 236–46. Woodbridge: Boydell, 1986.

Stone, Charles Russell. "Chaucer's Alexander the Great and the *Monk's Tale*: Reconsidering the Fourteenth-Century Reception of a Pagan's Tragedy." *Mediaevalia et Humanistica* NS 42 (2017): 23–42.

Stone, Charles Russell. *From Tyrant to Philosopher King: A Literary History of Alexander the Great in Medieval and Early Modern England.* Turnhout: Brepols, 2013.

Stone, Charles Russell. "Investigating Macedon in Medieval England: The *St Albans Compilation*, the *Philippic Histories*, and the Reception of Alexander the Great." *Viator* 42, no. 1 (2011): 75–111.

Stone, Charles Russell. "'Many man he shal do woo': Portents and the End of an Empire in *Kyng Alisaunder*." *Medium Ævum* 81 (2012): 18–40.

Stoneman, Richard. *Alexander the Great: A Life in Legend.* New Haven: Yale University Press, 2008.

Stoneman, Richard, Kyle Erickson, and Ian Richard Netton, eds. *The Alexander Romance in Persia and the East.* Groningen: Barkhuis, 2012.

Strickland, Debra Higgs. *Saracens, Demons, and Jews: Making Monsters in Medieval Art.* Princeton: Princeton University Press, 2003.

Sturges, Robert S. *Medieval Interpretation: Models of Reading in Literary Narrative, 1100–1500.* Carbondale: Southern Illinois University Press, 1991.

Suard, François. "Alexandre est-il un personnage de roman?" *Bien dire et bien aprandre* 7 (1989): 77–87.

Szkilnik, Michelle, "Conquering Alexander: *Perceforest* and the Alexandrian Tradition." In *The Medieval French Alexander*, edited by Donald Maddox and Sara Sturm-Maddox, 203–17. Albany, State University of New York Press, 2002.

Tabacco, Giovanni. *The Struggle for Power in Medieval Italy: Structures of Political Rule.* Translated by Rosalind Brown Jensen. Cambridge: Cambridge University Press, 1989.

Takayama, Hiroshi. "Law and Monarchy in the South." In *Italy in the Central Middle Ages, 1000–1300*, edited by David Abulafia, 58–81. Oxford: Oxford University Press, 2004.

Taylor, Jane H.M. "Alexander Amoroso: Rethinking Alexander in the *Roman de Perceforest*." In *The Medieval French Alexander*, edited by Donald Maddox and Sara Sturm-Maddox, 219–34. Albany, State University of New York Press, 2002.

Taylor, Jane H.M. "The Sense of a Beginning: Genealogy and Plenitude in Late Medieval Narrative Cycles." In *Transtextualities: Of Cycles and Cyclicity in Medieval French Literature*, edited by Sara Sturm-Maddox and Donald Maddox, 93–123. Binghamton: Center for Medieval and Early Renaissance Studies, 1996.

Taylor, Jane H.M. "The Thirteenth-Century Arthur." In *The Cambridge Companion to the Arthurian Legend*, edited by Elizabeth Archibald and Ad Putter, 53–68. Cambridge: Cambridge University Press, 2009.

Taylor, John. *English Historical Literature in the Fourteenth Century*. Oxford: Oxford University Press, 1987.

Thomas, Hugh M. *The English and the Normans: Ethnic Hostility, Assimilation, and Identity 1066–c 1220*. Oxford: Oxford University Press, 2003.

Thomson, R.M. *Manuscripts from St Albans Abbey 1066–1235*. 2 vols. Woodbridge: Brewer, 1982.

Thomson, R.M. *England and the Twelfth-Century Renaissance*. Aldershot: Variorum, 1998.

Tristram, Hildegard. "Der Insulare Alexander." In *Kontinuität und Transformation der Antike im Mittelalter: Veröffentlichung der Kongressakten zum Freiburger Symposion des Mediävistenverbandes*, edited by Willi Erzgräber, 129–55. Sigmaringen: Thorbecke, 1989.

Tristram, Hildegard. "More Talk of Alexander." *Celtica* 21 (1990): 658–63.

Tronzo, William. "The Mantle of Roger II of Sicily." In *Robes and Honor: The Medieval World of Investiture*, edited by Stewart Gordon, 241–53. New York: Palgrave, 2001.

Trotter, D.A. Review of *Le roman d'Alexandre, ou, Le roman de toute chevalerie*, translated by Catherine Gaullier-Bougassas and Laurence Harf-Lancner. *Medium Ævum* 73, no. 1 (2004): 178.

Tubach, Frederic C. *Index Exemplorum: A Handbook of Medieval Religious Tales*. Helsinki: Suomalainen Tiedeakatemia, 1969.

Tudor-Craig, Pamela. "The Painted Chamber at Westminster." *Archaeological Journal* 114 (1957): 92–105.

Turville-Petre, Thorlac. *England the Nation: Language, Literature, and National Identity, 1290–1340*. Oxford: Clarendon Press, 1996.

Turville-Petre, Thorlac. "A Lost Alliterative Alexander Romance." *The Review of English Studies* 30, no. 119 (1979): 306–7.

Tyson, Diana. "The Epitaph of Edward the Black Prince." *Medium Ævum* 46 (1977): 98–104.

Vale, Juliet. *Edward III and Chivalry: Chivalric Society and Its Context, 1270–1350.* Woodbridge: Boydell Press, 1982.

Van Bekkum, W. Jac.. "Alexander the Great in Medieval Hebrew Literature." *Journal of the Warburg and Courtauld Institutes* 49 (1986): 218–26.

Vaughan, Richard. *Matthew Paris*. Cambridge: Cambridge University Press, 1958.

Verner, Lisa. *The Epistemology of the Monstrous in the Middle Ages*. New York: Routledge, 2005.

Warren, Michelle R. *History on the Edge: Excalibur and the Borders of Britain 1100–1300*. Minneapolis: University of Minnesota Press, 2000.

Webber, Teresa. "The Patristic Content of English Book Collections in the Eleventh Century: Towards a Continental Perspective." In *Of the Making of Books: Medieval Manuscripts, Their Scribes and Readers: Essays Presented to M.B. Parkes*, edited by P.R. Robinson and Rivkah Zim, 191–205. Aldershot: Scolar Press, 1997.

Weiler, Björn. "Reasserting Power: Frederick II in Germany (1235–1236)." In *Representations of Power in Medieval Germany 800–1500*, edited by Björn Weiler and Simon MacLean, 241–71. Turnhout: Brepols, 2006.

Weiss, Judith. "Emperors and Antichrists: Reflections of Empire in Insular Narrative, 1130–1250." In *The Matter of Identity in Medieval Romance*, edited by Phillipa Hardman, 87–102. Woodbridge: D.S. Brewer, 2002.

Weiss, Judith. "Ineffectual Monarchs: Portrayals of Regal and Imperial Power in *Ipomedon*, *Robert le Diable* and *Octavian*." In *Cultural Encounters in the Romance of Medieval England*, edited by Corinne Saunders, 55–68. Woodbridge: D.S. Brewer, 2005.

Weiss, Judith. "Insular Beginnings: Anglo-Norman Romance." In *A Companion to Romance from Classical to Contemporary*, edited by Corinne Saunders, 26–44. Malden: Blackwell, 2007.

Weitzmann, Kurt. *Art in the Medieval West and Its Contacts with Byzantium*. London: Variorum Reprints, 1982.

Welter, J.T. *L'Exemplum dans la littérature religieuse et didactique du moyen âge*. Geneva: Slatkine Reprints, 1973.

Weynand, Johanna. *Der Roman de Toute chevalerie des Thomas von Kent in seinem verhaltnis zu seinen quellen*. Bonn: C. Georgi, 1911.

Whatley, Laura Julinda. "Romance, Crusade, and the Orient in King Henry III of England's Royal Chambers." *Viator* 44 (2013): 175–98.

White, Jr., Lynn Townsend. *Latin Monasticism in Norman Sicily*. Cambridge, MA: Mediaeval Academy of America, 1938.

Williams, David. "Alexandre le Grand dans la littérature anglaise medievale: de l'ambivalence à la polyvalence." In *Alexandre le Grand dans les Littératures Occidentales et Proche-Orientales: Actes du Colloque de Paris, 27–29 novembre 1999*, edited by Laurence Harf-Lancner, Claire Kappler, and Françoise Suard, 355–65. Nanterre: Centre des Sciences de la Littérature Université Paris X-Nanterre, 1999.

Williams, Steven J. "Roger Bacon and His Edition of the Pseudo-Aristotelian *Secretum secretorum*." *Speculum* 69, no. 1 (1994): 57–73.

Williams, Steven J. *The Secret of Secrets: The Scholarly Career of a Pseudo-Aristotelian Text in the Latin Middle Ages*. Ann Arbor: University of Michigan Press, 2003.

Wogan-Browne, Jocelyn, Nicholas Watson, Andrew Taylor, and Ruth Evans, eds. *The Idea of the Vernacular: An Anthology of Middle English Literary Theory, 1280–1520*. University Park: Pennsylvania State University Press, 1999.

Wood, Juanita. *Wooden Images: Misericords and Medieval England*. Madison: Fairleigh Dickinson University Press, 1999.

Zink, Michael. *Medieval French Literature: An Introduction*. Translated by Jeff Rider. Binghamton: Medieval & Renaissance Texts & Studies, 1995.

Zink, Michael. "The Prologue to the *Historia de Preliis*: A Pagan Model of Spiritual Struggle." In *The Medieval French Alexander*, edited by Donald Maddox and Sara Sturm-Maddox, 21–7. Albany, State University of New York Press, 2002.

Index

www.ingramcontent.com/pod-product-compliance
Lightning Source LLC
LaVergne TN
LVHW090155080826
844660LV00013B/821/J

* 9 7 8 1 4 8 7 5 0 1 8 9 1 *